SHAKESPEARE SURVEY

SHAKESPEARE SURVEY

AN ANNUAL SURVEY OF
SHAKESPEARIAN STUDY & PRODUCTION

2

EDITED BY
ALLARDYCE NICOLL

Issued under the Sponsorship of

THE UNIVERSITY OF BIRMINGHAM
THE SHAKESPEARE MEMORIAL THEATRE
THE SHAKESPEARE BIRTHPLACE TRUST

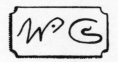

CAMBRIDGE
AT THE UNIVERSITY PRESS
1970

Published by the Syndics of the Cambridge University Press
Bentley House, 200 Euston Road, London N.W. 1
American Branch: 32 East 57th Street, New York, N.Y. 10022

ISBN 0 521 06415 5

First published 1949
Reprinted 1966 1970

Printed in Great Britain
at the University Printing House, Cambridge
(Brooke Crutchley, University Printer)

CONTENTS

Notes are placed at the end of each contribution

v

CONTRIBUTORS

R. C. BALD
Professor of English, Cornell University, U.S.A.

M. ST CLARE BYRNE
Lecturer in the History of Theatrical Art, Royal Academy of Dramatic Art

HARDIN CRAIG
Professor of English, The University of North Carolina, U.S.A.

UNA ELLIS-FERMOR
Professor of English, Bedford College, The University of London

HENRI FLUCHÈRE
Director, Maison Française, Oxford

ROSAMOND GILDER
Formerly Editor of 'Theatre Arts Monthly'

D. J. GORDON
Lecturer in English, The University of Reading

LESLIE HOTSON
Formerly Professor of English, Haverford College, U.S.A.

JAMES G. McMANAWAY
Deputy Director, The Folger Shakespeare Library, Washington, U.S.A.

MIKHAIL M. MOROZOV
Professor of English in Moscow University

ELIZABETH M. POPE
Research Fellow, The Folger Shakespeare Library, Washington, U.S.A.

I. A. SHAPIRO
Lecturer in English, The University of Birmingham

J. DOVER WILSON
Formerly Professor of English, The University of Edinburgh

LIST OF ILLUSTRATIONS

LIST OF ILLUSTRATIONS

Thanks are due to the Arts Council of Great Britain for permission to select the illustrations used for Miss St Clare Byrne's article from material collected by her for their
Exhibition on the History of Shakespearian Production in England.

FIFTY YEARS OF
SHAKESPEARIAN PRODUCTION: 1898-1948

BY

M. St CLARE BYRNE

To attempt an interim report upon Shakespearian production during the last fifty years is not quite so presumptuous an undertaking as the title might seem to imply. It is a good moment for taking stock of the situation, because we have now reached a position which can be apprehended and defined and can see how and why we have arrived there. Development goes on, but in the main we are working with assurance in an accepted mode. Practical experiment in the theatre, inventiveness and ingenuity have for the time being made their important and sufficient contribution, and are incorporate now in a new and vigorous tradition. It is, in fact, one of those propitious moments when mastery of technique and of material means is so assured that it should enable the fullest concentration of energy to be focused on essentials—in this case, upon the fundamental brain-work applied to the author's text to discover meaning and dramatic structure and purpose.

THE SCENIC HERITAGE: CHARLES KEAN AND HENRY IRVING

To understand the methods and achievements of Shakespearian production in the first half of this century we must turn to the last fifty years of the nineteenth. The work of Beerbohm Tree at His Majesty's represents the culminating point in the history of spectacular Shakespearian presentation, which goes back by way of Irving and the Lyceum in the eighties and the nineties to Charles Kean and the Princess's in the fifties. Granville-Barker's Savoy productions and the first fifteen years of the Old Vic take us back to William Poel and the early work of F. R. Benson, and so back to Samuel Phelps and Sadler's Wells. No one is likely to ignore or undervalue the influence of European ideas in general in the English theatre since 1900, more especially the influence of Germany and Reinhardt in Shakespearian production; but our roots to-day are still, as they always have been, deep in our own past.

John Philip Kemble, and later his brother Charles, were responsible for the effective introduction of specially designed and appropriate scenery for Shakespeare. Following the precedent of Charles Kemble's much-praised *King John* in 1824, Macready's 1837-9 Covent Garden seasons made it the accepted thing for London productions; and with Charles Kean, spectacle, based upon archaeology and social history, established itself as the dominant consideration. With scenery went an insistence upon correct costume for the plays which could be assigned to definite historical epochs and countries. Shakespeare in modern dress, or in theatrical fancy costume, was not therefore banished from the Victorian theatre; but as Ellen Terry points out in *The Story of My Life* (1908), on the London stage in her childhood, carefully mounted historical productions were the norm under Kean's management: "in some respects they were even more elaborate than those of the present day." By 1860 Shakespeare had acquired all the material resources at the command of the English theatre, but the appeal of spectacle was so much stronger than that of the full text that Macready was moved to describe Kean's productions as scenes annotated by the texts. Generally speaking the plays had been purged by then of most of the early 'improvers' passages; but the singing witches of *Macbeth*, removed by Phelps, were put back by Kean in 1853; Irving achieved one of the spectacular triumphs of his 1888 *Macbeth* with his "black spirits and white spirits" chorus, "Over woods, high rocks and mountains", which ended the witches' cavern scene; and it was not until 1911 that they made what seems to have been positively their last appearance in Tree's production.

Kean's spectacles determined the main trend in English Shakespearian production for sixty years: this was the tradition inherited by Irving at the Lyceum from 1878 to 1902. Irving still cut the texts freely and interpolated bits of spectacular business which took up precious minutes. If the present generation of playgoers is astonished to find a great actor cutting Hamlet's revenge soliloquy, it must be remembered that we have only just emerged from the period in which one of the critics' first-night excitements was to see how the text of a Shakespeare production had been 'arranged'. It was possible for *The Athenaeum* in 1901 to describe Irving's *Coriolanus* as "a virtual reconstruction of the play".

It is generally said that his productions, though in the Kean tradition, were less spectacular, more imaginative and more beautiful. Although his lighting effects were often severely criticized by his contemporaries, he was both a lighting pioneer and a lighting artist, and Antoine of the Théâtre Libre, who saw his *Macbeth* in February 1889, considered that the lighting of the discovery of the murder of Duncan and of the banquet scene went far beyond anything of the kind then known in France. He was equally enthusiastic about the settings: "Je ne me suis point emerveillé de ce grand acteur...mais ce qui est incomparable c'est sa mise-en-scène, dont nous n'avons guère la notion en France" (*Mes Souvenirs*). It is instructive to put this beside his comment on the Meiningers whom he had seen and admired in Brussels a few months earlier: "Notez que je ne suis pas du tout emballé, comme on dit, par eux. Leurs décors très criards, mais curieusement plantés, sont infiniment moins bien peints que les nôtres." His opinion, in fact, amply corroborates that of *The Graphic*'s critic, who wrote of this production: "In scenic art England may now be fairly said to stand pre-eminent. With the exception of the Meiningers, who now and then, when at home, are worthy rivals, there is nothing to be seen on continental stages which will compare for *mise-en-scène* with the Lyceum productions."

THE SCENIC HERITAGE: SAMUEL PHELPS AND F. R. BENSON

The other nineteenth-century tradition from which the modern impulse derives some of its rooted strength was the tradition of simpler scenes and better texts as maintained for eighteen years (1844–62) by Samuel Phelps at Sadler's Wells. Macready is reported to have said: "I believe we must look for the drama, if we really wish to find it, in that remote suburb of Islington." Phelps did more than anyone, before William Poel, to restore a fuller text to the stage. His treatment of *Macbeth* is typical: in 1847 he dropped the music and the interpolated words, restored Lady Macduff and her son, killed Macbeth off-stage and brought on his head on a pole. His artistry of setting and lighting drew high praise from such discriminating critics as Henry Morley and Douglas Jerrold: while sufficiently decorative in the accustomed realistic historical manner of the time it was definitely a background and not an end in itself. He kept

Shakespeare alive in the theatre for a popular audience; and no one among his contemporaries and immediate successors approached as nearly to the modern conception of the proper relationship between the text and the facilities and the conditions of the picture-frame stage.

In the last years of the century and until the outbreak of the 1914 war F. R. Benson did for Shakespeare in the provinces and at Stratford in his thirty years of repertory playing very much what Phelps had done earlier at Sadler's Wells. His work was a constant reminder to a country without a national theatre for the performance of its own classics that Shakespeare could and should be something more than the annual offering to the London public of a spectacular production of one of the most popular of the plays. In 1900 at the Lyceum he challenged London with his repertory company and a repertory programme, including the *Hamlet* in its entirety which he had presented at Stratford the previous year. His settings were mostly the fairly simple and ordinary theatrical stock of his time, but they were not designed to give unbroken continuity of playing and were realistically localized, so that in *The Merchant of Venice*, for example, the text had to be transposed in order that all the early Venice scenes could be played in succession, followed by all the early Belmont scenes. He took liberties with the text of the kind associated with the spectacular tradition, and in the tragedies in particular the pace of his productions was often too slow. His real achievement was other than technical, and something greater: it was the creation and maintenance, through three decades, of the company that bore his name, and the widespread love and knowledge of Shakespeare fostered throughout the country by its work. It is easy to decry his production methods as old-fashioned, and to forget that the presentation of the modern plays of his time would seem equally old-fashioned nowadays: it is better to remember that his methods were conditioned by and suited to the theatre, the audience and the standards of his own time; and that for many years his company was the only real nursery of Shakespearian talent in England.

The historical method of presentation was, in origin, an integral part of the nineteenth-century movement towards realism in the theatre. *Décor* and detail must be credible and accurate, whether it was a reproduction of the Rialto or a drawing-room in Grosvenor Square. Shakespeare and Tom Robertson, in production, were linked by a common theory: the one supreme commandment was; "Be thou real—to look at." In this the English theatre, from the time of Addison's sparrows to Tree's real rabbits, has rightly gauged the predilections of its audience. It was one of the major triumphs of Tree's 1898 *Julius Caesar*, which played from 8.15 to 12.15 although the text was drastically cut, that the audience was so literally transported to ancient Rome that a considerable portion of the *Telegraph*'s scholarly review could be devoted to pointing out in some detail just what elements in the scenery, costume and colouring made it a replica not of the last days of the Republic but of the hey-day of the Empire. Tree's instinct was theatrically sound: his scene was Rome: to make his Rome superbly, theatrically itself, he had to give back to his audience their idea of Rome made bigger and better and three-dimensional: for an audience raised on Alma Tadema and Academy paintings of classical subjects he had no real alternative. In Tree's 1898 Rome, as in Reinhardt's completely real forest in his 1905 *Midsummer Night's Dream*, spectacular realism reaches its culminating point, and reaches it for Shakespearian production as effectively as for modern plays.

The Influence of William Poel

"What's come to perfection perishes." In the nature of things, spectacle would have been bound to decline in the present century. But even before its apotheosis, cutting across at a tangent, there came in 1881 the ideas of William Poel, who advocated a complete break-away from normal theatrical methods for sixteenth- and seventeenth-century plays. His first demonstration was a performance of the First Quarto of *Hamlet*, on which occasion, at the St George's Hall, as later in other halls and in theatres, in London and elsewhere, he reproduced as far as was physically possible all the conditions that modern scholarship believes to have governed the performances of Shakespeare's plays in his own theatre and time.[1]

Poel realized that the picture-frame stage, as then used for Shakespeare, completely destroyed the vital speed and continuity of the action, broke the tension when it was essential to preserve it, distorted the fundamental dramatic structure, and made savage cutting a necessity. He found the whole tradition of Shakespearian acting as corrupt as the texts used by the theatre: it was cluttered up with traditional business, inserted, as often as not, to bridge a gap in the thought created by some cut in the lines; its presentation of the minor characters was almost entirely conventionalized; and in general the delivery of the verse was slow and declamatory. Ignorance of the Elizabethan social background and a facile readiness to identify secondary characters, as for example Maria or Polonius, with stock theatrical types such as the pert serving wench or the elderly dotard, had falsified their relationships and their dramatic functions and associated them with ludicrously inappropriate costumes.

Poel thought in terms of practical Elizabethan theatre-craft, and was at his best when producing, talking or lecturing: he was less good at embodying his sound theatrical common sense and his great knowledge of the Shakespeare plays in writing, so that the little he has left gives no real measure of the importance and the inspiration of his work in his own time as a practical corrective of the weaknesses of the old tradition, as an entirely new and original stimulus to actors, producers and scholars, as a continuous and consistent demonstration of the proper method of studying a Shakespeare text for production, and as a startling demonstration of the difference between the authentic Shakespeare and Shakespeare in the theatre. Between 1887 and 1914 not a year passed without a Poel production (see *William Poel and his Stage Productions: 1880–1932*), including not only Shakespeare but also an amazing number of other sixteenth- and seventeenth-century plays; and among the list of his actors will be found such names as Granville-Barker, Herman Vezin, Lillah MacCarthy, Ben Greet, Robert Loraine, Lewis Casson, Nugent Monck, Esmé Percy, Sara Allgood, Edith Evans and Robert Speaight, to mention only some of the most distinguished. His principles were of profound influence in the work of Granville-Barker, the first modern Shakespearian producer of the commercial theatre; and although his Elizabethan stage with its purely architectural background has not, ultimately, been adopted for general use, it still lives and flourishes in Nugent Monck's Maddermarket Theatre at Norwich, which began as The Norwich Players in 1911, was broken up by the 1914 war, reorganized in 1919, and has now an international reputation. Modern producers, on the whole, believe it is not necessary to give up the technical advantages of the modern theatre in order to regain the speed and continuity of Elizabethan playing; but the impetus, the principles and the methods which have determined the nature of our present tradition at its best all stem directly from Poel's insistence upon the vital relationship between the play and its own stage. In the face of the evidence of two centuries of theatrical practice he demonstrated the fact that Shakespeare was a practical man of the theatre and knew his own business best.

THE ADVENT OF THE TWENTIETH CENTURY: BEERBOHM TREE

In Germany the kindred impulse to Poel's found expression in the professional theatre. Under the influence of the ideas of Appia, Craig and Fuchs, realism for the staging of Shakespeare and the poetic drama in general was being rapidly abandoned and being replaced on the new 'Raumbühne' by simplified settings, permanent or semi-permanent, free of all superfluous detail and of wings and perspective scene painting, equipped in most cases with a cyclorama for open-air scenes, and in some cases—as at the Munich Kunstlertheater—with an arrangement of fore-, middle- and rear-stages that was almost Elizabethan.

At the beginning of the century, however, neither Poel nor the German simplified setting exercised any influence over English production in general. The fifty years under consideration begin, appropriately, with Tree's *Julius Caesar* in January 1898—the first of his great Shakespearian spectacles at the newly built Her Majesty's, which for the next fourteen years was to take the place of the Lyceum as "a home for Shakespeare". Tree's productions varied considerably in scale and elaborateness, and contemporary criticism and recollection make it clear that while his public and the critics admired the great shows, such as *Julius Caesar, Midsummer Night's Dream, Antony and Cleopatra* and *Henry VIII*, they enjoyed even more the simpler but beautifully staged *Twelfth Night* and *The Merry Wives*. These were the items in his repertoire which were most frequently revived, and which give a better idea of the general standard of good London production at the time. The staging of Forbes-Robertson's 1897 *Hamlet*, for example, or of Oscar Asche's 1906 *Measure for Measure*, though elaborate to us, should not be confused with Shakespearian spectacle: but George Alexander's second (and last) excursion into Shakespearian management with *Much Ado* in 1898 was elaborate even for its own time.

At Her Majesty's, Tree produced *Julius Caesar* (1898), *John* (1899), *A Midsummer Night's Dream* (1900), *Twelfth Night* (1901), *Merry Wives* (1902), *Richard II* (1903), *Tempest* (1904), *Much Ado* (1905), *Winter's Tale* (1906), *Antony and Cleopatra* (1907), *Merchant of Venice* (1908), *Henry VIII* (1910), and *Macbeth* (1911). The student who wishes to see for himself the amazing contrast between representative work of the English and German stages at the end of the first decade of the century will find in the *Stage Year Book* for 1910 and 1911 some typical photographs of current German productions in juxtaposition with two scenes from *Twelfth Night* as presented by Tree in Berlin. The bare, stripped style of the former, in which all superfluous detail has been eliminated, makes the latter look as if the cast must have been almost crowded off the stage by their realistic garden set, which includes the famous grass carpet so much admired by Odell. Even at their simplest, Tree's settings involved severe cutting of the text, and the transposing and telescoping of scenes: at their most elaborate they necessitated what must really be described as an abridged version, the cuts amounting to as much as a third of the play. Gordon Crosse (*Fifty Years of Shakespearean Playgoing*, 1940) recalls that on one occasion he timed the intervals while the sets were built up and found that forty-five minutes were lost in this way; and as an example of the way Tree played havoc with the texts cites his omission of the whole of Act v, Scene 2, in *The Winter's*

Tale—a vital piece of construction frequently cut as dull, which, as Granville-Barker demonstrated in 1912, was genuinely amusing if properly handled. Tree also lost playing time with his elaborately worked-up entrances and his invented stage-business.

It would be unfair to give the impression that all production previous to Granville-Barker was equally unscrupulous in its handling of the text; Forbes-Robertson's 1897 *Hamlet* will still stand comparison with any cut version. He was the best Hamlet of his time, and gave a rendering of the character which for beauty, grace and charm of manner, and nobility of spirit is still generally held by those who knew it to remain unsurpassed. His sound critical perception of the author's intention was never more triumphantly manifested, however, than in his restoration of the end of the play. Other star Hamlets had always ended it themselves with "The rest is silence": Forbes-Robertson, with the producer's more balanced instinct for total effect, restored the entry of Fortinbras, and though he omitted the English ambassador's announcement of the deaths of Rosencrantz and Guildenstern and cut down Horatio's two speeches to one of three and a half lines, kept the concluding speech intact save for "such a sight as this Becomes the field, but here shows much amiss". Hamlet was then hoisted on to the shields of Fortinbras's soldiers, and borne slowly away—an extremely fine and effective piece of business invented by his brother Ian Robertson. Such independence of the traditional acting cuts was rare, however, and this particular restoration was still matter for debate when he staged his last revival in 1913.

How long, but for the war of 1914, the tradition of elaborate mounting would have held its own in the English theatre, in the face of modern Continental methods, it is impossible to say, but reading the notices of Tree's 1910 and 1911 productions one is aware that saturation point had already been reached; and that even without Granville-Barker's Savoy productions there would have been some kind of a reaction against spectacle. The stage had never seen anything more elaborate and gorgeous than Tree's 1910 *Henry VIII*: it was a great success and the talk of the town: the furniture, the costumes and the banqueting hall of Wolsey's palace had all been designed by Percy MacQuoid, an acknowledged authority: from the point of view of pageantry, as *The Times* allowed, he had done the thing as well as it could be done...and there was really nothing more anybody could say about it.

Then, in 1911, came *Macbeth*, with the bad old business of the singing witches, and all Tree's usual bits of invention. Gordon Crosse describes the elaborate episode of escorting Duncan to bed: "His train includes a harper, and there is singing which turns to a hymn as the king blesses the kneeling company. When the stage is empty the witches enter and indulge in a few malevolent cackles." The most significant comment, however, was the ironic tone of *The Times* review:

Beauty is the thing this revival aims at, first and last. There is nothing ugly in the representation—not even the witches.... The sleep-walking scene was a scene of beauty. Flights of steps zig-zagged precipitously from the base to the very top of the scene. Evidently in an incident of sleep-walking it is appropriate that the sleep-walker should really have some walking to do. Lady Macbeth went slowly up and up, always beautifully. There was beauty again in the banqueting scene, barbaric beauty (including a fierce dance of retainers), and even the ghost of Banquo was a beautiful ghost.... Of course, we were never shaken with terror. Terror (on the stage) has had its day.

FIFTY YEARS OF SHAKESPEARIAN PRODUCTION

THE NEW SPIRIT AT WORK: HARLEY GRANVILLE-BARKER

The time was ripe for change when *The Times* could greet a well-mounted and not unduly spectacular *Macbeth* in this fashion. Not that the younger generation knocking at the door exactly a year later was to be allowed to get away at once with all its new ideas: it had to face prejudice and dislike, especially in theatrical circles, and some sharp banter in *The Times*. "It was bound to come", was the national organ's greeting to Granville-Barker's production of *The Winter's Tale* in September 1912:

Here, like it or lump it, is post-impressionist Shakespeare...the costumes are after Beardsley, and still more after Bakst: the busbies and caftans and deep-skirted tunics of the courtiers come from the Russian ballet, and the *bizarre* smocks and fal-lals of the merry-makers at the sheep-shearing come from the Chelsea Arts Club Ball....Squads of supers have symmetrical, automaton-like movements which show the influence of Sûmûrun....The Old Shepherd inhabits a model bungalow from the Ideal Home Exhibition, with Voysey windows.

The Bohemian peasants were described as "genuine Thomas Hardy", with dresses "superfluously, wantonly ugly"; but the final verdict was: "It is very startling and provocative and audacious, and on the whole we like it."

A month later, with practically the same company, *Twelfth Night*, with 'decoration' and costumes by Norman Wilkinson, was the success of the season. *The Tatler* hailed it as "a breath of fresh air over a world super-stuffy with the theatrical conventions of centuries". *The Referee* wrote in the same vein: "Mr Granville-Barker serenely continues his task of spring-cleaning Shakespeare and of dusting the stage of some of its close-clinging cobwebs of convention." *The Times* critic found it the most enjoyable performance of the play he had ever seen—an opinion still generally maintained by all who had the same good fortune. He praised its beauty of line, colour, posture and movement, while finding it "great fun" and rejoicing that the usual exaggerated playing had been abolished, so that Henry Ainley as Malvolio was quietly and reasonably Shakespeare's Malvolio. The pace of it was also commended: "The main thing about it is its 'go'. It *goes*, if we may use the word, slick, but not too fast."

Then, in February 1914, with again many of the same company, came the famous *Midsummer Night's Dream* of the golden fairies. If its predecessors had been provocative and original, this was sensational and called forth gibes and enthusiasm in almost equal measure. "Artistically disappointing" was the verdict of *The Manchester Guardian*: "decadent" and "Barkerized Shakespeare" were two of the milder descriptions. Once again, however, the historian of the theatre will be well advised to refer to *The Times* review with which the late Harold Child completed his triad of judicious notices of this birth of modern English Shakespearian production. It is a fine piece of critical writing, and captures for those who did not see it the atmosphere and enchantment of that fabulous evening which held the first-night audience spellbound, to break, at last, into overwhelming enthusiasm. "The mind goes back to the golden fairies, and one's memories of this production must always be golden memories."

Whether the golden fairies were an inspiration, as Harold Child thought, or whether they were as ugly as others alleged, the methods employed by Barker in the staging of these three plays were revolutionary in England, even if they admittedly derived more than a hint from what had already become the commonplaces of the German theatre. His arrangement of the stage was very similar to the average simplified Shakespearian setting already popular abroad. A false proscenium, fixed in the actual arch, reduced the depth and width of the stage proper, which was then raised by the height of a couple of steps and thus provided an acting area which could be used for set or furnished scenes in much the same way as the Elizabethan inner- or rear-stage but was at once larger and more useful. The front of the stage and the portion actually spanned by the arch made a wider but shallow middle acting area, at a lower level; and this was enlarged, again at a slightly lower level, by having an apron built out over the orchestra pit. Proscenium doors (restored) gave entry to the middle and down-stage areas: set speeches were delivered from the very edge of the stage directly to the audience. The footlights were abolished and the forward areas lighted from the front of the dress-circle by what *The Times* notice calls "search-lamps converging on the stage".

The general plan of the *décor* was the same in all three productions, and before the first Barker, in a letter to the *Daily Mail*, had explained his aims and paid tribute to Gordon Craig for having opened his eyes to the real beauty and dignity of 'stage decoration' and freed him from reliance upon the "stuffy, fussy, thick-bedaubed canvas" of the traditional nineteenth-century scenery. In each case only two main scenes were used, varied when necessary by painted curtains decorated with formalized designs or formal patterns. For the first part of *The Winter's Tale* the setting was "a simple harmony of white pilasters and dead-gold curtains": for *Twelfth Night* a formalized Elizabethan garden and a simple formal design of gates and walls were used. The wood near Athens and the Palace of Theseus were the two set scenes in *A Midsummer Night's Dream*: the former had "very tall, draped curtains for a background, of greens, blues, violets and purples, changing much in tone according to the lights played upon them", and the floor was covered with a "very rough green velvety material, swelling to a hillock in the centre, on which are white spots indicating flowers" (*Westminster Gazette*). Over the hillock was suspended "a giant wreath of flowers from which depends a light gauze canopy in which fire-flies and glow-worms flicker" (*Evening News*). The *Telegraph* describes the palace as "a place of massive white columns with black decorations and a background of star-spangled black yielding to glimpses of a reddish-purple".

Granville-Barker presented unabridged texts. For this to be possible, in what was, after all, an evening's entertainment and not a test of scholarly endurance, the whole tempo of production had to be speeded-up. The methods he employed have given the present-day producer his ABC of Shakespearian stage-craft. He allowed only one break in the action: having learnt from William Poel "how swift and passionate a thing, how beautiful in its variety, Elizabethan blank verse might be when tongues were trained to speak and ears acute to hear it", he insisted on a much more rapid delivery than was usual in Shakespearian playing, and helped his actors by bringing them into closer contact with their audience for the set speeches; and finally he created physical conditions which gave him facilities similar to those of the Elizabethan playhouse for uninterrupted transition from scene to scene. Other precious minutes were saved by his ruthless excision of bits of traditional business and clowning; and H. M. Walbrook in the *Pall Mall Gazette* singled out for praise the straight performances of Bottom and his fellows, expressing the hope that this would "set up a new standard for the English stage, and that the old depressing imbecilities sacred to 'acting versions' have at last and forever been swept away".

PLATE I

A. CHARLES KEAN'S *Macbeth*. Princess's Theatre, 1853
(Victoria and Albert Museum)

B. HENRY IRVING'S *Henry VIII*. Lyceum Theatre, 1892
(*Black and White* 'Souvenir')

PLATE II

A. WILLIAM POEL's *Hamlet* (First Quarto). St George's Hall, 1881
(Enthoven Collection, Victoria and Albert Museum)

B. BEERBOHM TREE's *Macbeth*. His Majesty's Theatre, 1911
(*Daily Mirror* and Messrs Newton)

PLATE III

A. FORBES-ROBERTSON'S *Hamlet*. Drury Lane, 1913
(*Daily Mirror* and Messrs Newton)

B. HARLEY GRANVILLE-BARKER'S *The Winter's Tale*. Savoy Theatre, 1912
(*Daily Mirror* and Messrs Newton)

PLATE IV

A, B. *The Merchant of Venice*, 1920

C, D. *Macbeth*, 1923

E, F. *Coriolanus*, 1933

Six designs by W. BRIDGES ADAMS for productions at the Shakespeare
Memorial Theatre, Stratford-upon-Avon

(Reproduced by J. B. Charlesworth from the original drawings)

PLATE V

A. SIR BARRY JACKSON'S *Macbeth*. Court Theatre, 1928

(Enthoven Collection, Victoria and Albert Museum: Copyright Lenare)

B. MICHAEL MACOWAN'S *Troilus and Cressida*. Westminster Theatre, 1938

(Angus McBean)

PLATE VI

A. John Gielgud's *Romeo and Juliet*. The New Theatre, 1935
(Bertram Park)

B. Tyrone Guthrie's *Hamlet*. Old Vic, 1938
(Angus McBean)

PLATE VII

A. Komisarjevsky's *Comedy of Errors*. Shakespeare Memorial Theatre, 1938
(Daniels, Stratford-upon-Avon)

B. John Burrell's *Henry IV, Part 2*. Old Vic, New Theatre, 1945
(John Vickers)

PLATE VIII

A. *Hamlet*. Shakespeare Memorial Theatre, 1948
(Angus McBean)

B. *King John*. Shakespeare Memorial Theatre, 1948
(Angus McBean)

PLATE IX

A. *The Taming of the Shrew*. Shakespeare Memorial Theatre, 1948
(Angus McBean)

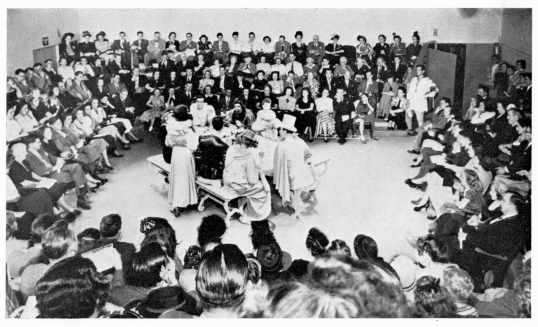

B. *The Taming of the Shrew*. 'Theatre-in-the-round' production by
the Dallas Theatre '48, Dallas, Texas
(Associated Press)

PLATE X

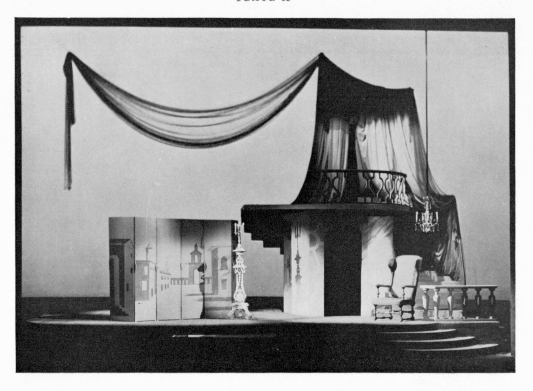

A, B. *Twelfth Night*. Royal Dramatic Theatre, Stockholm, 1945
(Studio Järlas)

PLATE XI

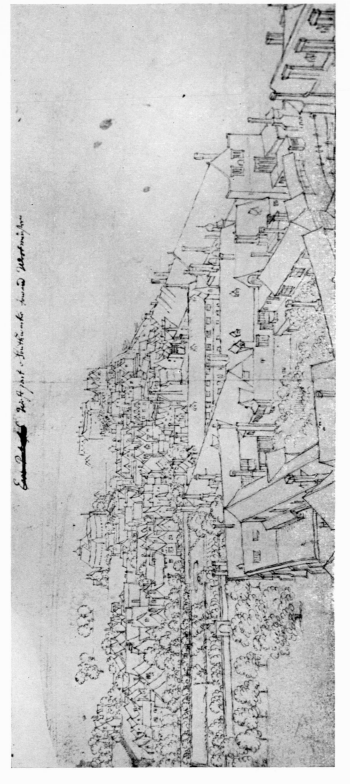

Hollar's drawing of the "West part o[f] Southwarke toward Westminster".
Pencil, mostly inked over, 5 by 12⅛ in.

(Collection of Iolo A. Williams, Esq.)

PLATE XII

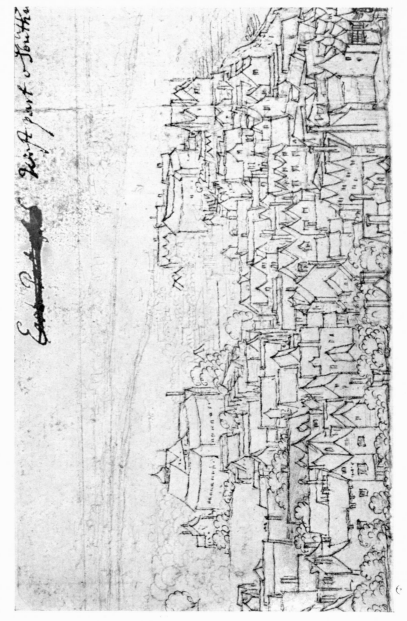

THE SECOND GLOBE THEATRE AND THE BEARGARDEN, c. 1640.
Full-size detail of HOLLAR'S drawing of "West part of Southwarke"

It is hardly possible for those who did not see them to assess the merits of the 'decoration' of these productions. In each there was obviously much beauty of colour and of formal pattern, and the best contemporary criticism recognized and welcomed the deliberate avoiding of realistic effects—nothing, "thank Heaven", says the *Evening News*, "that is imitatively the least like a tree—none of those tiresome, flat, gauze-tethered bough-and-blossom cut-outs". It was an entirely practical contribution towards the solving of the problems of speed and continuous action, and it was a happy compromise between the severity of the architectural or curtained stage of the scholarly enthusiasts and the elaborate scenery to which the ordinary playgoing public was accustomed. Judging by the photographs, however, what was not fully achieved by the 'decoration' was that unity of emotion and atmosphere throughout, which was already the explicit aim of the newer aesthetic theory of the time.

Granville-Barker retired from active work in the English theatre in 1914. For at least a decade England had been lagging far behind the best that Germany had to offer in the way of Shakespearian production; and in August 1912 William Poel had roundly condemned English Shakespearian acting as still entirely artificial: "In the interpretation of Shakespeare's characters and in the intelligent reading of his text there seems to be no progress made and no individuality shown." The plays, he averred, were not taken seriously by the actors, and the characters were treated as theatrical types: "Oh, hang Shakespeare!" was what one of the popular Shakespearian actors of the day said to him. Within sixteen months Granville-Barker had applied practical correctives to the outstanding weaknesses of the sixty-year-old English tradition, and had effectively demonstrated that our Shakespearian production could once again hold its own in the rapidly advancing experimental European theatre—an achievement which was nowhere more warmly recognized and applauded than in Germany. His modified and modernized Elizabethan stage was as practical and pleasing as any of the best German projects, and though as a structure it has not established itself in the English theatre it suggested the wisdom of compromise between antiquarianism and the ineluctable fact of the proscenium arch of the modern theatre. The unabridged texts, the simplified settings, the livelier pace and natural speech, the teamwork instead of star performances, the discarding of the back-slapping, the unmotivated laughter and the rest of the conventional cluttering 'business' traditionally attached to 'Shakespearian acting', the resolute coming to grips with real problems such as the presentation of the fairies—all these were given practical demonstration, not in an uncommercial venture such as Poel's but in the West End theatre. With the loss of Irving and the Lyceum in 1902 what had been a bias in favour of reading the plays had become almost a bias against seeing the plays acted—with reservations, of course, in favour of one or two star players. For those who prized the authentic Shakespeare there was more of genuine revelation, more substantial and satisfactory mental pabulum in the subtleties of romantic criticism, and in particular of A. C. Bradley's studies of the tragedies, than in the frequently crude simplifications of romantic spectacular production. Granville-Barker at the Savoy gave the theatre the chance to see how it was possible to reorientate its endeavours. Itemize his reforms, analyse his methods, they all add up to the one supremely important aim—the theatre in search of authenticity, learning to come to terms with the author's text, and unlearning a great many bad habits in the process.

Within the period under discussion two major misfortunes befell not only Shakespearian production but the English theatre in general. The withdrawal of Granville-Barker after these productions was a loss we could ill afford; and though Edward Gordon Craig has always exercised a potent influence upon stage design, and must rank with Appia as one of the two greatest sources of inspiration from which modern stage-craft has drawn, the contrariness of fate has kept this English genius from that active participation in the practical work of the English theatre by which the last three decades should have profited. No one, however, can study his designs for *Hamlet* and *Macbeth*, or read what he has to say on the subject, without realizing how vitally he has affected the principles which have governed our Shakespearian experiments throughout the last quarter-century; and one particular instance has been noted by John Gielgud, who points out that he himself and Martin Harvey and John Barrymore have all been influenced by Craig's *Hamlet* designs in their use of the unlocalized setting.

THE OLD VIC AND THE BIRMINGHAM REPERTORY

The year 1914 brought to the West End the war-time theatre, which banished Shakespeare and left the modern enterprise to be taken up elsewhere on what was for years practically a non-commercial basis. Throughout the war the only real strongholds of Shakespearian production were the Old Vic, which opened in 1914, and the Birmingham Repertory, which gave seventeen of the plays between 1914 and 1923. In 1919 the New Shakespeare Company began work at Stratford-upon-Avon with W. Bridges Adams as producer, and in all three organizations simple settings, speedy playing, continuity of action, reliance on teamwork, and unabridged texts bore witness to the growing acceptance of Granville-Barker's ideas. At Birmingham Sir Barry Jackson always used a permanent set, together with the three acting areas of Granville-Barker's stage, retaining the apron and the inner-stage with its own proscenium but giving more space and prominence to the middle section. His inner-stage was raised by two or more steps, and in some productions was divided vertically into halves, which in *Henry IV*, for example, gave him uninterrupted transitions between palace and tavern. As a rule the inner proscenium was used as part of the period decoration—a Tudor archway in *The Merry Wives*, a heavy Norman arch on short, thick pillars for *Macbeth*. As he had equipped the theatre with the Fortuny lighting system his productions had the advantage of the true sky-dome for outdoor scenes—one of the accessories which had contributed so largely to the beauty of the German simplified settings.

At the Old Vic, inevitably, the settings were much more austere—under Robert Atkins (1920–5) plain curtains, with perhaps one or two set scenes. Bridges Adams' settings, generally of his own design, were admirably suggestive and at the same time economical of means and material, so that no time was lost over scene changes though the pictorial effects were often extremely beautiful. Differences between the respective achievements of these three producers still seem significant: W. A. Darlington, comparing the Old Vic and Stratford in 1920 and 1921, found the chief aims of both "speed and simplicity", the production and settings at Stratford better conceived, "but for team work and acting ability the Old Vic has it nine times out of ten". To future historians of the theatre, however, the outstanding fact will be the establishment and maintenance, in these years, for regular annual Shakespeare seasons, of two companies, and the maintenance, despite lukewarm support, of regular Shakespearian repertory work in the annual programme of the most enterprising repertory theatre in the country.

At the Old Vic the playing of unabridged texts, with no transpositions of scenes and only verbal or linear cuts, together with performances of the rarely-seen plays such as *Troilus and Cressida*-and the annual offering of *Hamlet* in its entirety as the most booked-out event of the season did much to bring back into the audience the more discerning element. A good audience in London, however, did not, in those days, mean a better audience in the provinces; and W. A. Darlington described the enthusiasts, the "Shakespearian ritualists" of the Stratford audience, who chorused approval alike for good, bad or indifferent work, because "it is all Shakespeare—therefore perfect", as one of the worst menaces with which Shakespearian production had to contend. By their lack of judgment they confirmed the average man in his boredom with Shakespeare: actors and producers know Shakespeare is not dull, "but they generally despair of ever being able to persuade the public of this". And of this, he warns us, is begotten the producer who treats Shakespeare as a peg on which to hang his own fantastic ideas so that the boredom may be overcome, whereas the real need is for "pure and undiluted Shakespeare" and good acting.

The Decline and Revival of Shakespearian Acting

Good acting—the crux of the matter, once you had ceased to rely on spectacle. There was good teamwork and acting ability at the Old Vic in the early twenties, but a new production roughly every fortnight did not give scope for much more. And a very curious thing had happened—so curious and so subterranean as a process that it is doubtful if in the future the historian will find any trace of it, except by accident. With the return of the audience—or rather, an audience—to Shakespeare had come the retreat of the actor. The modern Shakespeare audience was springing to life in London, but for various reasons the actors were setting their faces against Shakespearian work. Young men and women, at the beginning of their stage careers, were warned against it as fatal to their chances of success. Once labelled a Shakespearian actor you were done for: managers would not look at you for modern plays. To be able to act Shakespeare was equivalent to being 'ham'—the word then used indiscriminately to describe bad acting and any kind of acting that was larger than life or anything other than purely naturalistic. Inaudibility could be forgiven you, and many other sins against the audience; but to be able to take the stage and remind the audience that there had once been such a thing as the limelight, or to be able to discriminate between entering and making an entrance—these things were not to be forgiven: you might just as well spring off with a glance at the pit or exit kneeling. Realism in production was at its zenith with Basil Dean at the St Martin's: du Maurier's genius for understatement in acting was more highly esteemed than ever before or since. And after all, the Old Vic was only one company, paying very low salaries: there was no other real Shakespearian opening in London.

As a phase this cannot be said to have done any harm: it was probably a good thing for plays, players and audience, to get Shakespeare in London dissociated entirely from the star system and firmly associated with repertory instead of with the isolated production. The rot was stopped by a combination of circumstances. Acting at the Old Vic was good and the theatre's prestige grew steadily: the audience grew; and in 1925 and 1926 Sybil Thorndike and Lewis Casson put on handsomely mounted productions of *Henry VIII* and *Macbeth* in the West End. Dame Sybil had played all the main women's parts and many others besides in the 1914–18 seasons at the Old Vic: her return at this juncture to Shakespeare was an encouraging sign, and although the *Henry VIII* was much in the older tradition scenically, the text was not sacrificed to the spectacle, and she herself gave one of the finest performances of her career, which James Agate unhesitatingly described as touching the sublime in the trial scene. Two other events, separated in point of time, finally restored the position. Edith Evans, with a West End reputation behind her and her triumphs as Millamant and Mrs Sullen, went to the Old Vic for the 1925–6 season. She played all the great roles and established herself beyond any question not only as one of our leading actresses but as a great English actress in a great tradition. She had proved her quality before 1925, but at the Old Vic it was the people's voice that acclaimed. Shakespeare may, perhaps, be 'dull' or 'boring' to the average man; but with his usual inconsistency he still regards Shakespearian work as the diploma piece by which he measures stature in the theatre; he may enjoy the naturalistic, but he still admires largeness. Shakespeare might not spell wealth, but he still spelt fame: he was still the touchstone of greatness. Then, in 1929, John Gielgud went to the Old Vic for a couple of seasons, and left in 1931 with the well-earned reputation of the leading young Shakespearian actor of his time. For young genius waiting to spread wings nothing could have been more salutary and instructive than these examples; and by the end of the 1920's not only had the prejudice against Shakespearian acting been well and truly disposed of, but apprenticeship at the Old Vic had become the first ambition of a high proportion of the most talented beginners and the first thing to be recommended to them.

SHAKESPEARE IN MODERN DRESS

This decline and revival of the prestige of Shakespearian acting cannot be overlooked in any account of post-1918 Shakespearian production. Historically, however, the next important landmark was the London production in 1925 of Barry Jackson's modern-dress *Hamlet* at the Kingsway. In spite of the "Hamlet in plus fours" headlines, it was in general taken seriously by the Press and intelligently received. For its audiences—average man and Shakespearian scholar alike—it was a profoundly exciting experience, and the best critics of the day were unanimous in praise. One of the things which surprised people most was to discover what an extraordinarily good play it was, and that all the characters were as real and vital as Hamlet himself—they saw it, in fact, as a play for the first time. It had always been one of the most unsatisfactorily costumed plays, and the mere getting rid of the theatrical fancy dress which did duty for most productions would have helped to bring the play to life; but on to the scrap heap, with the incredible clothes and the wigs and the beards, went the whole accumulation of conventional characterization which had been stifling everybody except the star performer who had used it as his vehicle. Everything had been as freshly considered and was as freshly interpreted as if the play were being put on the stage for the first time. And far from its 'Elizabethanism' suffering under this treatment, never—as William Poel pointed out in the *Manchester Guardian*—had the revenge motif been so well-handled or made more explicit. The incongruity of blank verse and modern dress was felt by some, but the verse was quickly and naturally delivered, and most of the audience, already accustomed to the speedy modern tempo of the Old Vic productions under Robert Atkins, took it in their stride.

Despite the success of the 1925 *Hamlet* the whole question of "Shakespeare in modern dress" remains fraught with difficulties. The idea does not yet meet with general, critical or theatrical acceptance, though it has received informed and discriminating support. Disregarding the usual contention that it is a mere stunt, an exercise in ingenuity, it is worth while to assume that most producers and actors who care for Shakespearian work and who try this experiment are at heart simpler and more simply sincere than their critics believe, and are attempting it in good faith. It is never an easy solution of the producer's problem, but the terms of reference it offers are wide—including the Ruritanian magnificence of Tyrone Guthrie's 1938 *Hamlet*—and provided the emotional associations are sensitively and truly keyed and that the acting is first class, then, as *The Times* critic said of the original experiment, there is "a clear gain in freshness and life and vigour". Whatever its future, it has earned the right to be regarded not as a stunt but as a serious excursion in search of authenticity, and one for which there is every theatrical and scholarly justification. After the work of Granville-Barker, therefore, Barry Jackson's *Hamlet* may be regarded as the most important single contribution to the history of modern Shakespearian production, which it has influenced in a similar and equally vital fashion. It stressed again, at a moment when such inspiration was much needed, the necessity for the fresh and original approach to the problem of production—the flight from Shakespearian acting in the twenties was at least partly due to the lack of any really outstanding Shakespearian producer. If the intellectual basis of Barker's approach to the text had to some extent been masked by the picturesque and pictorial qualities of the stage spectacle, now, in the Barry Jackson production, the intellectual approach and the realization were unmistakably identified. Translation into the idiom of modern life forces you to make your meaning clear to yourself: your understanding may be right or wrong, but you must make up your own mind and express yourself accordingly. By the "Shakespearian ritualists" your manner of proceeding is viewed from the start with the gravest suspicions: if you throw away tradition you must have the author: your scrupulous interpretation of his text in the entirety of its statement and implications is your only strength. For an engineer of a modern-dress production of *Hamlet* it must be "back to the text" with a vengeance, or he will be hoist with his own petard: he has forced his audience back to the text and the pursuit of the authentic Shakespeare. He has shocked them into thinking.

THE ADVENT OF THE PRODUCERS

Although the replacement of the star-actor-manager system for Shakespeare by repertory and teamwork in 1914, together with the new approach to the text, had already given a new prominence to the producer, there was nothing else in the immediate post-war circumstances to favour the work of another Granville-Barker, even if the theatre had been able to produce such a man. But in 1925 the lesson of the modern-dress *Hamlet* was plain enough: it was a triumph of production, in the truest sense, in that the play came over more effectively than ever before. It had the drive and the sense of direction that only the producer's unifying concept can give. The new audience, already well-grounded by performances which had given them speed, simplicity and good acting, now saw interpretation take charge as it would with a modern play. The worst faults of the old tradition had gone, but with them had gone something of the vitality, the vigour, the high spirits of the actor's theatre: dullness would keep breaking in. Edith Evans,

Sybil Thorndike, Baliol Holloway were reminding us that Shakespearian acting must be an affair of evident largeness: things were ready for the producer as the dominant factor, and when Harcourt Williams took over at the Old Vic in 1929, and quickly proved that he had imaginative grasp and subtlety, Gordon Craig wrote to him: "The Producers are going to save the English stage and have already begun." It should remain to their everlasting credit that in the thirties and the forties, and allowing for freaks, backslidings and fallings-off, their main endeavour has flowed steadily on in the channel originally pointed out by Poel, Granville-Barker and Jackson.

Harcourt Williams remained four years at the Old Vic, with John Gielgud as his leading man for the first two seasons. His work marked the transition between the first phase of the Old Vic's Waterloo Road career and its last. His aim of a better all-round standard of production was made possible by a more reasonable allowance of rehearsal time, and there was a general improvement in the variety and adequacy of the settings, though they still had to remain essentially simple. His own account of his methods lays stress upon the first rule he made for himself, which was to work throughout with the Folio text and ignore all previous 'acting versions', with their cuts and act- and scene-divisions. He found it an important aid to his own perception of the play's continuity, and he succeeded in playing his first production (*Romeo and Juliet*) with only one interval and no waits between scenes, and his second (*Julius Caesar*) in its entirety. This meant a speeding up of the Old Vic's already speedy playing and evoked the criticism, "Harcourt Williams-non-stop Shakespeare". He was determined to get rid of the last vestiges of the old slow and deliberate speaking of the verse, the old tricks of Shakespearian pronunciation such as 'me' for 'my', and above all what he calls the "absurd convention of the Shakespearian voice". He also set himself to eradicate "unnecessary and meaningless gesture" and any bits of traditional business that still slowed down the action. He was accused at first of letting his players 'gabble': so, too, was Granville-Barker over the *Midsummer Night's Dream* of 1914. But as the actors settled in and got the measure of their task the complaints soon ceased, and under his direction the speaking of the verse remained brisk, lively and natural, without losing beauty and rhythm. Finance was, of course, always a limiting factor, but in so far as this permitted, the design of his productions was soundly imaginative and enterprising. In his first season, for example, he presented a Jacobean *Midsummer Night's Dream* with Inigo Jones fairies and real English yokels and, as Ivor Brown phrased it in the *Manchester Guardian*, "put it straight where it belongs—into the very heart of moonstruck Warwickshire". In his second season he made what was for that time the even more daring experiment of presenting *Antony and Cleopatra* according to the general Renaissance conception of classical scenes and costumes, following up the suggestion made by Granville-Barker in his *Prefaces* that this was more or less the mode in which it must originally have been conceived. It was under stimulating conditions of this kind, playing full texts, in the modern manner, with an actor-producer who had been for five years a member of the Benson company and was himself an experienced and sensitive interpreter of Shakespearian characters, that a very considerable number of the actors and actresses who are now in the front rank of their profession served their original apprenticeship to Shakespearian work.

In the 1930's the historian's task becomes more complicated. Behind us are the milestones, recognizable as such—Benson's 1900 *Hamlet* in its entirety, with Sidney Lee's comment: "There should be no difficulty in restricting the hours occupied by the performance to four and a half"—

a milestone pointing us on to 1937, when Tyrone Guthrie at the Old Vic was to put on *Hamlet* in its entirety for a run, with the playing time reduced to under four hours, no rush or gabbling of the verse, but "a feeling of spaciousness and of being led not driven": 1912 and the second milestone, Granville-Barker's productions at the Savoy, and the birth of a new tradition: 1914 and the start of the Old Vic: 1925, Barry Jackson's modern-dress *Hamlet*: then, at the end of the twenties, the return of the actor to Shakespeare and the arrival of the producer; and behind it all, from 1891 to 1932, the productions of William Poel, a steady, running accompaniment from the days of Irving to the rise of a third generation of actors. But once we are in the thirties everything seems to happen at once. At the Old Vic the various seasons under Tyrone Guthrie as producer stand out: John Gielgud produces Shakespeare in the West End: at Stratford the new Memorial Theatre opens in 1932, Bridges Adams resigns in 1934, visiting producers—among them, notably, Komisarjevsky—startle and provoke, and the critics grumble steadily about the low standard of the acting. One thing, however, is clear: the 1930's meant primarily the acceptance, by actors and audience, of the producer. Instead of going to see *X*'s performance people went to see *Y*'s production.

Summing up the situation in 1934 the late Harold Child wrote:

At present the age shows signs of wanting merely to find some way of playing Shakespeare that has never been tried before...and tricks are played with the construction and the tone of the plays every whit as daring as those of Tate or Cibber.... The best possible base for all experiments would be a strong and active tradition that Shakespeare, as playwright, knew what he was about. The maintenance of that tradition is too much to ask of the theatre as at present conducted.

It was fair comment: with specific performances in mind he was speaking of what then seemed to be a general tendency, at a time when considerable notoriety still attached to the Shakespearian productions of our one English specimen of the producer's theatre, Continental model, and when two of Komisarjevsky's productions at Stratford in 1933—*Macbeth* and *The Merchant of Venice*—had drawn copious protests from almost every critic save himself. The recent visit to London of the Habima Players must have emphasized still further the danger that production for its own sake might overwhelm both the plays and the players.

This phase, however, was short-lived. The 'producer's Theatre'—Terence Gray's Festival at Cambridge—had ceased to exist in 1933, and already little was remembered of 'producer's Shakespeare' save its misdeeds—the Duke in the trial scene of *The Merchant of Venice* playing with a yo-yo while Portia spoke "The quality of mercy" speech, and the baby tossed to the audience at the end of *Henry VIII*. Such things remain to plague their inventors. Gray probably had, as he claimed, the best stage in England for Shakespearian productions, and he certainly had something to contribute to the theatre; but his itch to express himself instead of his author meant that his productions were not interpretations but criticism gone wrong: they brought out not what the author meant but what the producer thought, and by their extravagance were a timely warning to other producers. So, too, were the Habima Players, with their ingenious but crude devices: one could sympathize with the determination to get rid at all costs of the stock (mis)-casting for Olivia of mature ladies of matronly build and regal beauty, but it is not necessary to turn an actress into a painted doll with automaton-like movements in order to convince the audience that in her exaggerated grief for her brother's death and her infatuation for Viola she is living in a childishly unreal world.

Over-emphasizing as they did the producer's function, these and similar novelties in the early thirties were probably a useful corrective: they taught us, quite quickly, that mere theatrical inventiveness was not enough, and that if stylized productions were to prove acceptable to the public they must not be arbitrarily conceived, for the fun of it, but must have some reasonable justification simple enough to make itself apparent in performance. An outstanding success in this kind was Esmé Church's production of *As You Like It* (Old Vic, 1936; New, 1937) with Edith Evans as Rosalind, and scenes and costumes *à la Watteau*, designed by Molly McArthur. It gave pictorial and emotional unity to the whole play: never had it appeared so enchantingly fresh and lively. No one can pretend that nowadays we take naturally to the pastoral convention, and it was a bold stroke of production to emphasize both the pastoral and the conventional elements by setting the play in the period which, because of Watteau's pictures, is, above all others, associated in people's minds with this particular form of artificiality; but the device was fully justified, because, by transferring it from the less-known Elizabethan convention to the better-known eighteenth-century convention, it was made more essentially itself for the average spectator.

THE PRODUCER AND THE FULL TEXT

It would be difficult to say precisely when it was that the idea "that Shakespeare, as play-wright, knew what he was about" began to make itself felt in the productions of the thirties, but its most obvious manifestations were to be found in the increasing desire to play as full a text as possible, and in the search for settings that would provide facilities equivalent to those of the Elizabethan stage in order to secure speed and continuity. For various reasons the apron or fore-stage seems to be the least acceptable feature, but the use of different levels is much more frequent; and in two recent productions—notably Michael MacOwan's 1946 *Macbeth* at Stratford and Glen Byam Shaw's *Antony and Cleopatra*—effective equivalents of the Elizabethan upper- and inner-stages were provided for by the permanent set. John Gielgud in 1934 and Tyrone Guthrie in 1937 both used for *Hamlet* a large rostrum with ramps and varied levels to diversify and point the action; and for *Romeo and Juliet* in 1935 Gielgud used a permanent set which was a valiant and in many ways successful attempt to solve the complex problem of general background plus the special demand made by this play for Juliet's bed-chamber 'above', for the balcony and for the vault of the Capulets. Its only drawback was that it made the brilliant lighting required for the dog-days in sun-drenched Verona almost impossible. But it dealt handsomely with 'above', which is one of the worst problems for line-of-sight in any theatre with an ordinary proscenium.

That it was the "Hamlet in its entirety" habit which was largely responsible for convincing producers and actors that the author knew his business there seems little doubt. In any abridgement the story bristles with difficulties which are resolved in the complete version, as Sidney Lee pointed out in 1900 after seeing Benson's entirety: "the events are evolved with unsuspected naturalness. The hero's character gains by the expansion of its setting." Harcourt Williams in his *Four Years at the Old Vic* comments: "Queerly enough, as a distinguished critic wrote the other day, the less that is cut of *Hamlet* the shorter it seems." In 1937, when it was put on for a run, everybody began to say how much easier it was to understand than the cut version. The naïve astonishment at the idea that the author should be right in his calculations is entertaining, but the fact remains that the continued performance of this one important text was driving home the lesson of dramatic structure in the place where it most needed to be learnt—the theatre. When Gielgud played *Lear* at the Old Vic in 1940, with the production by Lewis Casson based on Granville-Barker's *Preface* and his personal advice, the text was practically uncut. And so, after experiments with the theatrical, the more experienced producers begin to come down whole-heartedly on the side of the angels with Poel and Granville-Barker, and to transfer their allegiance to dramatic values in their search for authenticity. It is here that they still have most to learn, as the adjustment between drama and the theatre is one of the subtlest and trickiest in the whole artistic creation that we call the play produced. But it is of the utmost significance for the general understanding of the modern attitude and approach that Tyrone Guthrie, the most adventurous and unconventional of our English producers, should be prepared to state unequivocally his belief that when a scene or a passage fails in the theatre to hold or to get across, it is not because the author is at fault but because we do not yet know how to tackle it. Of all our producers he has the liveliest invention and the greatest sense of the theatrical—things which are held against him by those who dislike his Shakespearian work. It is well to remember that the producer may take as many years as the scholar to come to a ripe understanding of his matter and his own discovery of the wholly appropriate manner; may take, indeed, half a lifetime of learning by doing, taking buffets and rewards with equal thanks, before he succeeds in satisfying that last and most exacting critic of all—himself.

THE ENGLISH BIAS IN PRODUCTION

What the historian of A.D. 2000 will have to say of us is anybody's guess, but there are a few facts which can be put down already. Imprimis: that after nearly three centuries of cutting and arranging, the theatre is beginning to come to terms with Shakespeare's texts in their fullness. Atrocities are still perpetrated in the name of the theatrical; but the idea that the author knew his business is now a serious factor in every good producer's calculations. Secondly, this has happened because when things were ripe for change and we might have gone off, in company with the Continental theatre, in single-minded pursuit of modes and theories of theatrical presentation, the work of William Poel and Granville-Barker gave a characteristic bias to our reforms, so that ultimately we have concentrated on matter rather than manner and have sought first, by re-creating the original conditions of performance, to understand Shakespeare's dramatic technique in order fully to comprehend what it was the plays had to say. Thirdly, by reason of his increased understanding of this dramatic technique, typically the modern producer asks from his scenic designer the help of a setting which, without foregoing the natural advantages of the modern stage and its technical resources, will at the same time provide him with facilities equivalent to those enjoyed by the Elizabethan theatre. Finally, tackling his play as he would if it were newly written, it is the producer who will decide what it is he believes the play has to say and how he believes the dramatist tried to say it—who will, in fact, decipher and then make explicit by his control and co-ordination of casting, setting, costuming, balance, proportion and tempo that emotional-cum-intellectual statement and atmosphere which is real 'unity'. He is not going to upset the balance of a Shakespeare play simply because he has a star actor. We saw an admirable instance of this in John Burrell's production of *Henry IV*, Part 1, in 1945, when Ralph Richardson and Laurence Olivier kept the balance between Falstaff and Hotspur intended by the author. Had the Old Vic's resources afforded a Prince Hal of full weight it is not too much to say that perfection would have been achieved.

That if he is unwilling to subordinate himself to the play and its methods the producer may force upon it a fictitious unity far more destructive than the most haphazard or, at best, stage-managerial production, goes without saying. It is the real danger of the producer's theatre. There are, of course, many weaknesses in some of the productions which are, as production, best conceived, and this was especially noticeable in the thirties at Stratford, where impossibly heavy programmes of repertory work, inadequate supporting casts, and inadequate rehearsals justifiably provoked severe criticism. Individual producers, moreover, have their individual weaknesses: too often the poetry is sacrificed to bad verse-speaking as ruthlessly as Charles Kean sacrificed it by cutting for the sake of his scenery: crowds too often remain what they are—ten or twenty supers: we still need much greater appreciation of the authority and evident largeness that was taken as a matter of course in the older Shakespearian acting, the lack of which can make a play seem a bloodless, impoverished thing; and in spite of all we know about speed and continuity most producers can nearly always take a lesson from Nugent Monck and his Elizabethan stage.

THE PRESENT-DAY AUDIENCE FOR SHAKESPEARE

What, finally, of the theatre in which the modern Shakespearian producer is to function? Is it yet so constituted as to give him the opportunities he needs? The real Old Vic that won the inter-war Shakespeare audience by giving it six or eight Shakespeare plays in a season no longer exists: apart from Stratford there is no longer any genuine Shakespeare repertory. But the circumstances attending one fairly recent production give grounds for hope. In October 1944 James Agate wrote of the Haymarket production of *Hamlet*: "Mr Gielgud is now completely and authoritatively master of this tremendous part....This is, and is likely to remain, the best Hamlet of our time." Ivor Brown hailed it as "*Hamlet* indeed, the play, nearly the whole play, and nothing but the play. No nonsense, no affectations, no stint of energy, no stunt of production". What they were describing was a West End production, backed by a West End management and by the Arts Council of Great Britain. It was expertly designed, staged and lit: it was played by a distinguished cast, headed by the leading Shakespearian actor of the day; and it was produced by George Rylands, an English scholar and University lecturer, Fellow and bursar of his college, and director and trustee of the Arts Theatre at Cambridge. The lion and the lamb lying down together was in itself a portent—the theatre and scholarship, professional and amateur, the commercial theatre and state-aided Shakespeare. Nor was this all. The production had already played to packed houses on its provincial tour, and in London the playgoing public, during the V 2 bombing, in the last year of the Second World War, kept it running until August 1945. We have only to try to imagine this happening at the end of the First World War to realize the full nature and extent of the inter-war achievement. Here was its symbol—and a summing-up of endeavour, and a gathering-in of all the threads—and finally, the conclusion of the operation "Back to Shakespeare", which had begun in that very theatre in

October 1844, precisely a hundred years earlier, when Benjamin Webster, with the help of Planché, had staged his uncut *Taming of the Shrew* in the Elizabethan manner. In face of such a production, so designed, so sponsored and so received, we have surely reason to believe that the theatre to-day is ready for this pooling of talents, energies and resources which has been already found possible even under war conditions.

The tradition is there, and it is our own. As in the history of our literature, we have borrowed from abroad, and been enriched by our borrowing, turning it into "blood and nourishment". We have not thrown over our own past; we have gone on, in the light of modern knowledge and modern technical developments in theatrical art which have modified but not fundamentally altered our taste. As an audience we still prefer a pictorial to an abstract background: we accept decoration instead of realism, presentational instead of representational methods, and permanent settings, but we prefer them to be beautiful in a pictorial manner. We appreciate the admirably functional quality of a stage composed entirely of sweeping flights of steps, as used by Komisarjevsky for *Lear* at Oxford and Stratford, but we enjoy more naturally the simpler, less intellectual appeal of a setting such as Reginald Leefe's for Peter Brook's 1946 Stratford production of *Love's Labour's Lost*, or of Oliver Messel's scenes and costumes for Tyrone Guthrie's 1937–8 Old Vic production of *A Midsummer Night's Dream*. The historically associative manner, deriving from antiquarian realism, still seems to us more suited to the romantic playwright than the severity of significant form. The associative values were and always will be fundamental: the over-elaboration was an initial but incidental excess.

In Search of Authenticity

The demand for textual authenticity also has roots in our own past. We meet it in the theatre when Macready restores the Fool in *Lear*, when Phelps cuts away spurious and restores genuine material in *Macbeth*, or when Forbes-Robertson restores the ending of *Hamlet*. But there are reasons why its main impact should have been felt most strongly in the theatre in the present century. Poel and Granville-Barker formed an effective link between the theatre and scholarship, and the main trend of our Shakespearian scholarship since the first decade has been textual and bibliographical. The transmission of the text and the provenance and authority of the early editions are the problems which have occupied our best modern scholars until recent years. With this, inevitably, has gone detailed study of the relationship of the transmitted texts to contemporary performance, accompanied by an increasing knowledge of the physical conditions of the Elizabethan stage. When scholarship itself took a jaundiced view of the authenticity of the text, the theatre might well be excused if it cut and trimmed to suit its own purposes, but the vindication of the Folio editors and of the good Quartos by Pollard, Greg, McKerrow and others altered the whole position. There is always a certain parallelism between Shakespearian scholarship and the presentation of Shakespeare in the theatre: a general bias of interest, concentrating upon the somewhat romantic interpretation of character, is as distinctive a mark of acting from Kemble, Kean and Mrs Siddons to Irving, Forbes-Robertson and Ellen Terry, as of criticism from Maurice Morgann, Coleridge and Hazlitt to Dowden and A. C. Bradley. At no time, however, have these two aspects of Shakespearian study shown a greater tendency to converge upon an intellectual level than in this period under review; and paradoxically, it is the producer, whom the English distrust by instinct, who has, in fact, brought about their union, and as the heir of Poel and Granville-Barker confirmed the decisively English bias of our modern theatre tradition by acknowledging an artistic control that is basically intellectual rather than aesthetic. For some three hundred years the stage—his own included—has cut and hacked and trimmed and interpolated, paying Shakespeare the dramatist the two-edged compliment of treating his plays as superb theatrical material. They have been used for "what the actor wants", for what the actor thinks the public wants: now, the best producers, who have accepted the idea that the author knew his job, are prepared to concentrate their energies upon what the author wanted.

NOTE

1. This was not actually the first experiment of its kind, though probably the most complete: cf. p. 19, and see *Shakespeare Survey*, 1, 1–2.

[In connection with the above article it should be noted that Miss St Clare Byrne has prepared for Common Ground Ltd. a series of film-strips richly illustrating the development of "Shakespearean Production in England". The first part deals with the period 1700–1800 and is accompanied by a valuable brochure in which the separate pictures are fully described and in which attention is drawn to points of special interest. In all, this series of film-strips will contain eight parts, covering the entire field of Shakespearian production up to the present day. ED.]

AN ORIGINAL DRAWING OF THE GLOBE THEATRE

BY

I. A. SHAPIRO

In last year's *Shakespeare Survey*, after reviewing all the known pre-Restoration pictures of the Bankside theatres, I argued that Hollar's 'Long View', published in 1647, is the most trustworthy of these. I pointed out that there was every reason for supposing that Hollar etched it from drawings made for that purpose before he left England in 1644, but that in it he must accidentally have interchanged the names of the Globe and Beargarden.[1] This argument has since received strong corroboration. The Librarian of the Barber Institute of Fine Arts has drawn my attention to the existence of two Hollar drawings of Southwark which seem to be studies for the foreground of the 'Long View'. These are in the possession of Iolo A. Williams, who in 1933 reproduced and described them in *The Connoisseur* (XCII, 318–21), but they have apparently escaped the attention of historians of the stage. The drawing of the "West part of Southwarke" is reproduced in our Plate XI; the full-size detail of the theatres in Plate XII should be compared with the equivalent portion of the 'Long View' reproduced in the first volume of *Shakespeare Survey*, Plate XIII.

In these drawings of Southwark no building is named. Presumably Hollar in Antwerp etched from them or similar studies; if so he would have had to insert names of buildings from memory, and thus might very easily have interchanged the theatre labels. The corrections in Hollar's inscriptions on both these drawings indicate some uncertainty of memory and suggest also that the drawings were inscribed some time after they were made, perhaps in Antwerp when Hollar came to review the material he had collected for his 'Long View'.

While the drawings show that the labelling of buildings in the 'Long View' may require occasional correction, they confirm our opinion of its pictorial accuracy. Since neither drawing was made exactly from the standpoint adopted for the 'Long View' it is especially instructive to compare them with the etching. The layout is identical, and the relative proportions of buildings are nearly always the same; the foreground of the 'Long View' must have been based on more than one careful study of the Southwark scene. The differences in detail, with one or two exceptions to be noted presently, are just such as one would expect from the difference in viewpoint. Iolo Williams has noted two in the representation of St Olave's Church in the 'East part'[2]; in one case the drawing seems correct, in the other the etching. In the drawing both theatres appear taller in relation to surrounding houses, the Beargarden markedly so. The whole line of windows round the Globe is visible in the drawing; in the etching, though its viewpoint seems no lower, some of these are masked by a nearby roof. In both pictures the width of the Globe is about three times the height of the main structure; the Beargarden has the same proportions in the etching but in the drawing is only twice as wide as its height. Both drawings are in pencil, mostly inked over. Whether the inking is by Hollar himself or by a later hand has not been established; it appears occasionally to disregard the pencilling. The Beargarden flagpole and flag have been left in pencil, but are clearly visible. The pole seems to be fixed not on the inside of the Beargarden, as in the etching, but on the outside, nearly where one would locate the western staircase projection on the hidden side of the building. Was it perhaps the custom for playhouse flags to be fixed above one of these projections, where they would be more promi-nently displayed than a flag inside the theatre? It is noteworthy that the drawing also shows something like a flagpole above the western staircase of the Globe. This is much too tall for a chimney, though it may have been mistaken for one and inked in as such.

Whether the drawing presents a more reliable picture than the etching must remain uncertain. It is certainly first-hand evidence, made on the spot; on the other hand it is probably only one of several studies of this view, perhaps not the latest or most careful. Moreover, Hollar almost certainly etched the 'Long View' not only from small-scale drawings but also from larger studies, many still extant, of individual buildings; he may have made more detailed sketches of the theatres than those in this drawing. In any case the discrepancies between the two pictures are slight and insignificant, and thus strengthen our confidence in the general trustworthiness of the 'Long View' as pictorial evidence.

It seems to be generally accepted that the second Globe theatre was shaped as Hollar portrays it, but my contention that the first Globe was also cylindrical has so often evoked the same two objections that it seems desirable to discuss them briefly here. First, it is argued that we know some of the timbers of the Theatre were used in building the first Globe. This is correct, but it is all we know about the matter. It may be that the timber transferred from the Theatre to the Globe was chiefly that of the stage; moreover, a great deal of timber would be required for an Elizabethan theatre of any shape, and we must not assume that the old Theatre timbers were used without being reshaped or cut. But much more important than these considerations is the fact that we know nothing about the shape of the Theatre; it may itself have been cylindrical.

The second objection assumes that it would have been impossible, or at least very difficult and unnecessarily expensive, to build round theatres with wooden-framed walls. This objection would have greater strength if there were any justification for the further assumptions implicit in it. The little evidence I have been able to collect about the outer walls of the Bankside theatres points to their having been built of flint. Flint would do admirably for building a curved wall; it is especially plentiful in the southern counties and presumably therefore was inexpensive. But it does not follow that because the outer walls were circular the inner walls were necessarily circular also. De Witt's drawing of the Swan[3] shows a circular inner wall, and is corroborated by the 1627 map.[4] It also shows a large number of supporting pillars under the galleries, which is what some have argued an Elizabethan audience would not have tolerated. Hollar's picture of the Beargarden and second Globe also suggests a circular inner wall. But practice may have varied. It would be quite easy to build a theatre with outer wall circular, and inner wall poly-gonal. This plan would presumably be easier and cheaper to work to than one which used curved timbers[5] and the more closely spaced vertical supports this would entail, and my own opinion is that it may have been adopted in some theatres. Perhaps confused memories of a polygonal inner wall explain the pictures of polygonal theatre exteriors which we find in some engravings.

A further note on Norden's *Civitas Londini* may be added here. This is the engraved panorama of London from the south, with inset maps of London and Westminster, published "By the industry of Jhon Norden" in 1600. Noting that errors in its view of Southwark do not occur in

Norden's inset map, and recalling his deservedly high reputation as a careful surveyor and cartographer, I suggested that at least the Southwark foreground of the panorama must be by another hand.[6] The inscription on the 1624–5 reissue of Norden's "East Prospect of London Bridge" proves that the 1600 panorama was engraved from a careful drawing by Norden himself of the west side of London Bridge and the view of London at least north of the river. This seems to leave only one explanation of the misrepresentation of Southwark, namely that Norden drew his panorama from the *statio prospectiva* indicated on the tower of St Mary Overie[7] and that the foreground thus excluded was supplied from another source. The errors in its picture of Winchester House and St Mary Overie's Church are immediately obvious when we compare drawings of the same buildings made fifty years earlier by Antony van den Wyngaerde, and by Hollar and other artists fifty or more years later. Since these contradict the 1600 version but agree among themselves and also with the documentary evidence, we must continue to regard the foreground of *Civitas Londini* as a blend of fancy and convention, useless for the historian of the Elizabethan stage.

NOTES

1. *Shakespeare Survey*, I, 34.   2. *The Connoisseur*, XCII (1933), 320.
3. *Shakespeare Survey*, I, Plate III.   4. *Ibid.* Plate IV.
5. The frequently expressed objection that Elizabethan carpenters would have avoided cutting or shaping curved timbers seems to ignore their experience in ship-building, and also the many surviving examples of curved beams in sixteenth-century buildings. There are several in the roof of the Grammar School at Stratford-upon-Avon.
6. *Shakespeare Survey*, I, 30.   7. See *ibid.* Plate IV B.

THE PROJECTED AMPHITHEATRE

BY

LESLIE HOTSON

Ever since Collier published his *History of English Dramatic Poetry* it has been known that under James I and Charles I attempts were made to establish an amphitheatre or arena for shows in or near London. It is curious that historians of the English stage have been content to quote the three letters printed by Collier, without seeking more light on this grandiose scheme, so characteristic of the period, first set on foot four years after Shakespeare's death, and without studying the illuminating documents on the proposed amphitheatre first printed by 'G.E.P.A.' in *Notes and Queries*, 11th ser., x, 481, 502, December 1914.

What Collier printed was one letter (29 September 1620) from the King to the Privy Council, and two others (12 August and 18 September 1626),[1] from Lord Coventry to Lord Conway. By the first letter, James says that three of his servants, Cotton, Williams, and Dixon, have been licensed under his signet to build an amphitheatre. Yet since certain provisions gave them too much latitude, he instructs his councillors to cancel the grant, and to have a new one drawn according to accompanying instructions. These instructions Collier did not find. The two letters from Lord Coventry, a year after the accession of Charles, showed not only that the Jacobean grant never passed the great seal, but that by the new licence Williams and Dixon (Cotton having dropped out) were to be allowed greater monopolistic power over theatrical London. As Lord Coventry notes, the first project

was intended principally for Martiall exercises and extraordinary shews and solemnyties for Ambassadors and persons of honour and quality, with a Cessation from other shews and sports for one daie in a Moneth onlie, upon 14 daies warning; wheras by this new graunt, I see little probability of any thing to be used, but common plaies or ordinary sports now used or shewed at the Beare-garden, or the common playhouses aboutes London, for all sorts of Beholders, with a restraynt to all other playes and shewes for one day in the weeke upon two daies warning: with liberty to erect their Buildings in Lincolns Inne fields, where there are too many buildings already....

Conway's endorsement on this reads: "That it is unfit the grant for the Amphitheater should passe."

These tantalizingly brief notes left most of our questions unanswered. How large was the amphitheatre to be? Of what material was it to be constructed? What was the estimated cost, and how was it to be raised? What kinds of shows and plays were to be given? What artists and engineers were to provide the technical theatrical skill? Who was behind the plan? Answers to queries such as these, as well as the knowledge that the scheme was still being pressed as late as 1634—fourteen years after the first proposal—are to be found in the discoveries of 'G.E.P.A.' in the Tanner collection at the Bodleian, supplemented by fresh finds in the Lambeth Manuscripts and the State Papers.

Before coming to them, however, it may be recalled that James's notion of statecraft and the dignity of the English Crown included efforts to entertain the many ambassadors and envoys he

24

welcomed more strenuous than any Elizabeth had ever put forth. Confronted in 1603 with the arrival of seven embassies and ten ambassadors, he created the office of Master of the Ceremonies, held successively by Sir Lewis Lewkenor, Sir John Finett, and Sir Balthazar Gerbier. Of course masques, plays, and tilting at court satisfied part of the demand for entertainment of these dignitaries; but a need was felt for more and more varied spectacles and "noble and martial exercises"; and further, since most of the foreigners could not understand English, for plays in the common language of civilized Christendom, Latin.

Well aware that the expenses of entertainment made a severe drain on the royal purse, the projectors of the amphitheatre represented their scheme as a relief, in supplying diversions for foreign visitors by private enterprise. Their first plan, which James approved without sufficient consideration, was ambitious and inclusive in the extreme, as appears from the following newly revealed document from the Privy Seal Office, dated 30 July 1620.

This licence is granted to John Cotton, John Williams, and Thomas Dixon, sergeants at arms, for their services to James and Elizabeth, allowing them "to build and prepare an Amphitheator upon some convenient peece of ground neere our City of London for the exercise and practize of Heroique and Maiestique recreacions aswell tending to the delight and enterteynment or [*read* of] forraigne Princes and Ambassadors and strangers and the Nobility and Gentry of this realme as for the exercise of all manner of armes and martiall discipline"; the period of the licence, thirty-one years. The lords of the Council had certified the approval of the Mayor and Council of the City of London. John Cotton was willing to release his interest to Williams and Dixon. The ground purchased was to be fit in every respect for the building of "a house and Amphitheator". The rent was to be forty shillings per annum. The grantees were, at their own costs,

to erect, build, and sett upon the same parcell of ground one sufficient messuage, house, or Amphitheator of free stone, brick, and strong tymber with all necessary outhouses stables and other edifices... as may be most gracefull and fitt to accomodate all the exercises and pleasure hereafter mencioned... that is to say the ryding and mannaging great horses, with the exercise of Tilte, Turney, course of field, Barriers, running at the ring and other martiall and manly exercises on horse-backe, the true use of all manner of Armes for foot (vizt) the Pike, Partizan, Holberd, swords, muskett, pistoll, or any other usuall or necessary armes whatsoever, the manner of Seafightes with Shippes and Gallies, embatelling of horses and foote, the rights to be performed in Campe, seige or garrison with other documentes and instruccions belonging to the honor and danger of a Martiall Court with mathematicall and arithmeticall readinges necessary for martiall men. And likewise maskes or other shewes or invencions, dancing, musique of all sorts, high and lowe winde instruments and others, prospectives, exercises of the Olimpeyades, wrastling in oyled skins for prices or otherwise, fightes with pike, partizan, and holbert, heroique and maiestique playes in latin or in English and other pleasant delightfull and convenient shewes whatsoever...fitt for the more stately and delectable publishing and setting forth of the same, with a prohibicion to all Players within the City of London and the Suburbes thereof to suspend and restraine them from their playes one day in every month throughout the yeere, giving them notice thereof fowerteene dayes before every such day of restraint....[2]

First, as to the recipients of this astonishing grant, Cotton, Williams and Dixon. They were sergeants at arms, members of the royal household, and had formerly served Elizabeth. At

James's funeral more than ten such officers walked in the procession, and two were described particularly as "the Lord Treasurer's Sergeant at arms" and "the Lord Keeper's Sergeant at arms". Thomas Dixon may have been the Treasurer's sergeant, and at about this time the tool of the hated Sir Giles Mompesson; for in the Commons on 21 February 1620/1, "Drake of Devonshire proved that Sir Giles Montpesson had acted unjustly and rigidly against Inn-keepers and Alesellers by his overseers, the servants of the Treasurer and Chancellor, Dixon and Almond".3

As for Williams, he is perhaps the John Williams who in March 1626 was allowed by the King £270 a year "for the custody and keeping of an Elephant sent out of Spayne", the allowance to commence as from Christmas 1624 "and to continue so long as he shall have the keeping of the said Beast." John Cotton, who by the grant is said to be ready to resign his interest to his two fellow-sergeants, evidently withdrew from the amphitheatre business, for he is heard of no more.

Such men can have had small experience in mounting spectacles and military shows. No doubt they were energetic "project-mongers monopolitan" and promoters of a joint-stock company to finance the amphitheatre. As we shall see, however, from a later document, the brain behind them was that of a certain Captain Robert Hasell, described as "the first inventor and professor of the business of the Amphitheatre". In Robert Hasell we are presented with a most interesting Jacobean theatrical planner of whom nothing further is known.

When James came to look more closely at the provisions of the grant he had signed, his eye was arrested by several objectionable features. First, he found the projectors proposing to build their huge fabric partly of timber. This he vetoed as neither durable nor safe. The materials must be brick and stone only, and the specifications approved by his commissioners for buildings. Further, he found plans for "the exercise of Tilte, Turney, course of field, Barriers" and "documentes and instruccions belonging to the honor and danger of a Martiall Court with mathematicall and arithmeticall readinges necessary for martiall men". These likewise he ordered struck out. The first infringed prerogative, and the second smacked of an attempt to set up an "academy of honour" under guise of a show. There is no space here to discuss the latter phenomenon, beyond mentioning that Sir Balthazar Gerbier claimed to have acted for Prince Henry in working before 1612 to establish such an academy, and later outlined to Buckingham a detailed and interesting prospectus for erecting "King James his Academ, Societie heroick, or College of honor" which James seems to have had at heart. The 'Museum Minervae' under Charles, whose constitution was prepared for the Press in 1636, was no doubt a continuation of the same project.4

Possibly as a consolation for thus cutting down privileges already granted, James quadrupled the projectors' monopolistic rights over theatrical London. Instead of one day in every month, he grants them one day of monopoly in every week. In view of the inveterate opposition of the London authorities to the establishment of theatres, it is amazing to read that the Lords of the Council had certified the approval of the Mayor and Council of the City of London of this proposed amphitheatre. No other record of such a vote or of the Privy Council's certification has been found; and I suspect very strong pressure was exerted to extract the City's consent.

Following is "the Coppye of the Kings Direction Included in the kings letter".5 Obviously some delay had occurred. The letter to the Council was dated 29 September 1620; the accompanying direction, signed by Secretary Calvert, is dated some months later, 10 February 1620/1:

First That the Peticioners at theire owne chardg purchase a peece of Ground, in such a Convenient Place, as shall be alowed by our Commissioners for Buyldinges as perticularly that it fall not in such a Place as may hinder the intended Walkes in Lincolnes Inne Feilds; or some such other publique Worke; and that [they] assure the Inheritance of the same vnto vs by firme Deed in Lawe./

Wee are then pleased to giue them License to set there on vpon a new Foundacon, such an *Amphitheator* as is by them desired, namely to hould Twelue thousand Spectators at the least, *Prouided* it be buylt all of Bricke and Stone, the Walls to be of such thickness, as shalbe of necessitie for the continuance of such a Worke, and for the safetie of so many People, which shall be approued allso by our Commissioners for buyldinges, and that they shall not employ this, nor any parte thereof to dwelling houses, Stables, or otherwise whatsoeuer, but only to receiue the People in; at Tymes of Showes or Spectacles except one convenient Place of Dwelling in it for the *Man* which shall keepe yt, which shall be set out by our Commissioners for buylding, Neither that they erect any other house; Shedd, or buylding whatsoeuer; there being enough to be hired of all vses, and the motive to permit this vpon a new foundačon being that none such can be found readie buylte./

Wee are likewise pleased, according to theire humble Suite to graunt them a Lease thereof for Thirtie yeares With License (at all lawfull Tymes) to shew to theire best advantage all kindes of Bayteing or Fighting of Beastes, Fenceing with all Weapons, Wrestling in any Sorte, Tumbling, danceing on Ropes, All kindes of Musick, all kindes of Playes, in what Languadge soeuer, the Prohibition which they desire but one day in euery month to be enlardged to one day in euery Weeke, with all kindes of Shewes whatsoeuer which they can deuise, pleasant or delectable to the People Excepting Tilte, (which no Subiect can set vp without our License) Torney, Cou[rse] at the Feild, Barriers and such like reserued for [   ] Solempnities and Trivmphs of Princes, and not to be vilified dayly in the Eyes of the Vulgar for money offered./

That they practise all these thinges only for Spectacle to the People, not pretending to make yt an *Academy* to instruct, or teach the Nobilitie or Gentrie of this *Kingdome* a worke onely possible and fitt for Princes to *Vndertake*, and not to be mixed with *Mercenary* or *Mechanick* Endes; much less to have a worke which is so Noble, and hath been so long in our *Princely* resolučon to be blasted, by being made the cau[se] to delude wholy the good effects of our *Proclamation* and bringe in all kinde of Sordide houses vpon new Foundations wherewith the Cittye allready aboundes.

Geo Caluert

Februarie 10th 1620:

His Ma*iestie*s Attourney Gennerall is to prepare a Grant readie for his Ma*iestie*s Royall Signature, giueing License vnto John Cotton, John Williams and Thomas Dixon Seriantes at Armes to his Ma*iestie* to buyld an Amphitheator according to the directions and reservacions aboue wri[tten]

Pembroke

J. Degbye

Arundell

Geo Caluert

James signed this second grant, but certainly it never passed the great seal. Protests may have been entered by the actors and the owners of theatres, perhaps also by the commissioners of

3-2

buildings, the City, the justices of the peace for Middlesex, and the Society of Lincoln's Inn, although it must be confessed that none such has been found.

Canny, not to say grasping, are James's conditions as set down. The grantees are graciously permitted to buy the ground out of their own pockets, but must assure the inheritance of it to the Crown. Of the great amphitheatre to be built thereon at their own expense, the King is pleased to grant them a *lease* for thirty years only. Upon expiration of this term he will become the owner. Not without reason did they plan to call their structure "His Majesty's Amphitheatre"! To modern Western ears absolutism to this tune sounds an Oriental note. Yet supported by that word of power, *monopoly*, and the vision of vast profits pouring in for three decades, the resolute sergeants at arms were not dashed by James's bargain. While they were still confidently expecting letters patent to be passed, and the necessary capital to be raised, they put out a detailed prospectus, complete with bombast, superlatives, and seductive snob-appeal, which revealed much of their plans and preliminary preparations. It is true circus literature, the Jacobean grandfather of a P. T. Barnum bill announcing the Greatest Show on Earth. By good fortune a copy of this prospectus is found joined to the document just given from MS. Tanner 89. It is in manuscript, but the headings and the leading words of the paragraphs are heavily thickened for bold-face, and italics are thickly sown:

The Exercise of many Heroick and Maiestick Recreations at his Maiesties Amphitheator.

Imprimis *Tragedies*, *Comedies*, and *Histories*, *Acted* both in *Latine* and *English*, full of high State, and Royall Representmentes with many variable and delightfull properties, with Showes of great *Horse*, and riche *Caparisons*, gracefully prepared to Entertaine Foraigne *Princes*, and to giue content to the most *Noble* and *Worthyest* of his Maiesties *Admired* and happie *Kingdomes*.

There shall be Showne the manner of *Sea Fights* with the resemblance of Shipps and Gallies in very Exquisite and Singuler order, worthy the view of the most Noble and Generous beholders./

There shall be showne the true vse of all manner of *Armes*, and Weapons for *Foote*, faire and richly Armed with *Pike*, *Partizan*, *Holbert*, *Sword*, *Rapier*, *Muskett*, *Pistoll*, or any other vsuall or necessarie *Armes* whatsoeuer.

There shall allso be demonstrated many Excellent & Ingenious Experiences belonging to a *Campe*, *Seidge*, or *Garison* with the *Manly* order, and Posture of a Souldier.

There will be allso, for delight and Recreation, *Musick* of all Sortes, *Winde Instrumentes*, high and Lowe, *String Instrumentes*, *Voices*, the best this Kingdome, or any other Nation can aford./

Masques of very Exquisite and Curious *Inuentions* with the best *Dauncer*[s] that can be, *Mummeries* allso, and *Moriskors*./

Curious *Prospectiues* in this Kingdome vnnvsuall, of singuler rarietie, and high Invention, all possible Exercises of the *Olympiades*, as *Wrestling* in Oyled Skynnes for gold and siluer Collers, with other Inferiour prizes, *Wrestling* two or three against one, *Running*, *Jumping*, *Vauteing*, *Tumbling*, *Daunceing* on the Ropes, Gladiators in equall and vnnequall Combate two or three against one, to approue the singularitie of *Weapons* with the true and rightfull vse of them./

Strange and vnvsuall *Padgeantes* with very admirable and rare Inventions, neuer as yet brought forth to any Speculacõn in theise *Partes* of yᵉ World, with all manner of *Pleasures* that may either delight the Eare, or content yᵉ Eye in them./

There shall be seene the liuely *Figures* & pleasant demonstrations of yᵉ *Driades*, theire *Pastimes*, Natures, quallities and prime derivations./

The nymble *Naides* in their proper Natures, and delightfull pleasures, in and about yᵉ *Springes*, *Fountaines*, and *Waters*./

Nocturnalls of vnexpressable *Figures*; *Visions*, and *Apparitions Figureing deepe Melancholly* and vnusuall Representations./

Pastimes vsed in *Spayne*, called *Joco del Tauro* and *Joco del Cano*./

All manner of *Fightings* of *Wilde Beasts* whatsoeuer can be procured for *Pastime*, Recreation and veiwe. Besides an Infinite nomber of vnexpressed properties of singuler Order & composure.

Meanes to accomadate all the expressed properties are these./

At all Tymes When *Wee* shall stand in neede of Fortie or Fiftie Great Horse to *Ornifie* with high State the *Sceane*, *Historie*, or *Subiect*, A Gentleman his Maiesties Seruant and Commaunder in his *Highnes Stables* will be readie for vs./

Wee haue allso a *Captaine* of *Foote*, and his Officers of Excellent Experience, and direction, readie at all Tymes./

Cornelius the *Dutchman* the *most admired man* of *Christendome* for singuler *Invention* and *Arte* with diuers others of our *Nation*, that will vndertake for our *Sea Fightes, Prospectiues, Nocturnalls, Driades, Naides, Fire, and Water-workes*./

For *Masques* and all other properties belonging to them, *Wee* are allreadie prepared with Admirable Dauncers.

For our seuerall kindes of *Musick*, M.ʳ *Alphonso*, Mʳ *Innocent Laneire*, Mʳ *Bird*, Mʳ *Johnson*, and others great M.ʳˢ in *Musick*./

Gladiators and *Sword* men, good & sufficient store you all knowe./

For all Exercises of the *Olympiades* (being practized) no Nation is better to performe them, for high Courage *Activitie* and Strength./

For *Latine Playes*, the helpe of both the *Vniuersities*, when *Tyme* shall require for the Entertainment of *Princes*, or any *Embassadours* from foraigne *Nations*./

The *English Actors* you knowe Sufficiently./

Consideracõns *for the Vndertakers*, and *all Patentees*./

1. What chardge may buyld the said *Amphitheator* and how soone.
2. How, and by what sufficient, and Excellent *Men*, all seuerall properties may be fitted, and made *Gracefull* according to the former Expressions, and to continew the concourse of *People*, by which money may be still comeing in./
3. As reasonable as may be coniectured what proffitt may arise to the vndertakers to giue them satisfaction./

It is concluded by diuerse and Judicious *Artizans* that haue conferred, and long consulted herein, that ten or Eleauen thousand poundes in *Bancke* may buyld yᵉ said *Amphytheator* strong and faire, and that it is necessarie, to haue two thouzand poundes in *Bancke* when the *House* is buylt to furnish all properties *Gracefull* therevnto belonging.

Wee are alreadie prepared with all *Men* of Excellencie for the vndertakeing of each seuerall *propertie* whatsoeuer.

While the *House* is in buylding, all *Playes* and properties may be prepared, that there may be no Tyme lost, for it is the most pretious thing that belongeth thereunto./

It is desired that all those Gentlemen that resolue to be Vndertakers in this *Busienes* may aduise with the best, and most Learned Councell they can, for the best Assureance of all theire proportions, Shares, and Rates./

Whereas it may be Imagined the chardge wilbe great, to accomodate, and furnish these Showes with properties, and all other materialls, *It* will be so indeed, for some of the first and greatest Showes; But they will, or may be made continew many Yeares after for Exchange of *Sceanes*, and *Subiectes*, being well ordered, and preserued in the *Wardropp*. And thereby saue a great quantitie of money./

There is no Laudable *Way* or course that can deliuer vnto the *Vndertakers*, so easie, so great and so certaine a gaine as this doth offer, When you haue well aduised, and considered therevppon./ It is therefore requisite to hasten theire Accordance and Contractes the sooner. For halfe a yeare Tyme will proue to be the losse of asmuch money as will buyld the whole *House*, Which materiall *Pointe*, I could wishe that euery *Vndertaker* would well consider of./

This extraordinary document raises a crop of fascinating and important questions. In the present paper I cannot hope to do more than touch briefly on a few of them.

First, of course, the *idea* of an amphitheatre with gladiatorial combats, fights with wild beasts, *naumachia*, and the like, reflects the time's desire to emulate the greatness of Rome, as the plan for tragedies and Olympiads shows the admiration for Greece. The detailed antiquarian treatise, Lipsius *de Amphitheatris*, with its impressive and lively plates, was widely read; and every traveller to the Continent felt he must see the classical amphitheatre of Verona and especially the Roman Coliseum, no matter what Gothic masterpieces he missed. Tom Coryat waxes enthusiastic in his description of the grand structure at Verona. Reckoning in the marble for the seats, he estimates its cost as that of twenty English cathedral churches.

The Veronese circus held about 24,000 spectators. "King James his Amphitheatre" was to accommodate at least half that number, 12,000. This comparison may give a rough idea of its size. The oval arena enclosed by the building must have been planned large enough to allow for lists for the tilt, for the evolutions of a respectable body of infantry, for the mock cavalry fight of the *juego de cañas*, for the free manœuvres of the Spanish bull-fight or *corrida*, and for the running track for Olympic races, not forgetting room sufficient to show the paces of a troop of fifty 'great horse'. I shall not venture an estimate of the dimensions, but they must have been considerable.

As to the cost of the fabric, it is estimated at £10,000 or £11,000 in 1620. By 1634, as we shall see, this figure had risen to £12,000: a building charge, in round numbers, of a pound a seat. This works out not far from the relative cost of the Second Globe and the Fortune, though the latter were not "all of brick and stone". Nothing is said of the proposed prices of admission to the amphitheatre, or of the frequency of performances, though the projector fancies he could show a profit of £11,000 in half a year. But the request for a restraint on all plays and shows for one day in every week hardly reflects supreme confidence in meeting open competition. Nevertheless, the very fact that they planned to accommodate so huge a crowd is impressive.

Does not 12,000 for Jacobean London represent a far larger slice of the population than a full house at Wembley takes from the London of to-day?

Leaving aside the arrangements for the horses, the cavalrymen, the infantry, the rope-dancers, the animal fights, sham battles, the athletes, and the well-known London gladiators or swordsmen, let us come to the technical scenic side of the proposed spectacles and plays. Here the projectors say that for their "Sea Fightes, Prospectiues, Nocturnalls, Driades, Naides, Fire, and Water-workes" they have secured the skill of divers unnamed Englishmen, but principally that of "Cornelius the Dutchman the most admired man of Christendome for singuler Invention and Arte"—to wit, the celebrated Cornelis Drebbel of Alkmaar (1572–1633), scientist, inventor, and mechanical engineer, a favourite with King James, in whose service he had spent a number of years. His latest employment had been in Bohemia as tutor to the Emperor's son, which had ended disastrously on the capture of Prague by Frederick V. Stripped and imprisoned, Drebbel was freed to return to England only at the personal request of King James, in this very year 1620. Doubtless the projectors made a flattering offer to secure his services (possibly also by an application to the King), and certainly his genius and amazing skill were for them a cardinal acquisition.

Music too was an essential. The impresarios claimed to have engaged a number of the greatest composers and masters: William Byrd, Alphonso Ferrabosco, Edward Johnson,[6] Innocent Lanier, and others.

Clearly, some of the performances were to be at night. The splendour of the dresses and changing scenes of masques, the glamour of 'nocturnals', 'visions', and 'apparitions'—these could never endure the flat light of day, any more than could the fireworks, the simulated sea-fights, or the (doubtless illuminated) waterworks, to say nothing of the dryads and naiads. Further, scenic masques and 'prospectives' can be viewed properly from one side only, which would reduce the possible audience to a mere 6000 or even less.

Most important to us, and indeed the *Imprimis* of the prospectus, is the announcement of "Tragedies, Comedies, and Histories". The projectors had evidently come to terms with one of the best companies: probably (since this was to be King James's Amphitheatre) the King's Men of Heminges and Condell—"the English Actors you knowe Sufficiently". How frequently stage-plays were to be given in the arena is not revealed. As for the audience, perhaps somewhat more than half the encircling 12,000 seats would command a view of platform and inner-stage.

Of those who dealt with the matter, including King James and Lord Coventry, no one seems to have anticipated any difficulty in 'putting across' regular plays to such far-flung and high-banked rings of auditors. This fact is important testimony as to the *kind* of acting which Shakespeare knew and practised. With witchcraft of his wit, the late Harley Granville-Barker strove to make us believe that something very like the modern, intimate, 'interpretative' style of acting was developed under Shakespeare. Yet here we see Shakespeare's own company, or a rival, bespoken to act his plays or those of his fellow-dramatists in a great open-air amphitheatre before an audience perhaps twice or three times the size of the largest houses at the Globe or the Fortune. Under such conditions not even a Granville-Barker could find room for slight gesture, subtle facial expression, or the nuances of conversational tone. At the amphitheatre, acting would have had to be a simplification and an emphasis of what I take to be the standard Elizabethan style: large unmistakable gesture and declamatory tone, with a minimum of reliance upon facial expression. What is more, plays for the amphitheatre in Latin, though given for smaller and more select audiences chiefly to entertain ambassadors and their retinues, would unquestionably demand of the actor large effects and strong delivery, the rather as the English pronunciation of the language (with diphthongized *i*, for example) differed markedly from that current on the Continent.

Despite all these far-reaching plans and preparations, in which, we must remember, Captain Robert Hasell was a prime mover, we have seen that nothing was brought to fruition under James. As Collier discovered, in the second year of Charles's reign the projectors tried again, and again failed to carry their grant as far as the great seal. But it has not been known upon what powerful ally Williams and Dixon leaned to press this second attempt. We now find a copy of their new "Licence to build an Amphitheatre", dated 7 July 1626, preserved among the State Papers,[7] bearing the forbidding memorandum 'Stayed'. It is similar to the King James grant, but carries at the end the notes following: "...his Majesties pleasure signified by Mr Alisbury Subscribed by Mr Attorney generall Procured by Mr Endymion Porter."

Evidently the influential courtier who obtained Charles's authorization for building the amphitheatre was the King's companion and personal agent Endymion Porter, a patron of poets who counted among his friends Shakespeare's testamentary overseer Thomas Russell and Sir William Davenant. This is a significant discovery. Yet in spite of his Majesty's pleasure and Porter's recommendation, Lord Coventry ruled that it was "unfit the grant for the Amphitheator should passe", and it did not pass.

Nevertheless, the project was not allowed to die. It has been observed that in 1631, five years after this second rebuff, Shackerley Marmion's *Holland's Leaguer* (II, iii) carries a lively reference:

> Twill dead all my device in making matches,
> My plots of architecture, and erecting
> New amphitheatres to draw custom
> From playhouses once a week, and so pull
> A curse upon my head from the poor scoundrels.[8]

We now come to the discovery of two further attempts to put the amphitheatre scheme through. The first of these is a petition of Williams and Dixon to the King, dated 1634,[9] which runs as follows:

It hath formerly pleased your most graceous father of blessed memory to grant licence unto your Majesties servants John Williams and Thomas Dixon Sergeants at armes for recompence, and reward of theire longe service to build an Amphitheatre on some convenient peice of ground nere to the Citty of London for presenting many noble, and worthy exercises mencioned therin

And uppon your petitioners humble suite your Majestie hath beene likewise pleased to signe another bill to Confirme the said graunt but with some few words of alteracion which hath alsoe passed your Majesties Royall Signature.

In which bill there is nothinge desired (as wee can iudge) but may bee conveniently permitted in this kingdome by reason of many such like propertyes are dayly practised by others albeit wantinge the grace, and excellency by us intended.

These three followinge reasons (as wee conceave) may be motives for the furtherance of his Majesties graunts to the petitioners

The chardge of the purchase of the ground	— 1500[li]
The house or Amphitheator	—12000
The rent per Annum duringe the time of the graunt	40[s]

[1] Profitt to the Crowne

After the expiracion of the terme to be left fully, and wholy to the Crowne for ever/

[2] Honor to the Kingdome

In all Christendome is not now in use any place soe prepared to accommodate soe many variable, and delightefull recreations and speculacions as this Amphitheator may afford, for the entertainment of Princes Embassadors or strangers of any forraine nation which will be a graceous ornament to the Citty honor to the Kingdome and Content to honourable natives and others

[3] Benefitt to the Commonwealth

The excercises in that place may quickly enable the nobler sorte of gentry and others to many excellent, and lawdable services of theire prince and Cuntry: withdrawe many licentious, and unlimited disposicions, from drunknes lacivousnes, and such base or unworthy inclinations. Besides it may bee an occasion to embusy divers private consultacions and Conventickles, with matters of pleasant levitye, and s[p]eculacions A pollecy oftentymes permitted in the beste, and most flowrishinge Commonwealthes

Latyne Scœnes also beinge presented for forrayne intertainmentes there wilbe demonstrated the delicacy of nature [?nurture] and educacion of gentlemen students in the universities whereby choise may be made of the most ingenious schollers, and pregnant disposicions for the service, and attendancy, peeres, or Cuntry [sic]

By meanes also of the excercises of the Olimpiads may bee perfected, and enabled many tryalls for honourable Cumbattes single, or otherwise so to renew the auncient, and honourable reputacion of his Majesties Kingdome that were never formerly inferiour to any other Kingdomes, or nations of the world for activity, courage and strength.

This house beinge magnificen[t]ly built to accomodate a number of excellent propertyes, and inventions to entertaine Princes Embassadors Strangers, and honourable Natives and Subiects

It is therfore most humbly desired that the said Amphitheator may be dedicated to the memorable honor of the Queens most excellent Majestie, for it hath beene the auncient custome of greate Princes to be honored with the memory of sumptuous buildinges bridges Colledges and such like.

This house likewise will save his Majestie much money in entertaynment of princes Embassadors or Strangers for this place may content them with many convenient and pleasant accomodacions

Among these persuasive 'motives' for the King, besides the bribe of future ownership of the structure, the relief to the great expenses of entertainment, which were raising deep growls in the Commons, the flattery of naming it "Queen Henrietta Maria's Amphitheatre", and the appeal to national pride, we perceive the notion of an academy again slyly insinuated. The "excercises...may quickly enable the nobler sorte of gentry and others to many excellent, and lawdable services", and 'Colledges' have been named for princes. Further, the provision of plays, circene games, and 'speculations' is put forward as a deft move of policy to distract and "embusy divers private consultacions and Conventickles". Within a few years the latter were to swell the storm of revolution that blasted Charles off his throne.

The latest document on the Amphitheatre which I have been able to discover is another petition.[10] It is undated, but it mentions Dixon as dead. Four new projectors are joined with the 'very aged' Williams, among them Captain Robert Hasell, and they ask to have their names inserted as grantees:

To the Kinges most Excelent Majestie

The humble peticion of Sir Richard Young knight and baronet Sir Richard Darley knt Henry Murrey esq: attending his Majestie in his bedd Chamber John Willyams gent: And Capten Robert Hasell the first Inventor and profeser of the busines of the Amphitheater

Sheweth

That whereas your Roiall father of Blessed Memorie was plesed to grant leave unto John Willyams and Thomas Dixon, in recompence of their longe and faithfull service to build an Amphitheatre in or nere unto the City of London to present therin many Heroique & Maiestick recreations as in the sayd grant is mentioned. And that it hath bene likewise plesing to your gracious and princely goodnes to confirme the said grant admitting some fewe wordes of alteracion, as appereth by two grantes alredy passed the roiall Signature: And wheras Thomas Dixon one of the grantees is lately decessed, and the other very aged Your petiticioners moste humbly pray that this being a busines of so plesant, and famous a conscequence That it may not perish or fall for want of able and carefull prosecution: That your Majestie would be so graceously plesed as to grant that your petitioners may be Joyned in your Majesties grant with the Surviving John Willyams for the building of the said Amphitheatre and for the better strengthning and expeditinge therof, who have allso with chardge, and humble patience longe expected the same, and prepared their good frendes with great summs of money for the building therof & fittinge many other necessarie accomodacions therunto belonginge. Humbly allso beseching (your roiall Majestie) would be so graceously plesed to give orderes to the right honorable the Lord Keper, the Lord Chamberlaine of your Majesties house and the Secretarie Windebanke, that they three, or any twoe of them, To take their twoe grantes into their honorable Consideracions and to passe one of the twoe bookes immediately, which of them shall seme moste fittinge to their honorable Wisdomes

And your petitioners shall ever pray &c.

Here for the first time we find the projectors asserting that they have gone to expense in their preparations, and that their friends are ready with capital: though how much of the requisite grand total of £15,500 is in hand or promised they do not offer to say. And also for the first time they beg Charles to *order* his ministers to pass a patent at once.

Three of the new projectors (like Endymion Porter) are courtiers and Grooms of the Bedchamber—Sir Richard Young, Sir Richard Darley, and Henry Murrey. Charles must have recalled that Young once heroically rescued his royal father from drowning. On 9 January 1621/2, "his Majestie...ryding on horseback abroad, his horse stumbled and cast his Majestie into the New River, where the ice broke; he fell in so that nothing but his boots were seene. Sir Richard Yong was next, who alighted, went into the water, and lifted him out."[11] Young was a Londoner, Darley a Yorkshireman, and Murrey doubtless a Scot—a trio representative of the main regions of the United Kingdom. With them they joined (as Williams and Dixon had not done before) the amphitheatrical inventor and professor Captain Robert Hasell, and carried along the ancient Williams. For how many years more they continued to hope for a patent we cannot tell; but the subject survived into the Restoration to give point to the joke which Davenant wrote into the fourth act of *The Man's the Master* (? 1668):

Tis great pity there is not some Amphitheatre; built at the publicke charge of Butchers, for the honorable exercise of cutting men's throats.

What we need now is to turn up the architect's drawings for the London amphitheatre, complete with dimensions, and also to lay our hands on more facts about Captain Robert Hasell. But let us not be ungrateful. Already our discoveries have thrown a broad searchlight beam on this imperial castle in the air over Lincoln's Inn Fields.

Though the amphitheatre was to begin as a private enterprise, to review its scope is to see it as an unparalleled National Entertainment Centre, planned immediately after the death of Shakespeare, in the year in which the tiny *Mayflower* toiled westward with her freight of Pilgrim Fathers. This marvellous institution was to provide everything imaginable—West End drama by professionals, and on occasion Latin plays by University amateurs; Sadler's Wells (masque, dancing); cinema ("prospectives, visions, apparitions"); Covent Garden (under Endymion Porter's friend Davenant, opera would be taken in stride); Albert Hall concerts (instruments, voices); Aldershot Tattoo (martial exercises, sham battles); Greenwich Naval Pageant (sea-fights); Wembley (Olympic games); Watercade (naiads, waterworks); White City (prize fights); Olympia (horse shows, manège, circus acts); with fireworks, pageants, and how much more, not forgetting bear-baiting and bull-fights which now are forbidden! A monopolist's dream; even to-day, after three centuries of progress, "in all Christendom is not now in use any place so prepared to accommodate so many variable and delightful recreations and speculations".

NOTES

1. Misread by Collier as 28 September.

2. P.S.O. 2/44/14.

3. Camden, quoted in Nichols, *Progresses of James I*, III, 660.

4. For Gerbier's final effort in this direction under the Interregnum, see my *Commonwealth and Restoration Stage* (1928).

5. Bodl. MS. Tanner 89, f. 58. First printed, with the prospectus attached, by 'G.E.P.A.' in *Notes and Queries*, *loc. cit.*

6. 'G.E.P.A.' thought this Johnson was the lutanist Robert. He is far more likely to have been the composer Edward Johnson.

7. S.P. 38/13/180ᵛ.

8. Fleay (*Biographical Chronicle of the English Drama*, II, 66) makes the interesting suggestion that Marmion's rascally cheats Agurtes (ἀγυρτης, gatherer, collector; hence vagabond, mountebank, cheat) and Autolichus are satirical portraits of the projectors Williams and Dixon.

9. S.P. 16/281/44. I owe this find to the alert skill of my friend Miss Nellie O'Farrell.

10. Gibson Papers. MS. Lambeth 930, f. 131.

11. Mr Joseph Meade, quoted in Nichols, *Progresses of James I*, III, 749.

BEN JONSON AND *JULIUS CAESAR*

BY

J. DOVER WILSON

If we neglect *Titus Andronicus* as pseudo-classical, and only his by adoption and not by grace (of which it has little enough), *Julius Caesar* was Shakespeare's earliest attempt to try his fortune in the perilous arena of Roman tragedy. And a very bold attempt it was, made by a man equipped with but 'small Latin', under the keenly censorious eye of a learned friend alert for every slip or sign of weakness, to say nothing of a learned enemy, as many suppose Chapman to have been.

When the play was produced in the autumn of 1599 the friendship was probably little more than a year old; for in 1598 Ben Jonson's *Every Man in his Humour* had been performed by the Chamberlain's Company, with Shakespeare taking part; and it was Shakespeare who, according to a story which Rowe reports, had "by a remarkable piece of humanity and good nature" introduced the still comparatively unknown dramatist to his fellow-actors and induced them to accept the play.[1] "After this", Rowe continues, "they were professed friends, though I don't know whether the other ever made him an equal return of gentleness and sincerity." Rowe appears to have momentarily forgotten the magnificent *laudatio* which Jonson wrote for the posthumous edition of his 'beloved' friend's plays; but it cannot be denied that his immediate 'return' was rather sincere than gentle. In his next play, *Every Man out of his Humour*, performed in 1599, once again by Shakespeare's fellows, he mocks, not necessarily ill-naturedly, at two passages from *Julius Caesar*. First, in act 3 scene 4, a couple of coxcombs, Clove and Orange, talk 'fustian' philosophy together in the hearing of others to "make 'hem believe we are great scholars"; one of their scraps of spurious Aristotelianism being "Reason long since is fled to animals, you know", which is a patent fling at Antony's

> O judgment! thou art fled to brutish beasts,
> And men have lost their reason;

and, whether of malice prepense, or as I prefer to think because he missed Shakespeare's point, quoted out of its context as a serious 'philosophical' (that is to say scientific) observation. But Shakespeare was as learned as Jonson or anyone else in the science of his day and put it to better use in his plays than most dramatists. Antony's exclamation makes excellent sense when taken in its context and considered in relation to beast-lore. The best commentary on it is Hamlet's exclamation in the first soliloquy:

> O God! a beast, that wants discourse of reason,
> Would have mourned longer.

This proves that Shakespeare was well aware of the Aristotelian doctrine which ascribed the God-given faculty of reason and judgment to man alone;[2] but shows him equally aware that, despite this doctrine, beasts seemed capable of compassion, which was generally regarded as

36

one of the highest manifestations of reason. For as Anne remarks to the inhuman Richard Crookback:

> No beast so fierce but knows some touch of pity.[3]

It is just this paradox, this contradiction between scientific theory and a matter of common observation, that Antony has in mind, since like Hamlet and Lady Anne he too is referring to compassion. The passage begins:

> You all did love him once, not without cause.
> What cause withholds you then to mourn for him?

The exclamation follows naturally thereafter; and is itself followed by a moment or two's silence as Antony gives way to grief; while, when later he succeeds in moving the crowd to compassion, he returns to the same theme:

> O, now you weep and I perceive you feel
> The dint of pity: these are gracious drops.

But Jonson ignored all this, took the words out of their context and held them up to ridicule as 'fustian philosophy'. Yet it is not to be supposed that Shakespeare was without his defenders, even if he did not defend himself in one of those 'wit-combats' Fuller speaks of. And that the passage became the talk of the town is suggested by an echo of Jonson's gibe which appears in an anonymous play *The Wisdom of Dr Dodipoll* (pub. 1600), and runs "then reason's fled to animals, I see".[4]

Aristotelian psychology being long since out of date, this first of Jonson's jests is more obscure to us than it would have been to his contemporaries. His second no one can miss. In act 5 scene 6 of the same play, when Sir Puntarvolo, after beating the scurrilous Carlo Buffone to put him "out of his humour", proceeds to seal up his lips with wax, the victim's last pitiful cry is "Et tu Brute!" which he addresses to his friend Macilente who treacherously holds the candle for the execution of Puntarvolo's vengeance. And that the use of this tag was at once a good stage joke and a thrust at Shakespeare's ignorance is suggested by Dr Simpson, who notes that "Jonson, who knew his Suetonius, would be aware that what the dying Caesar said was something different",[5] and something moreover in Greek not in Latin.

Yet while Ben could mock at Shakespeare's history and 'philosophy' he was not above picking up a 'philosophical' crumb of the latter from under his table. When Shakespeare makes Antony say of the dead Brutus:

> His life was gentle, and the elements
> So mixed in him that Nature might stand up
> And say to all the world 'This was a man!'—

he drew upon the Galenic physiology, still orthodox in his day, which, based upon the notion that the life of man doth, as Sir Toby puts it, "consist of the four elements" (viz. earth, water, air and fire), declared that health, bodily and spiritual, depended upon a balance between them. Jonson avails himself of the same conception in the following description of Crites, a character in *Cynthia's Revels* (acted 1600), wherein he draws a picture of his ideal man and does not hesitate to give him features strongly reminiscent of his own:

A creature of a most perfect and divine temper. One in whom the humours and elements are peaceably met, without emulation of precedency: he is neither too fantastically melancholy, too slowly phlegmatic, too lightly sanguine, or too rashly choleric, but in all so composed and ordered, as it is clear Nature went about some full work, she did more than make a man when she made him.[6]

A commonplace of the age, implying no borrowing from either side, it may be said, while it may be argued that so far from the initial impetus coming from Shakespeare the lines just quoted from *Julius Caesar* were probably themselves inspired by *Every Man in his Humour*. Yet even if this last be true the wording of the eulogy on Crites is so similar to that of Antony's on Brutus, that an echo can hardly be questioned. And while Jonson echoed Shakespeare, Drayton in turn echoed both in the following stanza from the 1603 edition of *The Barons' Wars* in praise of Mortimer:

> He was a man, then boldly dare to say,
> In whose rich soul the virtues well did suit,
> In whom, so mixed, the elements all lay
> That none to one could sovereignty impute,
> As all did govern, yet all did obey;
> He of a temper was so absolute
> As that it seemed, when Nature him began,
> She meant to show all that might be in man.[7]

Here lines 4 and 5 clearly derive from Jonson's "without emulation of precedency", while "so mixed, the elements", a form of words Jonson does not use, seems with equal probability to point back to Shakespeare.

Finally, there is yet a fourth passage in *Julius Caesar* associated with Jonson and better known for being so than any of those already cited; a passage interesting, moreover, as affording in the opinion of many the only known instance in the Folio of an alteration made in deference to literary criticism. It forms the concluding portion of Caesar's speech rejecting the petition of the kneeling Metellus Cimber just before the assassination and runs as follows in the text as it has come down to us:

> Thy brother by decree is banished:
> If thou dost bend and pray and fawn for him,
> I spurn thee like a cur out of my way.
> Know Caesar doth not wrong, nor without cause
> Will he be satisfied.

And here is Jonson's comment which forms part of his reply, first printed in *Discoveries* (1640), to the players' boast that Shakespeare "never blotted out line":

His wit was in his own power; would the rule of it had been so too. Many times he fell into those things could not escape laughter: as when he said in the person of Caesar, one speaking to him: "Caesar thou dost me wrong"—he replied: "Caesar did never wrong, but with just cause", and such like, which were ridiculous.[8]

As thus quoted Caesar's words, though undoubtedly referring to the same situation, correspond with those of the Folio text neither in phrase nor in meaning. We are therefore faced with an alternative: either, as Steevens who first drew attention to the criticism supposed, Jonson "quoted the line unfaithfully" in order to ridicule Shakespeare, or, as Tyrwhitt suggested in reply to Steevens, "the players or perhaps Shakespeare himself, overawed by so great an authority, withdrew the words in question".[9] Steevens's explanation has found favour with good critics like Aldis Wright[10] and Mark Hunter,[11] who agree that but for Jonson's comment "no one would have suspected any corruption in the passage", a contention I find difficult to rebut, though some feel that the last line and a half in the Folio version follow those before with a certain inconsequence. Yet I am confident that Tyrwhitt offers the true interpretation and for three reasons.

First, any idea that Jonson invented out of sheer malice the line he criticizes seems to me quite incredible. Even if we accept in full and without question Drummond's well-known description of him as "a contemner and scorner of others, given rather to lose a friend than a jest",[12] that only means that he enjoyed retailing scandal or making unkind jokes at his friends' expense, not that he would go to the length first of concocting an absurdity and then of falsely attributing it to a fellow-dramatist in order to lampoon him. Such a piece of mean treachery is irreconcilable both with what we know of Jonson's frank if splenetic character and with the admiration and affection which breathe from the lines to Shakespeare already spoken of. As for the other two reasons, they would be valid whatever views we hold about him, since they are inescapable inferences from indisputable dates.

The criticism, I have said, is to be found in Jonson's *Discoveries*, a posthumous publication but compiled for the most part between 1626 and his death in 1637,[13] that is to say after the publication of the First Folio in 1623. Is it really conceivable that Jonson proposed to pass this absurdity off as Shakespeare's when the story could be checked and confuted by a simple reference to the printed text, a text moreover for which he had himself written two sets of commendatory verses? To do so would be to court instant exposure as a lying traducer, an exposure the more certain that, as he was aware, the dead Shakespeare had energetic partisans among literary men. One of these was Leonard Digges, who, having in his lines for the First Folio named *Julius Caesar* as unequalled among contemporary dramas, made the point still more explicit in an expanded version of these, printed a generation later, as follows:

> So I have seen, when *Caesar* would appear,
> And on the stage at half-sword parley were
> Brutus and Cassius, oh how the audience
> Were ravished, with what wonder they went thence;
> When some new day they would not brooke a line
> Of tedious, though well-laboured, *Catiline*;[14]

and so on, comparing play with play of the two authors and ever in Jonson's disfavour. This appeared in 1640, when Jonson too was dead; but it shows what some had long thought, and what Jonson must have known they thought.

The third reason is, I think, more cogent still. That the line as quoted in *Discoveries* was, at least in general tenor, well known to the theatre public is proved by its appearance in one of Jonson's plays; and, as with "O judgment, thou art fled to brutish beasts", he puts it in the mouth of a character to raise a laugh. The play is *The Staple of News*, first acted "by His Majesty's Servants" in 1626 and the allusion, which occurs in the Induction, is thus printed in the 1631 text:[15]

> EXPECTATION. *I can doe that too, if I haue cause.*
>
> PROLOGUE. *Cry you mercy*, you neuer did wrong, but with iust cause.

The difference of type shows that a quotation was intended, and there can be no doubt that the audience was expected to recognize it as such. It must have been a pretty familiar quotation too, since source and author are not even hinted at. And yet in 1626 *Julius Caesar* was already twenty-seven years old. The lines cited above from Digges explain the mystery. *Julius Caesar* retained its hold on the affections of playgoers long after its original production; and though our very imperfect theatrical records give no trace of a revival at the beginning of Charles I's reign, the allusion in *The Staple of News* is itself strong evidence that in 1626 Caesar's words were fresh in mind, that is to say had been recently heard on the stage; the same stage, for both plays belonged to the King's men. In face of all this, to contend that

> Caesar did never wrong, but with just cause

was a distortion of Shakespeare's meaning on Jonson's part not merely does wrong to Jonson's memory, it does a wrong for which no cause whatever can be shown. In other words, Shakespeare must have written what Jonson reports or something very like it, and what he wrote must have remained in the prompt-book and been spoken by the player taking Caesar's part at least three years after the other version had appeared in the First Folio.

It remains to inquire why the change was made, what precisely the change was, and who made it. None of these questions can of course be answered with absolute certainty, but one or two probabilities may be ventilated. As to the last, some have jumped to the conclusion that the change was made by Jonson himself, whose commendatory verses in the Folio suggest that he might have had a hand in the preparation of its text. If this means that *Julius Caesar*, in copy or proof, was passed on to him for correction as a classical expert, the supposition is disproved by the presence in the revised text of many other features which he would have considered solecisms and have amended, a glaring instance being the Italian form given to some of the Latin names. If, on the other hand, it means that the scribe who prepared the copy for the printer made the change at Jonson's instigation or in deference to his condemnation of the passage, that seems very probable, and is as far as we are likely to get with the answers to the first and the third questions. It is even possible that he asked Jonson to rewrite it for him, since it is hard to believe that a mere scribe invented the Folio reading. Tyrwhitt, it is true, suggested in 1766 that what originally stood in Shakespeare's manuscript was:

> Know, Caesar doth not wrong, but with just cause;
> Nor without cause will he be satisfied;

a reconstruction which ingeniously combines the meaning that Jonson recollected with the words of the Folio text; and if this be right then any scribe might have made the change by simply deleting four words. Tyrwhitt's solution, however, involves two difficulties: first, it implies that Jonson's verbal memory, well known for its accuracy, was less precise than usual; secondly, the line as he recollected it is so manifestly superior to the line and a half of Tyrwhitt's reconstruction that it is hard to believe the recollection anything but exact.

The first critic to bring out this last point, as far as I know, was the late John Palmer in 1945. He noted that the words

Nor without cause will he be satisfied,

which belong to the text both of Tyrwhitt and of the Folio, and imply that Caesar "might be satisfied if cause were shown", make a very lame conclusion to a speech the whole tenor of which is that the decree of banishment is irrevocable, and seems quite inconsistent with "constant as the northern star" in the speech that follows. On the other hand, Jonson's single line,

Caesar did never wrong, but with just cause,

is "dramatic, significant and in character". Its very isolation and abruptness give it just that hint of menace and air of inflexible finality which the end of such a speech demands. "It is Shakespeare's finishing touch to the portrait of a dictator. It is the last, if it be not also the first, assumption of the man who lives for power that the wrong he does is right."[16] I am of course aware that 'wrong' does not necessarily mean wrongdoing in Shakespeare, though Jonson evidently assumed it did, and that the line might be interpreted "Caesar never punished a man unjustly". The sense Palmer places upon it seems, however, the more likely because dramatically the richer; or Shakespeare, as often elsewhere, may have deliberately used an ambiguous word to allow his audience a choice of meanings. Anyhow, in neither case is the meaning the least 'ridiculous'. As with "O judgment, thou art fled to brutish beasts", Jonson has taken the passage as a logical or philosophical proposition without reference to context or character.

And that, I think, explains a point which Palmer has not squarely faced: the protest "Caesar, thou dost me wrong" which Jonson reports as the occasion of Caesar's contemptuous reply. Some critics have given it to Metellus Cimber and made the dialogue run:

> *Caesar*: ...I spurn thee like a cur out of my way.
> *Metellus*: Caesar, thou dost me wrong.
> *Caesar*: Caesar did never wrong but with just cause
> *Metellus*: Is there no voice....

But that, by associating 'wrong' with 'spurn' etc., would empty Caesar's line of its larger dramatic significance, to say nothing of degrading it from its position as an exceedingly effective close to the preceding speech. Moreover, as Aldis Wright objects, "for Metellus to interrupt Caesar with the petulant exclamation...is out of character with the tone of his speeches before and after, which is that of abject flattery". Take it how you will, such a protest cannot be fitted into the context. Yet what is there surprising in this? Is it inconsistent to suppose that Jonson's memory, so clear as to Caesar's 'ridiculous' words, was vague about the dramatic occasion on which they are used? His highly critical intelligence, prejudiced against the play directly he learnt that Shakespeare was attempting a theme so far, as he considered, out of his element, seized upon anything he could quote or laugh at as absurdities and paid little or no attention to the context, in which he was not interested. In the *Discoveries*, however, some kind of peg for the quotation was necessary and what he supplied was harmless and good enough for the purpose.

That we should have four instances of Jonson criticizing this one play, and that the criticisms should extend over a period of twenty-five years or more, suggest something of an *idée fixe*. It was Sidney Lee's belief that the famous 'purge' which according to *The Return from Parnassus*

41

Shakespeare had administered to Jonson was the writing of *Julius Caesar* in which he "proved his command of topics...peculiarly suited to Jonson's classicised vein and had in fact outrun his churlish comrade on his own ground".[17] However that may be, a play on such a theme by one who was no scholar could hardly have been anything but a standing offence in his eyes. That it brought throngs to the theatre would not surprise him; he knew the 'barbarism' of the London public. And when it continued to do so after he had shown in *Sejanus* and *Catiline* how plays on classical themes, based on the original historical sources not on some English translation of a French translation of Plutarch's *Lives*, ought to be written, he could console himself with

> Art hath an enemy called Ignorance.[18]

But when the players insisted on praising their Shakespeare for the wrong things he was bound to speak out. That he "never blotted out line" was the man's weakness; how much better the plays might have been had "he blotted a thousand", as anyone who knew his Horace[19] could have told them. And this, he protested, and honestly protested, was not malevolence on his part but sound criticism. Even to speak of it as "ridiculously patronising"[20] is unfair. After all, did not Matthew Arnold criticize Wordsworth and Shelley and Keats in much the same fashion and much the same spirit? Poets are apt to misapprehend each other, especially when they belong to the same period. The very brightness of their genius blinds them to the peculiar excellences of a genius differing from their own. Certainly Jonson quite failed to understand Shakespeare; his praise of him in the First Folio proves that. He even missed the point of the passages he picked out for laughter or censure in *Julius Caesar*. Misunderstanding, however, does not quite account for all. There was rancour in the cup; the unconscious realization by a proud spirit of another's superiority. Jonson won a great place for himself, a great following, and he deserved them.[21] But it was his fate to live from beginning to end of his career in the shadow of one by whom his genius was

> rebuked, as it is said
> Mark Antony's was by Caesar.

NOTES

1. Rowe does not mention the title of the play in question, but it can hardly have been any but *Every Man in his Humour*. See *Ben Jonson*, ed. Herford and Simpson, I, 18.

2. Cf. *Hamlet*, IV, v, 83–5:

> "poor Ophelia,
> Divided from herself and her fair judgement,
> Without the which we are pictures or mere beasts."

3. *Richard III*, I, ii, 71. See also *Henry VIII*, II, iii, 10; *Titus*, II, iii, 151; *Winter's Tale*, II, iii, 186–9.

4. First noted by E. Koeppel in *Shakespeare Jahrbuch*, XLIII (1907), 210.

5. *Notes and Queries*, 11 February 1899.

6. *Cynthia's Revels*, II, iii, 123 ff. I quote from *Ben Jonson*, IV, 74, modernizing the spelling.

7. Canto III, stanza 40. In her notes on this Mrs Tillotson cites *Julius Caesar*, v, v, 85–7 and adds: "the lines are not in *Mortimeriados* [1596], so there can be no doubt that Drayton is the imitator, and the verse is in fact nearer to its model in 1619 than in 1603. His collaboration in the lost play *Caesars Fall* in 1602 may have made him especially familiar with Shakespeare's play." (*The Works of Michael Drayton* (1941), v, 67.) She does not notice the link with *Cynthia's Revels*.

8. *Ben Jonson*, VIII, 583–4 (spelling modernized).

9. See Boswell's *Malone* (1821), XII, 75–6.

10. *Julius Caesar* (Clarendon Press Series), note on III, i, 47–8.

11. *Julius Caesar*, ed. App.D. This edition ("The College Classics", Madras, Srinivasa, Varadachari and Co., 1900), though little known in England, contains a full and interesting commentary, in which the editor's friend Dr Percy Simpson had a large share.

12. See *Ben Jonson*, I, 151.

13. *Ibid.* I, 104.

14. From *Poems: written by Wil. Shakespeare Gent*, 1640 (reprinted in Chambers, *William Shakespeare*, II, 232–4), in which 'Catilines' is misprinted for 'Catiline'. Again I modernize the spelling.

15. *Ben Jonson*, VI, 280.

16. John Palmer, *Political Characters of Shakespeare*, pp. 44–6. Harbage (*As they Liked It*, 1947, p. 83), who also accepts Jonson's version, finds a less sinister meaning in it. He cites "Bassanio's plea to Shylock's judge, 'To do a great right, do a little wrong'", and notes that Shakespeare constantly uses the moral dilemma in an experimental or provocative way.

17. *Life of Shakespeare* (1916), pp. 353–4.

18. *Every Man out of his Humour*, Induction, I, ii, 9.

19. See *De Arte Poetica*, ll. 291–4.

20. Hunter, *op. cit.* p. 390.

21. I do not think these concluding remarks are inconsistent with G. E. Bentley's monumental *Shakespeare & Jonson: Their Reputations in the Seventeenth Century Compared* (University of Chicago Press, 2 vols. 1945), or with his inaugural address, *The Swan of Avon and the Bricklayer of Westminster* (Princetown University), which came to my hand after this article was already in type.

THE BOOKE OF SIR THOMAS MORE
AND ITS PROBLEMS

BY

R. C. BALD

MS. Harley 7368 in the British Museum is the damaged and much revised manuscript of an Elizabethan play bearing the title "The Booke of Sir Thomas More". It is known to have been in the collection of a certain John Murray of London in 1728; thence it passed into the library of the second Earl of Oxford, and with the rest of his manuscripts came into the possession of the nation in 1753. Nearly ninety years later it was first referred to in print in John Payne Collier's edition of Shakespeare, but in 1844 the play was edited for the Shakespeare Society by Alexander Dyce. The manuscript had already suffered from decay, but Dyce's transcript was a careful and reliable one. Since his time not only has the decay progressed but the manuscript has been repaired in a particularly unintelligent fashion. Holes were patched with gummed paper, and the leaves that showed signs of crumbling—six in all—were pasted over on both sides with a semi-opaque tracing paper. As a result Dyce's edition preserves many words and even lines that are no longer legible. Dyce's edition, like Hopkinson's (1902), was a limited one, and not until 1908, with the publication of C. F. Tucker Brooke's *Shakespeare Apocrypha*, did the text become generally accessible. In 1911 a facsimile of the manuscript was included by J. S. Farmer in his series of Tudor Facsimile Texts, and later in the same year the play was edited for the Malone Society by W. W. Greg. Greg's edition is likely to remain the definitive one; not only was the text prepared with exemplary care, but the various hands in the manuscript were first clearly distinguished and the relationship of the revisions to the original text was clarified.

In 1871 Richard Simpson contributed an article to *Notes and Queries* with the title "Are there any extant MSS. in Shakespeare's handwriting?" He answered his own question in the affirmative by citing the revisions in *Sir Thomas More* and by quoting passages from them which had a Shakespearian ring. A year later James Spedding, the editor and biographer of Bacon, wrote in support of Simpson, but pointed out that the passages which Simpson had cited were not all in the same handwriting and presumably not all by the same author. Thereafter no great progress was made in the discussion of Shakespeare's possible share in the play until 1916, when the former Director of the British Museum, Sir Edward Maunde Thompson, fresh from the writing of the chapter on handwriting for *Shakespeare's England*, turned his attention to the play. In his *Shakespeare's Handwriting* he attempted to prove, on palaeographical grounds alone, that the writer of the six authentic signatures of Shakespeare also wrote the three pages of revision in *Sir Thomas More* which are in the hand that Greg had designated by the letter D. His argument immediately aroused great interest; after the appearance of his book and all through the early twenties the correspondence columns of *The Times Literary Supplement* are full of references to the play of *Sir Thomas More*. The case for Shakespeare's authorship was further strengthened in 1923, when a group of scholars joined with Maunde Thompson in a series of essays, collected by A. W. Pollard and entitled *Shakespeare's Hand in 'Sir Thomas More'*, in which every possible argument—palaeographical, 'bibliographical', and literary—on behalf of Shakespeare was elaborated.

It may fairly be said that there was a widespread inclination on the part of scholars and general public alike to be convinced. The manuscript of a scene from a play in Shakespeare's handwriting was something which, for a variety of reasons, they had all desired to see, and the weight of authority to justify their faith was great. Naturally the Baconians demurred at being shown the Stratfordian in the very act of composition, and raised what objections they could. A few others were not convinced, and the part of devil's advocate was played by the acute but erratic S. A. Tannenbaum, whose palpable errors sometimes blinded his opponents to his real contributions to the discussion. Controversy, often heated, raged till about 1928. Thereafter the topic showed signs of exhaustion and, with one or two notable exceptions, the next decade produced little of comparable interest to the writings of the previous years. Since 1939 there has been no new contribution to the subject. Lest it should be thought that the issues were left in mid-air, a survey of the whole discussion seemed worth attempting in order to state clearly the real advance in our knowledge of Shakespeare which it achieved.

Unfortunately the three pages in the handwriting claimed to be Shakespeare's cannot be studied in isolation from the rest of the play. Not only is it necessary to have some understanding of the confused state of the manuscript, but other problems, such as the authorship of the other parts of the play, the extent to which it was revised, the date, and the company for which it was written, are all relevant to Shakespeare's possible share in it, and must be considered for the light they may throw on the central problem.

THE MANUSCRIPT

In its original state the manuscript of *Sir Thomas More* probably consisted of sixteen leaves, or eight sheets. It was a fair copy in a single hand occupying thirty-one of the available thirty-two pages, the last being blank. At an early stage in its history, though how early it is impossible to say, it was supplied with a vellum wrapper—a fragment of a thirteenth-century Latin manuscript—on which the title "The Booke of Sir Thomas More" was inscribed in large gothic letters. Signs of drastic revision of the original text are frequent in the manuscript: extensive passages are marked for deletion; at least two, and probably three, leaves have been torn out; and, in all, seven extra leaves as well as two smaller scraps have been inserted at different places. None of these is in the handwriting of the original scribe; no less than five different hands occur in the inserted material. The play has also been censored by Edmund Tilney, Master of the Revels from 1579 to 1610, and contains various deletions and notes in his hand.

The contents of the manuscript as at present bound up may be itemized as follows:

Folios 1 and 2. These two leaves are the early vellum wrapper. They are bound so that the remains of the original Latin text are the right way up, with the result that the title of the play, written in the wide lower margin of one of these pages, is now upside down at the foot of fol. 2*b*.

Folios 3–5 (hand S) are the first three leaves of the play, in the handwriting of the scribe responsible for the original fair copy. Greg designated him S (scribe) in his edition, but later was able to identify him as Anthony Munday.

Except for the first sixteen lines, all of fol. 5*b* is marked for deletion. After fol. 5 at least one, and almost certainly two, leaves were torn out.

Folio 6 (Addition I, hand A). This is a single leaf, written on one side only. It is evidently in the handwriting of the author, since it contains corrections and alterations which were clearly made during composition. In order to get all his material on to one side of the sheet the writer wrote the last seven lines vertically in the left margin. Two passages are marked for deletion.

Greg designated the hand of this page by the letter A. It has since been identified by Tannenbaum as that of Henry Chettle.

This leaf has been bound up in the wrong position. It is intended to replace a deletion much later in the play, on fol. 19*a*.

Folios 7–9 (Addition II) are three inserted leaves to replace the deletions on fol. 5*b* and the missing leaves. They contain three separate scenes (or rather, two scenes and the major portion of a third), and each is in a different hand.

Folio 7*a* (Addition II*a*, hand B). This page contains an enlarged version of a short scene deleted on fol. 5*b*. This writer too has been anxious to crowd all his text on to a single page, and his last two lines are written upwards in the right margin. B has been identified by Tannenbaum as Thomas Heywood but, though the identification has been accepted by a number of competent authorities, it must, pending further evidence, remain uncertain.[1]

Folio 7*b* (Addition II*b*, hand C) contains another complete scene and, at the foot, the opening stage-direction for the following scene, which begins at the top of the next page without any preliminary direction. C, the writer of this page, is nameless, but he has been identified by Greg as the theatrical scribe who wrote the plots of *The Seven Deadly Sins* and *Fortune's Tennis*. There is little doubt that he also wrote the title of the play on the vellum wrapper. Tannenbaum has maintained that C was the dramatist Thomas Kyd, but the identification has not won general acceptance.

Folios 8 *and* 9 (Addition II*c*, hand D) are the three pages (fol. 9*b* is blank) which have been claimed for Shakespeare. Fol. 8*a* begins a new scene without any introductory stage-direction, and the writer has crowded in his concluding words at the foot of fol. 9*a*. The scene does not end here, but continues near the top of fol. 10*a*.

Folios 10 *and* 11 (hand S). The original fair copy again. The first three lines of fol. 10*a* are deleted so that the text will be continuous with the insertion on the previous leaves. Several short speeches in hand B are inserted on fols. 10*a* and 11*a*.

A new scene begins about a quarter of the way down fol. 11*b*, but the whole of it has been deleted. It was probably a long scene and continued throughout the whole of the following leaf, but a leaf has been torn out after fol. 11.

Folio 11* (Addition III, hand C) is a scrap, formerly pasted over the lower part of fol. 11*b*. It contains a single speech of twenty-one lines, and presumably was intended as the opening speech for the scene which begins on fol. 12*a*, but it is not clearly linked with it.

Folios 12 *and* 13 (Addition IV, hands C and E). These four pages seem to represent a revision of the scene which originally occupied fol. 11*b*, the missing leaf, and fol. 14*a*. As far as it is possible to estimate the number of lines involved, the revised version seems to be somewhat shorter than the original one.

C wrote three and a half of the four pages of this addition, but E inserted a few words in the upper part of fol. 13 b and added a closing episode to the scene on the lower half of fol. 13 b. E has been identified as Thomas Dekker.

Folio 14a (hand S). The whole page is marked for deletion; it contains the latter part of the scene replaced by Addition IV.

Folio 14★ (Addition V, hand C) is a scrap similar to fol. 11★, and was formerly pasted over the lower part of fol. 14 a. This scrap, like the other, contains only a single speech (eighteen lines), but eight lines, written vertically in the right margin, partly in the original margin and partly on the margin of the scrap, provide a setting for it, and its own last line links it with the opening words on fol. 14 b.

Folios 14b *and* 15 (hand S). Three pages in Munday's hand.

Folio 16 (Addition VI, hand B) contains an episode to be inserted at the conclusion of a scene which ends in the middle of fol. 17 a. That a passage of fifteen lines on fol. 16 a was deleted by the author during composition is shown by the fact that though the speeches in it are separated by short strokes they have no speakers' names prefixed.

The episode ends near the top of fol. 16 b. Further down on the page appears the original draft of the lines copied by C into the margin of Addition V.

Folios 17–22a (hand S). The rest of the manuscript is in Munday's hand. On fol. 19 a a long passage is deleted and was intended to be replaced by Addition I. On fol. 22 a a passage of nine lines is deleted and is followed immediately by an expanded version, which concludes the play. It is likely that here, at least, Munday in transcribing revised his own work.

On the face of it, the manuscript presents the rather surprising appearance of a play in the autograph of a well-known dramatist which has been rehandled by no less than five different revisers. In his edition of the play Greg pointed out that the error of 'fashis' for 'fashiõ' (l. 1847) was scarcely one which an author would make, and so he regarded hand S as that of a copyist, in spite of the possible example of author's revision on the last page. But the keen ear of E. H. C. Oliphant detected three different styles in the original parts of the play, and he suggested the more reasonable theory that when first written it was the work of more than one author; Munday, as one of the part-authors, had undertaken the responsibility of fitting together the composite material and providing a fair copy.[2] On this hypothesis some at least of the revisers would be revising their own work. Further, if C was a professional theatrical scribe, it followed that the passages in his hand would almost certainly be the work of other men. The number of revisers is thus reduced to four, and, with Munday added, there is no need to suppose that more than five authors were ever concerned with the play. Re-examining the evidence in 1923, Greg decided that "the following conclusions in regard to the additions are at least plausible. A [Chettle, Addition I] is an author revising his own work. B on fol. 7 a [Addition II a] is transcribing with small original additions the work of another writer; on fol. 16 [Addition VI] he is making an addition to a scene originally written by himself....D [Addition II c] is a writer producing an entirely new version of a scene [written by the same author whose work in an earlier scene was revised by B]. E [Dekker, Addition IV] is a writer making an addition to his own revision [transcribed by C] of another man's original scene".[3] It would seem, then, that Munday, Chettle, and B (Heywood?) first collaborated on the play; Dekker may also have done so, or may have come in later as a reviser; D (Shakespeare?) was never anything but a reviser.

It was formerly taken for granted that the extensive revisions were undertaken at the insistence of the Master of the Revels,[4] but Greg first pointed out that this was not necessarily so; they could all have been theatrical revisions. In the margin of fol. 11 b, at the beginning of the deleted scene which has been replaced by Addition IV, occur the almost illegible words: "This must be newe written." The hand is uncertain—possibly B's, according to Greg—but it is not Tilney's, and there is nothing in what remains of the cancelled scene to suggest anything offensive to the censor. The writer is much more likely to have been someone of authority in the theatre who may have been dissatisfied with the original scene.[5] We can also watch B at work in the first scene of Addition II and on fols. 10 a, b and 11 a of the original text. In Addition II a he was merely transcribing the earlier version and inserting speeches for a new character as he went along; in the following pages he was adding further short speeches for the same character. He was, in fact, trying to enliven a series of episodes by adding a comic part for the clown. These revisions at least have no demonstrable relation to Tilney's strictures, and there is no certain evidence that any of the other revisions were so related to them.

As theatrical scribe it was C's function, besides transcribing some of the additions, to fit them all clearly into their places and generally to prepare the manuscript for production. My impression is that C's first task was to transcribe on to a fresh sheet the part of Addition IV which is in his hand (the concluding episode in Dekker's hand was added later, but before the insertion of Addition V); the place of the new matter in the text was adequately indicated by the deletions on fol. 11 b and by the producer's note alongside it: "This must be newe written." Next B inserted the clown's part, some of it on a new leaf (fol. 7) and some of it in the original text. A large cross opposite a deleted scene on fol. 5 b and a similar one on fol. 7 a make the relationship quite clear. These two crosses are probably not C's, but C seems to have recognized the existence of the symbol when he was called on to fit in another group of additions, and to have marked them with a set of symbols following on in series from the one already in use. Addition V is linked to its place in continuation of Addition IV by a cross within a circle, Addition VI to the main text by a cross within a double circle, and Addition I by a double cross.[6] If the evidence of this symbol-series is accepted, two things seem to follow. First, Additions III, which is out of series, and, for reasons to be considered later, II b, and c, belong to a yet later stage of revision. Secondly, the direction apparently added by C at the beginning of Addition V, "Mess/T Goodal", must, since it is enclosed by a surrounding line that also encloses the identifying symbol (a cross within a circle), be genuine, in spite of the charge of forgery that has been brought against it.[7]

It was also C's practice to add any necessary stage-directions or speech-prefixes to the additions he edited, and to link the additions to the main text by means of stage-directions (repeated if necessary) as well as by symbols. A good example of these activities can be seen in connection with Addition VI. On fol. 17 a (original text), in the left margin alongside his cross in a double circle, he has inserted the direction "Enter To the players wth a reward"; at the top of Addition VI (a single leaf in B's hand without any original directions at all) he adds after the identifying symbol, with reference to the same entrance: "Enter A Servingman." Further down the page another necessary direction omitted by the author is inserted: "Enter Moore wth attendants w^t Purss & Mace." There is no exit at the end of the episode, nor has C troubled to supply one.

C's part in the three sections of Addition II is rather more complicated. Fol. 7 a, in B's hand, opens without any entrance, but this presumably is supplied on fol. 5 b, at the point at which the new scene is to be inserted, by a direction added in the left margin by C: "Enter Lincolne Betts williamson Doll." At the end of the first page (and of the scene) C has added: "Manett Clowne." But overleaf begins a new scene, transcribed by C, in which the clown has no part. This scene ends near the foot of the page, and the last two lines contain the opening direction for the next scene, since D's addition, which begins on the following page, contains, like both those of B, no opening direction. C has been carefully through D's three pages, adding one necessary entrance, and frequently altering the speech-prefixes which D, who seems to have lacked a very precise knowledge of the play, has from time to time left deliberately vague.

Addition II replaces the greater part of fol. 5 b and two other leaves, now missing, which followed it. As already explained, Addition II a is the mere rewriting with the insertion of the clown's part of a cancelled scene on fol. 5 b. This cancelled scene is followed by a fragment of another scene in which some apprentices begin playing at cudgels, but this too is deleted. Whether C's direction at the foot of fol. 7 a, "Manett Clowne", means that the clown was originally intended to intervene in the prentices' scene, or whether some other opportunity for his sallies was provided, cannot now be determined; subsequently D was called in to revise the insurrection scene, and the intervening matter has disappeared. But the gap between II a, the scene showing the beginning of the insurrection, and II c, showing its pacification, was bridged by a brief scene, II b, which is made up of reports of its spread and of the measures being taken to quell it. This scene I suspect C, who transcribed it on the verso of the leaf already used by B, salvaged from one of the leaves now missing. The opening lines let us know what had happened in the prentices' scene:

> ther was even now
> a sort of prentises playing at Cudgells
> I did Comaund them to ther m^{rs} howses
> but one of them Backt by the other crew
> wounded me in the forhead wth his Cudgell
> and now I feare me they are gon to Ioine
> wth Lincolne Sherwine and ther dangerous traine.

These lines are cut, partly it may be, as Greg has suggested, to meet the possible objections of the censor, but also, surely, because they contain a reference to an episode already deleted and involve a character who, though he had had a prominent part in the omitted scene, would now appear only in this one brief episode.

In summing up the state of the manuscript Sir Edmund Chambers remarked: "As it stands, the manuscript seems inadequate for prompt-copy. Besides perfecting the insertions, the book-keeper has still to supply a few missing entries and speech-prefixes....In the text itself, many ragged edges have still to be joined."[8] True, in order to help the prompter, C has transferred a few directions in the original text to the left margin, where they would be more prominent.[9] Munday's directions, either centred or at the right of the text, do not stand out very clearly, and one cannot help feeling that a prompter would have been grateful for a few more such repeated directions. The appearance of Goodal's name at the beginning of Addition V suggests that the play had been cast,[10] but when one compares Addition V with Addition III one perceives that C had never properly fitted the latter into its setting. The manuscript could, indeed, have furnished copy for a tidy transcript to serve as a prompt-book, but the evidence seems to show that it was itself in process of being made ready for the prompter. But C never properly finished his job, and the unfinished state of the manuscript suggests that plans for production were abandoned.

The activities of Edmund Tilney are the most puzzling of all the problems of the manuscript. Tilney's bold hand is easily distinguishable, and some at least of his deletion marks can be identified from his habit of adding a marginal cross to the line he put alongside the passages to be omitted. But there are no deletions definitely attributable to him in any of the revisions, or in any of the surviving portions of the original text which have been replaced by revisions. Tilney's attentions were confined to three scenes only. Nearly all the first scene, showing the outrages committed by privileged foreigners on London citizens, is marked for omission; the third scene, in which the Privy Council is discussing grievances against the foreigners, has two passages marked, and "Mend y^{is}" written against the first of them. In the same scene Tilney has in one place altered 'straunger' and in another 'ffrencheman' to 'Lombard'.[11] The other scene to which Tilney objected comes considerably later in the play, and is the one in which Fisher, Bishop of Rochester, and Sir Thomas More demur at signing certain articles submitted to the Council by the King. Amusingly enough, there is no hint in the play as to what the articles were about, and the episode has been made as innocuous as one would imagine it was possible to make it. Nevertheless, the very suggestion of resistance within the Privy Council to the sovereign's wishes seems to have offended Tilney so much that he marked some thirty lines for omission and wrote alongside them "all alter".

The specific passages marked by Tilney for deletion or alteration are not very extensive, amounting in all to about 120 lines, but a note in the margin at the top of the first page demands much more drastic revision: "Leaue out ye insurrection wholy & ye Cause ther off & begin w^t Sr Tho: Moore att ye mayors sessions w^t a reportt afterwards off his good servic don being shriue off Londõ vppo a mutiny Agaynst ye Lũbards only by A shortt reportt & nott otherwise att your own perrilles."[12] This would have allowed the second scene of the play to stand, but would have cut out everything else, including Addition II, up to the conclusion of the insurrection scene—a total of 497 lines—and presumably also the execution scene (sc. vii in Greg's numbering), since there would be no point in showing the rioters at the gallows if it was impossible to portray the events which had led up to their condemnation. This scene is 169 lines long, so Tilney's order would have involved the omission of a total of 666 lines, or over a quarter of the play.

There is no question that the revisions in Addition II do not carry out Tilney's instructions, and for this reason Greg believes that the play was censored after the revisions were made and abandoned because Tilney demanded such radical alterations after the many that had already been made. Sir Edmund Chambers admits the logic of this argument, but wonders at the temerity of the actors in submitting so chaotic a manuscript to the Master of the Revels. He continues:

My impression is that when Tilney had finished with sc. iii he realized that piecemeal reformation of this section of the play was hopeless, and that he then turned back to the first page, and wrote the note "Leaue out ye insurrection wholy...". He did not interfere with the harmless second section of the play, but in sc. x he crossed out the episode of More's resignation.[13]

This is helpful, and may well be a full explanation of what happened, but there is one odd feature of Addition II that has not previously been noticed. In the brief second scene (Addition II *b*) on the two occasions on which the aliens are mentioned they are 'Lombards' (ll. 82 and 104), whereas elsewhere they are, with one exception, either French or Dutch.[14] This discrepancy may merely be due to multiple authorship, though internal evidence seems to suggest that this scene (Addition II b) is by the same author as the earlier council scene (sc. iii)—the very one in which Tilney had altered 'straunger' and 'ffrencheman' to 'Lombard'. In other words, it looks as if either the author or the transcriber was already aware of Tilney's objections to references to any foreigners but Lombards. One is tempted, therefore, to surmise that the play was submitted to Tilney not once, but twice; the first time he made only a few minor deletions in the early scenes, but altered the references to the aliens' nationality, and confined his attention mainly to the scenes on the missing leaves. He might well have objected to the staging of an apprentices' riot, have been dissatisfied with the original handling of the insurrection, and have insisted on seeing that his instructions had been observed in the revisions. So all references to the prentices had to go, and a more skilful dramatist than any of the original collaborators (D) was called in to refurbish the insurrection scene. When the play was re-submitted, Tilney proved, perhaps owing to recent political developments, even more rigorous than he had been on the first occasion, and the actors, in spite of the fact that they had gone so far as to cast the play, decided that it was useless to attempt any further revision. This, admittedly, is almost all pure conjecture, but there is no specific evidence to contradict it. It is at least a possibility, and a possibility more satisfactory than the suggestion that the play was censored unrevised, "laid aside when Tilney sent it back, and taken up later by new writers, with different literary notions from Munday's, in the hope that the political cloud had blown by and that Tilney might now be persuaded to allow the main original structure to stand".[15]

COMPANY AND DATE

The men definitely known to have been connected with *Sir Thomas More* are Munday, Chettle, and Dekker, authors; C, scribe; and Thomas Goodal, actor. Heywood and Shakespeare must also be considered as possible part-authors.

Of the careers of C and Goodal little is known. The plot of *The Seven Deadly Sins*, in C's hand, dates from about 1590. According to Greg, it was written for Strange's men at the Curtain; according to Chambers, for the Admiral's men (or perhaps for a joint company) at the Theatre.[16] C's other extant plot, that of *Fortune's Tennis* was written for the Admiral's men at the Rose about 1597 or 1598. Goodal, whose name appears in the plot of *The Seven Deadly Sins*, was thus a member of the Admiral's or of Strange's men about 1590; he is mentioned as a player in the parish register of St Botolph in 1599, but there is no evidence of the company to which he then belonged.

Munday, Chettle, and Dekker were all members of the needy band of dramatists who did hackwork for Henslowe. Munday's literary career began in 1577, but he is not known as a playwright until a considerably later date. Weight must be given to Miss Byrne's contention that his other occupations probably gave him little time or opportunity for dramatic collaboration between 1588 and 1592,[17] and if we assign a date as early as 1592 or 1593 to his *John a Kent and John a Cumber* (which also survives in an autograph manuscript with a vellum wrapper, part of which came from the same Latin manuscript as that of *More*, and an engrossed title on it in C's hand), Maunde Thompson has argued on palaeographical grounds that *Sir Thomas More* must have been somewhat later.[18] Munday first appears in Henslowe's *Diary* in December 1597, and reappears on and off until December 1602. Chettle made his first appearance as a writer when he brought out Greene's *Groatsworth of Wit* in 1592 and followed it up in the same year with his *Kind Heart's Dream*. He is first heard of as a dramatist in Henslowe's *Diary* under the date 25 February 1598, but his autograph contribution to the manuscript play *John of Bordeaux* may be several years earlier. Chettle was at work for Henslowe with very few breaks from the beginning of 1598 until March 1603. Dekker, a younger man than either of these, also appears in Henslowe's pages for the first time at the beginning of 1598; he may have been writing as early as 1594, but it seems unwise to try to push back his career any further. And Heywood, who was twenty-one and fresh from Cambridge in 1594, published his first tentative effort in verse in that year, but makes his earliest appearance with Henslowe at an uncertain date towards the end of 1596.

The general trend of all this evidence is to suggest that *Sir Thomas More* was written for the Admiral's men, or at least for some company under Henslowe's management, at a date later than 1594, but it leaves unexplained how Shakespeare could have been connected with the play. This difficulty has caused Greg, in his most recent pronouncement, to push the date back to *c.* 1593, when Strange's men, to whom Shakespeare then belonged, were in temporary association or amalgamation with the Admiral's.

In point of fact, almost every possible date between 1586 and 1605 has at one time or other been suggested. The more extreme limits can doubtless be ignored, and it is surely significant that there is no mention of the play in Henslowe's *Diary*. Allusions within the play itself are not very helpful. Disturbances against foreigners, though not on the scale of the insurrection which More is alleged to have pacified, are recorded for the years 1586, 1593, and 1595–6, but one would expect the play to have been written at a discreet interval after, rather than on the heels of, such an outbreak. Ogle the wig-maker, alluded to in lines 1006 and 1148, is first heard of in 1571 and last heard of in 1600; he is "father ogell" in a note of Henslowe dated 10 February 1599/1600, so he was evidently then an old man. Another allusion, "Moore had bin better a Scowrd More ditch" (Addition IV, l. 215) has been taken as a reference to the scouring of Moorditch in May 1595, but it was also cleansed in 1603,[19] and doubtless at other times.

On the strength of such evidence, none of it really conclusive, the general tendency has been to date *Sir Thomas More c.* 1595–6. But it is difficult to ignore an objection raised by G. B. Harrison: if Shakespeare's hand is to be found in the play, the versification of the passages attributed to him is not that of the period of *Richard II*, but of *Julius Caesar* and *Troilus and Cressida*.[20] This argument, admittedly, involves assuming what is to be proved, but one way of testing a hypothesis is to inquire what its acceptance involves. Further, Harrison's evidence is not so rigid as to forbid a certain latitude; as valid a comparison could doubtless be made, say, with the versification of the choruses of *Henry V* as with that of Ulysses' speech on degree, but his general contention for a date *c.* 1600 rather than *c.* 1595 on metrical grounds is well founded.

Harrison's suggestion was followed up and elaborated by D. C. Collins,[21] who pointed out the significance likely to be attached to parts of the play in the period of Essex's rebellion. It is well known how the fall of Essex dashed the hopes of many Englishmen, and lines like these, to which Tilney has objected, almost certainly describe a widespread attitude at that time:

> I tell ye true, that in these daungerous times,
> I doo not like this frowning vulgare brow.
> My searching eye did neuer entertaine
> a more distracted countenaunce of greefe
> then I haue late obseru'de
> in the displeased commons of the Cittie. (ll. 318–23)

In the execution scene too there are lines, marked for omission, which could also have had a topical significance in February and March 1601, when first Essex and then his principal followers were led to the scaffold:

> God for his pittie help these troublous times
> The streetes stopte vp with gazing multitudes,
> Commaund our armed Officers with Halberds,
> make way for entraunce of the prisoners.
> Let proclamation once againe be made,
> that euery householder, on paine of deathe
> keep in his Prentises, and euery man,
> stand with a weapon ready at his doore,
> as he will answere to the contrary. (ll. 584–92)

Indeed, the political situation in February and March 1601 makes comprehensible not only Tilney's refusal to allow the stage to show two members of the Privy Council resisting the wishes of the sovereign—and Essex, of course, was a Privy Councillor—but also his insistence that the whole of the insurrection scene should be expunged from the manuscript of the play.

Theatrical history also tends to confirm a date of late 1600 and early 1601. The Admiral's men were acting at the Rose during the first half of 1600, but early in July they left it; presumably some at least of them went on tour. Meanwhile their new theatre, the Fortune, was being hurried to completion, but they were not able to occupy it until the end of November or beginning of December.[22] During this period Henslowe's payments for new plays are very few, and not until later do they pick up again. Chettle does not reappear in the *Diary* until 31 March, nor Munday until 10 October 1601. It seems that during the building of the Fortune and until the novelty of the new theatre had worn off Henslowe made no attempt to provide full employment for his staff of dramatists. It would be natural for a group of them to try to find a market for their wares with the Lord Chamberlain's men.[23]

According to this hypothesis, then, *Sir Thomas More* was begun in the latter part of 1600. The collaborators must have thought that by joining with Munday, the ex-pursuivant and associate of Topcliffe, they could safely handle so delicate a subject as the life of More, and in such a way as to avoid offending the censor by any suggestion of Catholic bias. But the play did not entirely satisfy the company to which it was offered, nor, probably, the Master of the Revels, and revisions had to be undertaken. Even then a crucial scene was inadequate, and Shakespeare intervened to see what he could do with it. But meanwhile political events were moving fast; Essex launched his brief and futile rebellion; the Chamberlain's men, who had played *Richard II* with its deposition scene on the eve of the rebellion at the instigation of Essex's followers, were doubtless temporarily under a cloud, and the theatres were being closely watched. When the manuscript was submitted (or re-submitted) to Tilney soon after the execution of the rebels, he demanded further changes so sweeping that the play was abandoned.

THE HANDWRITING AND SPELLING OF THE THREE PAGES

The parts of *Sir Thomas More* which it is possible with any show of reason to claim for Shakespeare are the three pages of Addition II*c*, which are in the hand of their author (D), and Addition III, which is in the hand of C. As has been shown, there are bibliographical reasons for suggesting that these two insertions may be related, in that they both belong to the final stage of revision, but any attribution of Addition III to Shakespeare must rest mainly on internal and stylistic evidence. That for II*c*, on the other hand, is based in addition on handwriting and on D's spelling habits as well.

The problem of identification of Elizabethan handwritings is complicated by the fact that most writers were accustomed to using at least two different hands—an English and an Italian one—and sometimes more. There was also a natural tendency in some writers to mix the forms of the two hands. In addition, certain writers used a signature notably different from their ordinary hands. When one adds the differences produced in a man's handwriting by lapse of time, and the difficulties resulting from the sparseness of the materials available for comparison, it will be seen that certainty is not always attainable.

The problem of Shakespeare's handwriting should be approached only after consideration of a number of other examples, such as can be found in Greg's *English Literary Autographs, 1550–1650*. One finds a writer such as Chapman signing his name indifferently in English or Italian script; others, such as Henry Porter or Sir John Davies, use signatures which furnish comparatively little information about the way in which they usually form the letters which make up their names. In other cases, such as those of Edmund Spenser, Gabriel Harvey, and Giles Fletcher the elder, only by reason of juxtaposition or authentication is it possible to identify two seemingly quite different hands as the product of the same writer. In yet others, like those of John Lyly and Joseph Hall, where the type of handwriting remains constant, causes such as lapse of years and variations in the degree of care in the writing, produce such differences even in signatures as would cause one, if there were any doubt as to the writer, to hesitate to make the identification. An extreme case, and one presenting in an exaggerated form some of the difficulties faced by the present investigation, is that of Christopher Marlowe. *The Massacre at Paris* scrap in the Folger Shakespeare Library is, if one accepts its genuineness, presumably an author's draft, yet its hand presents very little resemblance to the signature of Marlowe recently discovered.[24] The best one can say is that it is conceivable that the same hand wrote them both.

For a study of Shakespeare's handwriting there are only six unquestioned signatures and two other words: "By me." The earliest, of 11 May 1612, is attached to the deposition in the case of Belott *v.* Mountjoy in the Record Office; the next two, dated 10 and 11 March 1613, are affixed to the conveyance and mortgage of the Blackfriars property, and are preserved at the Guildhall and British Museum respectively; the other three are the signatures to Shakespeare's will, dated 25 March 1616: one signature is at the foot of each page, and the final one is prefixed by the words: "By me." All are considerably later than the manuscript of *Sir Thomas More*, and five out of the six were written in abnormal circumstances. The signatures to the will are clearly those of a man weakened by illness; they seem to have been written slowly and carefully, but with deliberate and perhaps painful effort. The signatures to the conveyance and mortgage have both been crowded on to the parchment strips (for the attachment of seals) inserted through slots in the deeds. Only the signature to the deposition was written with normal fluency. In the three signatures to the will the surname is written in full; in the other three it is abbreviated. The Christian name is unabbreviated in two of the signatures to the will and in that of the conveyance; in the others it is abbreviated to 'W^m', 'Wi⫟m', and 'Willm'. In all, these signatures contain seventy-six still legible letters; they give examples of the way in which Shakespeare wrote eleven minuscules and three majuscules.

Sparse as is this material for comparison with the addition to *Sir Thomas More*, it should be realized that the circumstances might be more desperate than they are. It can be fairly presumed that Shakespeare's signatures give us examples of his normal manner of forming the letters in his name;[25] this is evidenced by the signature at the end of the will, where there is no suggestion of any change of style from the words: "By me." Shakespeare and D both use the English hand with a minimum admixture of non-English forms, and there can be little question that the two hands are at least superficially alike in many respects. But it is clear that Shakespeare had no standardized form of signature to which he attempted to adhere. The signatures, even the three signatures to the will, vary considerably from one another; what is remarkable about them is the range of variant forms they display. They furnish more material for comparison than could be expected from such meagre specimens.

Several of the letters that can be compared, such as *e* and *y*, are of such standard forms that they show little individuality. In making his analysis, Maunde Thompson was on the watch for forms that might be regarded as showing personal peculiarities and in the signatures he found five which are also repeated in D:

(1) The 'spurred *a*', illustrated in the deposition signature and in D's 'that' at l. 105. Other *a*'s in D can be found approximating this form (e.g. 'are' in l. 107), but the one in l. 105 is closest to that in the signature. What distinguishes these two *a*'s is that "the pen, descending in a deep curve from the overhead arch, is carried to the left into the horizontal spur and then to the right *horizontally* till it ascends to form the second minim".

(2) "Shakespeare makes use in his few signatures of three out of the four forms of the letter *k* which appear in the Addition", and the unusual *k* in the second will signature, which is not the normal type of *k* with a crossbar, is paralleled by D's *k* in 'knees' (l. 110).

(3) Though the form of the *p* in the mortgage signature is common enough, its formation is exceptional. First the downstroke, with its initial serif and its terminal upward lift, was made; then, beginning to the left of the downstroke the pen made a cross-stroke to form the lower half of the loop, and the top of the loop was completed by a third stroke. The same formation can be observed in the initial *p*'s in each occurrence of 'peace' in l. 50 of the Addition.

(4) The one Italian form found in the signatures is the long ∫ of the conveyance and mortgage signatures, and presumably also of the third will signature. It may be contrasted with the English ∫ of the second will signature. In the speech-prefix 'seriant' at l. 17, D uses the Italian ∫, though of a somewhat different form. The ∫ and *r* in this word are the only Italian letters used by D.

(5) In the signature at the end of the will the *m* of 'me' and the *W* of 'William' have introductory upstrokes, in the lower part of which there is perceptible a preliminary downstroke which, in the *W*, is only partially covered by the upstroke and forms what has been called an "elongated needle-eye". A downstroke preliminary to a similar upstroke is visible in D at the beginning of such words as 'wretched' (l. 75), 'in' (l. 95), and 'noble' (l. 144), and in l. 130, at the beginning of 'needs', the identical needle-eye effect of the signature is reproduced.

The peculiarities singled out by Maunde Thompson have not escaped criticism, and certain facts have been brought to light which weaken, though they do not destroy, his case. It has been pointed out, for instance, that Chapman uses a form of the 'spurred *a*' capable of appearing in a form identical with that of the deposition signature;[26] Chapman, too, sometimes employs an initial upstroke preceded by a downstroke which produces the needle-eye effect,[27] though so far the phenomenon has only been found at the beginning of an initial *A* in his Italian hand. It is doubtful also if the *k* to which Maunde Thompson attaches importance is really a separate form. Further, it has been emphasized that Shakespeare's *W*'s are different from D's (l. 35 and 37), and that his *B* is unlike any made by D. In an effort to clinch the case against the identity of Shakespeare and D, Tannenbaum has drawn up what he calls "twenty-five points of essential difference" between the two hands.[28] They vary greatly in weight and importance, nor do they take any account of lapse of years or the abnormal circumstances in which five of the six signatures were written, though elsewhere Tannenbaum shows himself fully aware of the significance of these factors. He is capable too of citing for comparison forms in D as unlike those in the signatures as possible and ignoring those which resemble the signatures, as when, in stating that the upward curve at the end of D's *i*'s is "almost invariably" different from Shakespeare's, he cites the words 'this' and 'his' in ll. 101 and 102, but ignores 'willd' in l. 100, which furnishes a close parallel to the forms of the signatures.[29] The soundness of Tannenbaum's methods is thus open to suspicion, and he leaves one with the feeling that a really effective case on palaeographical grounds against Shakespeare's authorship of the Addition has yet to be stated.

Another argument in favour of the identity of the two hands has been advanced by Greg.[30] Five out of the eleven minuscules in the signatures and the Addition, he points out, assume several forms in both, and in both they are the same ones. "Such multiple agreement acquires considerable significance, even though the individual forms may be common." Of *e*, *h*, and *p*, there are two clearly marked varieties, as well as three *k*'s and three, or perhaps four, *a*'s. "Taken all together these agreements must be allowed to establish a case of some *prima facie* strength." How strong a case, however, is still not clear, for no information is available as to the probability of such agreements in more than one hand. Is it, in other words, a phenomenon for which the mathematical odds against its occurring twice are enormous, or is it something that might reasonably be expected to occur in the handwriting of a number of Elizabethans? But at least one does not have free scope to search for parallels for D throughout all England; D and Shakespeare were dramatists, and the range of search is restricted to the small group of dramatists writing at the end of Elizabeth's reign. On this fact the strength of Greg's case depends.

Greg has summed up his position in four propositions which may be accepted as the most authoritative statement yet made on the subject:

PLATE XIII

The Booke of Sir Thomas More, fol. 8*a*; Hand 'D'
(British Museum, Harl. 7368)

PLATE XIV

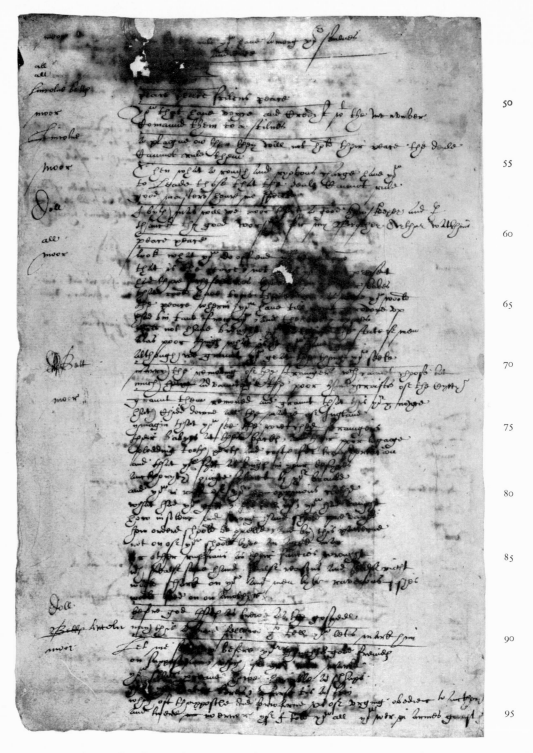

The Booke of Sir Thomas More (British Museum, Harl. 7368)

Above, fol. 8 *b*; Hand 'D'

Opposite, upper half of fol. 9; Hand 'D'

PLATE XV

9

all

Lincoln
wisdome god forbid that

nay certainly you ar
for to the king god hath his offyce lent
of dread of Iustyce, power and comaund
hath bid him rule, and willd you to obay
and to add ampler matie to this
he hath not only lent the king his figure
his throne his sword, but gyven him his owne name
calls him a god on earth, what do you then
rysing gainst him that god himsealf enstalls
but ryse gainst god, what do you to your sowles
in doing this o desperat as you are.
wash your foule mynds wt teares and those same hands
that you lyke rebells lift against the peace
lift vp for peace, and your vnreuerent knees
make them your feet to kneele to be forgyven
~~is safer wars, then euer you can make~~
~~in in to your obedienc~~
~~tell me but this what rebell captaine~~
as mutynes ar incident, by his name
can still the rout who will obay to braynd
or howe can well that proclamation sounde
when ther is no addicion but a rebell
to quallety, a rebell to a traytor
and euery there vayne~~r~~ ruffians~~was like~~
and lead the maiestie of law in lyom
to slipp him lyke a hound, ~~and that~~ say say the king
as he is clement, yf th'offendor moorne
shoold so much com to short of your great trespas
as but to banysh you, whether wold you go
what country by the nature of your error
shoold gyve you harber go you to ffraunc or flanders
to any Iarman province to spane or portigall
nay any where ~~that~~ that not adheres to Ingland
why you must needs be straingers, wold you be pleasd
to find a nation of such barbarous temper
that breaking out in hiddious violence
wold not affoord you, an abode on earth
whett their detested knyves against your throtes
spurne you lyke dogges, and lyke as yf that god
owed not nor made not you, nor that the elaments
wer not all appropriat to ~~their~~ your comforts.
but chartered vnto them, what wold you thinck
to be thus vsd, this is the straingers case
and this your mountainish inhumanyty

fayth a saies trew letts vs do as we may be doon by

Lincoln
wele be rulд by you master moor yf youle stand our
freend to precure our pdон

moor
Submyt you to thiese noble gentlemen
entreate their mediacion to the kinge
geve vp yor sealf to forme obay the maiestrate
and thers no doubt, but mercy may be found yf you so

PLATE XVI

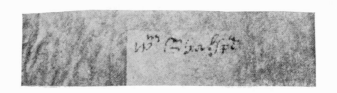

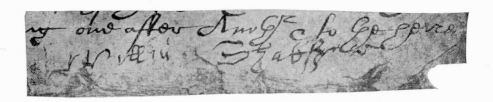

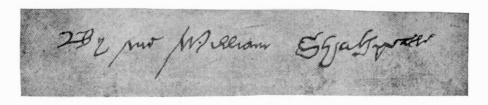

SHAKESPEARE'S SIGNATURES. (See the article by R. C. BALD)

(1) The palaeographic case for the hands of Shakespeare and D being the same is stronger than any that can be made out for their being different.

(2) The hand of Shakespeare is more nearly paralleled in D than in any other dramatic document known to us.

(3) Setting Shakespeare aside, it can be shown that D was not written by any dramatist of whose hand we have adequate knowledge.

(4) On purely palaeographical grounds there is less reason to suppose that all six signatures were written by the same hand than there is, granting this identity, to suppose that the hand of the signature also wrote the addition to *More*.

It is true that these propositions have been attacked, and it has been stated categorically that, on the materials available for comparison, as good a case could be made for C or for Chapman as the writer of the Addition as for Shakespeare.[31] But no such attempt has been made, for the simple reason that any experienced eye can see that these hands are not the same. It would seem that no infallible criteria have been found for the identification of handwritings and that, after all, insufficient specimens of Shakespeare's hand have survived to put the issue beyond doubt. The palaeographical argument, which might have been conclusive, depends more than any other on a delicate balance of probabilities.

A line of argument allied to the palaeographical one has been developed by J. Dover Wilson.[32] Assuming that D is Shakespeare, can the forms of the letters he uses and the characteristic spellings he employs throw any light on the early printed texts of Shakespeare's plays? In three respects they can. An elaborate classification of misprints in the 'good' Quartos which are probably due to misreading shows that similar misprints would be likely to occur from printer's copy in D's hand, and, in fact, modern editors of the Addition have been guilty of misreadings exemplifying four out of five of Dover Wilson's main classes. Secondly, misprints in the Quartos enable us to infer the spelling in the original manuscript which produced the misreading. For example, a misprint like 'pallat' for 'palace' (*Romeo and Juliet*, v, iii, 107) suggests: (i) That Shakespeare's *c* and *t* could under certain circumstances be mistaken for one another. How this could happen may be seen from a comparison of the *c* of 'thinck' in l. 138 of the Addition with the *t* of 'what' in l. 104. (ii) That Shakespeare, like many of his contemporaries, often omitted a final *e* after a palatal *c* or *g*. D does this frequently, though not invariably. Thirdly, spellings like 'Iarman' (German), which is found in l. 128 of the Addition, and the unusual 'scilens' (silence) in l. 50 have left traces in Shakespearian texts. 'Scilens' never occurs in the text itself, but in the speech-prefixes of the Quarto of *2 Henry IV* Justice Silence is either 'Scilens' or 'Silens'; the compositor would have normalized the spelling in the text, but when it was a proper name and a speech-prefix he left it as he found it.

Dover Wilson's method, in its concentration on a single hand, is much sounder than that of Leon Kellner in his *Restoring Shakespeare*, where Kellner illustrated his argument from a wide variety of Elizabethan hands, so that the reader ended up with the uneasy feeling that any letter might have been misread for any other, and that the liberty of emendation, instead of being restricted, was being granted new licence. Yet a great many of Dover Wilson's examples, as he is the first to concede, merely prove that Shakespeare, as we already know, wrote a fairly normal English hand and used spellings that are quite common in the period. But he is justified in stressing that the handwriting of the Addition is such as to be liable to cause the same groups of misreadings as are to be found in the Quartos, and that D's spellings reveal no habits at variance with those that can be inferred from the texts of Shakespeare. While the coincidence of the 'scilens' spellings is spectacular, it is the accumulation of numerous small details that gives force to his argument.

Tannenbaum has attacked Dover Wilson's conclusions also.[33] He has a point, I think, when he affirms that certain misreadings in the Shakespearian texts are caused by confusion between *e* and the symbol for final *s* or *es* which can be confused with it, but which is not used by D. He also points out that D does not use flourishes such as that which concludes the *m* of 'William' in the conveyance signature, though such flourishes have, he believes, been occasionally mistaken for signs of abbreviation by the compositors who set up Shakespeare's plays. But he seriously under-estimates one factor of which Dover Wilson is fully cognizant, and of which everyone is aware who has had to collate printed and manuscript versions of Elizabethan texts, viz. the extent to which compositors altered and normalized spellings found in manuscript. Once again we are justified in concluding that the case for the identity of D and Shakespeare "is stronger than any that has been made out for their being different", though Dover Wilson's evidence is admittedly only confirmatory and could scarcely be expected to stand by itself alone.

Finally, I have two crumbs to contribute to this part of the discussion. In order to parallel D's spelling 'Iarman' Dover Wilson cites from Shakespeare the misprint 'Iamanie' from a speech of Dr Caius in *The Merry Wives*; Tannenbaum retorts that 'Iamanie' is comic dialect and that "*Iarman* is not to be found either in the Quartos or in the Folio". A quick check with the aid of the concordance produced the following result: 'Iermane' (*Love's Labour's Lost*, III, i, 192, Q1598), 'Iarman' (*2 Henry IV*, II, i, 158, Q1), 'Ierman' (*Hamlet*, V, ii, 165, Q2), 'Iermans' (*Othello*, I, i, 114, Q1), and "a Iarmen on" for "a German one" (*Cymbeline*, II, v, 16, F.). We have no reason, then, to doubt that 'Iarman' was a Shakespearian spelling. Secondly, the likeli-hood of graphic confusion between *x* and *y* has not previously been considered, but anyone familiar with Elizabethan hands who examines D's *y*'s in 'Country' (l. 126) and 'gyve' (l. 127), or the first *y* in 'inhumanyty' (l. 140) will grant the possibility. It is therefore gratifying to find that in *Troilus and Cressida*, V, i, 16, the Quarto reads 'box' where the Folio corrects to 'boy'.

STYLE, THOUGHT AND IMAGERY

Simpson and Spedding first suggested that Shakespeare had had a part in *Sir Thomas More* because of the Shakespearian tone of certain passages. It was the evidence of style that originally drew attention to the play, and had there been no resemblances with Shakespeare's acknow-ledged works there would have been no attempt to marshal other kinds of evidence. The thought and expression of the Additions are therefore of fundamental importance, and evidence of hand-writing and spelling must be secondary to literary considerations. Unless the critical judgment is satisfied that these passages are such as Shakespeare could have written, there can be no question of admitting them to the canon, however Shakespearian the handwriting or spelling.

It would be easy to compile a list of earlier authorities who have been convinced that Shakespeare's style is to be found in the play, and oppose it with another list of names, equally authoritative, of those who have found no need to suppose that he had any part in it.[34] The early commentators like Simpson and Spedding were content to quote a few passages, cite an occasional parallel, and leave the rest to the reader. But a much more intensive examination was made by R. W. Chambers in 1923, and his conclusions were reinforced a few years later by Caroline Spurgeon.[35] In his essay Chambers concentrates on Shakespeare's concept of political order and his attitude to the common people, as expressed in the Jack Cade scenes of *Henry VI*, in *Richard II, Julius Caesar, Troilus and Cressida*, and *Coriolanus*, finding not merely striking parallels of expression and imagery with the Addition, but complete consistency of attitude and thought as well.

It is true that since 1923 further study has brought out a certain element of commonplace in the ideas behind Ulysses' famous speech on degree in *Troilus and Cressida*,[36] so that there may be a tendency to underestimate the force of part of Chambers's argument. But Chambers himself reworked and extended his material in a second essay[37] which, it seems safe to prophesy, will become a minor classic of Shakespearian criticism. This essay is readily accessible and involves few of the technicalities which have concerned us for the greater part of this paper, so there is no need to summarize it. It is sufficient to say that by means of a line-by-line commentary on the Addition, Chambers marshals his evidence to show not mere isolated parallels but whole sequences of thought and associated groups of images common to both D and Shakespeare.[38] Once again the emphasis is not on the isolated unit but on similar combinations of similar units. The validity of Chambers's method has only recently been strikingly confirmed in the results obtained by its application to the workings of Shakespeare's imagination as studied throughout the whole of the canon.[39]

Brief reference should also be made to the twenty-one-line speech of More which constitutes Addition III. It is in C's hand, but since C is known to be a scribe it is a fair assumption that he could have transcribed it from a scrap of paper in D's handwriting, just as he transcribed part of Addition V from the lines in B's handwriting on fol. 16b. But the argument for Shakespeare's authorship of this speech, which has been asserted by various writers,[40] depends almost entirely on stylistic evidence. An impressive number of parallels with Shakespeare's acknowledged work has been accumulated, and it seems reasonable, if the identity of D and Shakespeare is granted, to accept this speech also as his.

In conclusion, it may be said that if certain details of the argument for Shakespeare's share in *Sir Thomas More* seem less convincing than they did twenty years ago, the essential case remains substantially intact, and R. W. Chambers's paper of 1939 has given it added strength. With the increase of knowledge, too, not only of the handwriting, printing, and spelling of the Elizabethans but of their habits of thought as well we gain a fuller understanding of both Shakespeare and his fellow-dramatists. And with every such advance the argument by elimination for Shakespeare's authorship of the Addition becomes stronger: it is increasingly more difficult to propose from among the dramatists of whose work we have knowledge an alternative to Shakespeare. Shakespeare, we perceive, possessed in a unique degree the capacity for rising above the immediate situation to a sense of the human and ethical issues involved in it; he seems instinctively to be able to link it with the best and most characteristic thought of his age. D also shows signs of this capacity, but who else among Shakespeare's contemporaries possessed it? Marlowe and Chapman, in a sense, and perhaps Jonson; but certainly not the Heywoods and Dekkers, however affecting their interpretations of single events may be, nor any of the rest of Henslowe's needy tribe. And dramatists like Marlowe, Chapman, and Jonson are too individual in style and outlook—by comparison with Shakespeare, too doctrinaire—to have written the Addition. To vary an old phrase which is penned in the margin of one of the other additions, *et tu Shakespeare an diabolus.*

NOTES

1. The identification was considered and rejected by Greg, but has been accepted by C. J. Sisson, and by A. M. Clark in his study, *Thomas Heywood.* Difficulties in the way of accepting it are the differences in the length of ascenders and descenders in relation to the body of the letters in the two hands, and the fact that some of B's forms, notably his *th*, show certain signs of fluency and economy of effort absent from Heywood's. It is difficult to imagine a constant writer, as Heywood unquestionably was, abandoning these forms in later years, especially as there is no compensating gain in legibility. On the other hand, there is no question that the clown's part added by B is very much in Heywood's manner.

2. "Sir Thomas More", *J.E.G.P.* XVIII (1919), 226–35.

3. *Shakespeare's hand in 'Sir Thomas More'*, pp. 46–7.

4. E.g. Brooke, *The Shakespeare Apocrypha*, pp. xlvii–xlviii.

5. *If* the hand is B's and *if* B is Heywood, this would be an argument against an early date for the play. Heywood is not likely to have been in a position of such authority before 1600 at the earliest.

6. The statement in this sentence is an over-simplification but, I believe, a justifiable one. It should be noted that (i) owing to the damage at the foot of fol. 13 *b* only part of the cross within a circle is visible; (ii) the double circle surrounding a cross is not really double, as C takes the second circle only a little more than half-way round the first; (iii) the top of fol. 6 has been damaged and the identifying symbol lost, though what seems to be a fragment of it is just visible in the top left-hand corner of fol. 6 *a*. It was probably owing to the loss of the symbol that Addition I was bound up in the wrong place.

7. S. A. Tannenbaum, "More about *The Booke of Sir Thomas Moore*", *P.M.L.A.* XLIII (1928), 767–78; "Dr Greg and the 'Goodal' notation in *Sir Thomas Moore*", *P.M.L.A.* XLIV (1929), 934–8; *An object lesson in Shaksperian research* (1931).

8. *William Shakespeare: a study of facts and problems*, I, 512.

9. See W. J. Lawrence, "Was *Sir Thomas More* ever acted?", *Times Literary Supplement* (1 July 1920), p. 421, where these directions are listed.

10. Some surprise has been expressed at the appearance of Goodal's name at this point, though Chambers remarks that "there is equally sparse casting in other [manuscript] plays". It should be noticed that his name appears at the beginning of the scene which, of the whole play, would most have taxed the resources of the company. This suggests that Goodal was someone in the theatre whose ordinary occupation allowed only for occasional and exceptional appearances on the stage as a super; hence the note of his name. Was C himself Goodal? It is just possible.

11. Since the Battle of Pavia Lombardy had been under the control of Spain, and thus, in the latter part of Elizabeth's reign, was virtually enemy territory. During the same period, of course, England was in alliance with the French and Dutch against the Spaniards.

12. In the introduction to his edition of the play (pp. xiii–xiv) Greg modernizes and punctuates, "upon a mutiny against the Lombards, only by a short report and not otherwise", but in view of the ensuing discussion in the text it should probably be "against the Lombards only, by a short report and not otherwise".

13. *William Shakespeare*, I, 503.

14. It is somewhat surprising to find that in Addition II *a*, on the other side of the leaf on which this scene is written, the added clown's part increases the number of derisive references to the French and Dutch; but if one thing emerges from a study of Tilney's dealings with this manuscript it is that he did not mark every detail to which he objected, but was content to issue general covering instructions.

15. E. K. Chambers, *op. cit.* I, 511–12.

16. W. W. Greg, *Dramatic Documents from the Elizabethan Playhouses*, pp. 17–19 and 41.

17. "Anthony Munday and his Books", *The Library*, I (1920–1), at pp. 243–5.

18. "The autograph manuscripts of Anthony Mundy", *Transactions of the Bibliographical Society*, XIV (1919), 325–53.

19. See Percy Simpson, "*Sir Thomas More* and Shakespeare's hand in it", *The Library*, 3rd ser., VIII (1916–17), 79–96, and G. B. Harrison, *The Elizabethan Journals*, III, 317.

20. "The date of *Sir Thomas More*", *Review of English Studies*, I (1925), 337–9.

21. "On the date of *Sir Thomas More*", *Review of English Studies*, X (1934), 401–11.

22. *Henslowe's Diary*, ed. Greg, II, 63 and 94–5.

23. On this presumption C must also have been available to help with the preparation of the manuscript.

24. See J. Q. Adams, "The *Massacre at Paris* leaf", *The Library*, XIV (1933–4), 447–69; J. M. Nosworthy, "The Marlowe manuscript", *The Library*, XXVI (1945–6), 158–71; Marlowe's signature is reproduced by John Bakeless, *The Tragical History of Christopher Marlowe*, I, opposite p. 208.

25. There is perhaps one exception to this statement. D usually, though not invariably, dots his *i*'s; in the signatures Shakespeare omits them. It should be added, however, that photographs seem to show a dot over the first *i* of 'William' in the first signature to the will, but it does not appear in the early facsimiles and may therefore be only a flaw or stain in the paper.

26. See R. W. Chambers, "Shakespeare's handwriting in *Sir Thomas More*", *Times Literary Supplement* (27 Aug. 1925), p. 557, and Greg's *English Literary Autographs*, Pl. XIIb.

27. S. A. Tannenbaum, *Shakspere and 'Sir Thomas Moore'*, p. 16 and Pl. I.

28. The phrase quoted is from *Shakspere and 'Sir Thomas Moore'*, p. 15; the twenty-five points are in *Problems of Shakspere's Penmanship*, pp. 199–211.

29. *Problems of Shakspere's Penmanship*, p. 203.

30. "Shakespeare's hand once more", *Times Literary Supplement* (24 Nov. and 1 Dec. 1927), pp. 871 and 908.

31. Tannenbaum, *Problems of Shakspere's Penmanship*, p. 190, and *Shakspere and 'Sir Thomas Moore'*, p. 16. Cf. A. Green, "The apocryphal Sir Thomas More and the Shakespeare holograph", *Amer. J. Philology*, XXXIX (1918), 229–67 at p. 253.

32. "Bibliographical links between the three pages and the good quartos", *Shakespeare's hand in 'Sir Thomas More'*, pp. 113–41.

33. "More about *The Booke of Sir Thomas Moore*", *P.M.L.A.* XLIII (1928), 767–78 at pp. 774–8, and *Shakspere and 'Sir Thomas Moore'*, pp. 44–63.

34. See A. Green, *op. cit.* at pp. 255–7.

35. R. W. Chambers, "The expression of ideas—particularly political ideas—in the three pages and in Shakespeare", *Shakespeare's hand in 'Sir Thomas More'*, pp. 142–88, and Caroline F. E. Spurgeon, "Imagery in the *Sir Thomas More* Fragment", *Review of English Studies*, VI (1930), 257–70.

36. Cf. A. O. Lovejoy, *The Great Chain of Being*; Theodore Spencer, *Shakespeare and the Nature of Man*; E. M. W. Tillyard, *The Elizabethan World Picture*.

37. "Shakespeare and the play of *More*", in *Man's unconquerable mind*, pp. 204–49.

38. Of particular interest is Chambers's vindication of his 'sequences' against the mere collection and citation of isolated parallels, which renders untenable the arguments of L. Schücking, "Shakespeare and *Sir Thomas More*", *Review of English Studies*, I (1925), 40–59, and S. R. Golding, "Robert Wilson and *Sir Thomas More*", *Notes and Queries*, CLIV (1928), 237–9, 259–62.

39. E. A. Armstrong, *Shakespeare's Imagination*.

40. Simpson, in his original article, quoted part of this speech for its Shakespearian manner. For modern comment on it, see E. K. Chambers, *William Shakespeare*, I, 514–15; R. C. Bald, "Addition III of *Sir Thomas More*", *Review of English Studies*, VII (1931), 67–9; H. W. Crundell, *Times Literary Supplement* (20 May 1939), p. 297.

[*Note:* Deletions in the manuscript are printed between square brackets. Pointed brackets indicate readings supplied by Dyce for parts of the manuscript that are now illegible. Words in bold face type have been added by C.]

Lincolne	Peace heare me, he that will not see ⟨a red⟩ hearing at a harry grote, butter at a levenpence a pou⟨nde meale at⟩ nyne shillings a Bushell and Beeff at fower ⟨nobles a stone lyst⟩ to me	Fol. 8ᵃ
[other] **Geo bett**	yt will Come to that passe yf strain⟨gers be su⟩fferd marke him	
Linco	our Countrie is a great eating Country, argo they eate more in our Countrey then they do in their owne	5
[other] **betts clow**	by a half penny loff a day troy waight	
Linc	they bring in straing rootes, which is meerly to the vndoing of poor prentizes, for whats [a watrie] a sorry p̱snyp to a good hart	
[oth] **willian**	trash trash,: they breed sore eyes and tis enough to infect the Cytty wᵗ the palsey	10
Lin	nay yt has infected yt wᵗ the palsey, for theise basterds of dung as you knowe they growe in Dvng haue infected vs, and yt is our infeccion will make the Cytty shake which p̱tly Coms through the eating of p̱snyps	15
[o] **Clown, betts**	trewe and pumpions togeather	
Enter Seriant	what say yoᵘ to t⟨he⟩ mercy of the king do yoᵘ refuse yt	
Lin	yoᵘ would haue ⟨vs⟩ vppon thipp woold yoᵘ no marry do we not, we accept of the kings mercy but wee will showe no mercy vppõ the straingers	20
seriaunt	yoᵘ ar the simplest things that euʼ stood in such a question	
Lin	how say yoᵘ now prenty prentisses symple downe wᵗʰ him	
all	prentisses symple prentisses symple	
	Enter the L. maier Surrey	
	Shrewsbury	25
[Sher] **Maior**	hold in the kings name hold	
Surrey	frends masters Countrymen	
mayer	peace how peace I [sh] Charg yoᵘ keep the peace	
Shro.	my masters Countrymen	
[Sher] **Williamson**	The noble Earle of Shrowsbury letts hear him	30
Ge betts	weele heare the earle of Surrey	
Linc	the earle of Shrowsbury	
betts	weele heare both	
all	both both both both	
Linc	Peace I say peace ar yoᵘ men of Wisdome [ar] or	35

	what ar yo^u	

	what ar yo^u	
Surr	[But] what yo^u will haue them but not men of wisdome	
all	weele not heare my L of Surrey, [ ] no no no no no	
		Shrewsbury shr
moor	whiles they ar ore the banck of their obedyenc	
	thus will they bere downe all things	40
Linc	Shreiff moor speakes shall we heare shreef moor speake	
Doll	Letts heare him a keepes a plentyfull shrevaltry, and a made my	
	Brother Arther watchin⟨s⟩ Seriant Safes yeoman lets heare	
	shreeve moore	
all	Shreiue moor moor more Shreue moore	45
moor	⟨even⟩ by the rule yo^u haue among yor sealues	Fol. 8^b
	Comand still audience	
all	⟨S⟩urrey Sury	
all	moor moor	
Lincolne betts	peace peace scilens peace.	50
moor	Yo^u that haue voyce and Credyt w^t the [mv] nvmber	
	Comaund them to a stilnes	
Lincolne	a plaigue on them they will not hold their peace the deule	
	Cannot rule them	
Moor	Then what a rough and ryotous charge haue yo^u	55
	to Leade those that the deule Cannot rule	
	good masters heare me speake	
Doll	I byth mas will we moor thart a good howskeeper and I	
	thanck thy good worship for my Brother Arthur watchins	
all	peace peace	60
moor	look what yo^u do offend yo^u Cry vppõ	
	that is the peace, not ⟨on⟩ of yo^u heare present	
	had there such fellowes lyvd when yo^u wer babes	
	that coold haue topt the peace, as nowe yo^u woold	
	the peace wherin yo^u haue till nowe growne vp	65
	had bin tane from yo^u, and the bloody tymes	
	coold not haue brought yo^u to [theise] the state of men	
	alas poor things what is yt yo^u haue gott	
	although we graunt yo^u geat the thing yo^u seeke	
[D] Bett	marry the removing of the straingers wch cannot choose but	70
	much [helpe] advauntage the poor handycraftes of the Cytty	
moor	graunt them remoued and graunt that this yor [y] noyce	
	hath Chidd downe all the matie of Ingland	
	ymagin that yo^u see the wretched straingers	
	their babyes at their backs, and their poor lugage	75
	plodding tooth ports and costs for transportacion	

and that yoᵘ sytt as kings in your desyres
aucthoryty quyte sylenct by yoʳ braule
and yoᵘ in ruff of yoʳ [yo] opynions clothd
what had yoᵘ gott; Ile tell yoᵘ, yoᵘ had taught   80
how insolenc and strong hand shoold prevayle
how ordere shoold be quelld, and by this patterne
not on of yoᵘ shoold lyve an aged man
for other ruffians as their fancies wrought
wᵗʰ sealf same hand sealf reasons and sealf right   85
woold shark on yoᵘ and men lyke ravenous fishes
woold feed on on another

Doll	before god thats as trewe as the gospell
[Betts] **lincoln**	nay this a sound fellowe I tell yoᵘ lets mark him

moor   Let me sett vp before yoʳ thoughts good freinds   90
on supposytion, which if yoᵘ will marke
yoᵘ shall ℘ceaue howe horrible a shape
yoʳ ynnovation beres, first tis a sinn
which oft thappostle did forwarne vs of vrging obedienc to aucthory⟨ty⟩
and twere [in] no error yf I told yoᵘ all   yoᵘ wer in armes gainst g⟨od⟩   95

all	marry god forbid that	Fol. 9ᵃ
moo	nay certainly yoᵘ ar	

for to the king god hath his offyc lent
of dread of Iustyce, power and Comaund
hath bid him rule, and willd yoᵘ to obay   100
and to add ampler mařie to this
he [god] hath not [le] only lent the king his figure
his throne [his] sword, but gyven him his owne name
calls him a god on earth, what do yoᵘ then
rysing gainst him that god himsealf enstalls   105
but ryse gainst god, what do yoᵘ to yoʳ sowles
in doing this o desperat [ar] as you are
wash your foule mynds wᵗ teares and those same hands
that yoᵘ lyke rebells lyft against the peace
lift vp for peace, and your vnreuerent knees   110
[that] make them your feet to kneele to be forgyven
[is safer warrs, then euer yoᵘ can make]
[whose discipline is ryot, why euen yoʳ [warrs] hurly] [in in to yoʳ obedienc]
[cannot ℘ceed but by obedienc] **tell me but this** what rebell captaine
as mutynes ar incident, by his name   115
can still the rout who will obay [th] a traytor
or howe can well that ℘clamation sounde
when ther is no adicion but a rebell

    to quallyfy a rebell, youle put downe straingers
    kill them cutt their throts possesse their howses   120
    and leade the matie of lawe in liom
    to slipp him lyke a hound, [sayeng] [alas alas] say nowe the king
    as he is clement, yf thoffendor moorne
    shoold so much com to short of your great trespas
    as but to banysh yo , whether woold yo go   125
    what Country by the nature of yo error
    shoold gyve you harber go yo to ffraunc or flanders
    to any Iarman ꝑvince, [to] spane or portigall
    nay any where [why yo] that not adheres to Ingland
    why yo must needs be straingers, woold yo be pleasd   130
    to find a nation of such barbarous temper
    that breaking out in hiddious violence
    woold not afoord yo , an abode on earth
    whett their detested knyves against yo throtes
    spurne yo lyke doggs, and lyke as yf that god   135
    owed not nor made not yo , nor that the elaments
    wer not all appropriat to [ther] yo Comforts.
    but Charterd vnto them, what woold yo thinck
    to be thus vsd, this is the straingers case

all   and this your momtanish inhumanyty   140
              fayth a saies trewe letts [vs] do as we may be doon by

[all] **Linco**   weele be ruld by yo master moor yf youle stand our
              freind to ꝑcure our ꝑdon

moor   Submyt yo to theise noble gentlemen
              entreate their mediation to the kinge   145
              gyve vp yo sealf to forme obay the maiestrate
              and thers no doubt, but mercy may be found yf yo so seek ⟨yt⟩

THE RENAISSANCE BACKGROUND OF
MEASURE FOR MEASURE

BY

ELIZABETH MARIE POPE

When critics of *Measure for Measure*[1] are not staggered or repelled by the ethical presuppositions upon which the characters act, they usually try to justify and explain the work on the ground that its morality is specifically Christian. But while such scholars as Roy Battenhouse, C. J. Sisson and R. W. Chambers have thus defended Shakespeare's treatment of law, authority, justice, and mercy, they have not inquired what exact meaning was attached to these terms in the Renaissance, apparently because they assume that he thought of them very much as we do.[2] But did he? What doctrines of equity and forgiveness were actually taught to the Elizabethan layman? Would the first audience that saw *Measure for Measure* find them in the play? Can they explain anything in Shakespeare's presentation of the subject that we might otherwise overlook or misunderstand? And for the answers to these questions we must turn to the popular religious text-books of Shakespeare's own day—not to the Church Fathers or the Latin works of the great contemporary Reformers and Counter-Reformers, but to the annotated Bibles, the translations, the English commentaries, the sermons, and the tracts through which the teaching of the Church reached the individual without special training or interest in theology.

The first point to be noted is that *Measure for Measure*, unlike some of Shakespeare's comedies, has a highly significant title, a phrase which not only sums up the basic theme of the play, but is brought out and emphasized at the crisis in the last act, when the Duke condemns his deputy:

> 'An Angelo for Claudio, death for death.'
> Haste still pays haste, and leisure answers leisure;
> Like doth quit like, and Measure still for Measure. (v, i, 414–6)

Shakespeare is of course thinking of a verse from the Sermon on the Mount: "With what measure ye mete it shall be measured to you again." In both Matthew and Luke, however, the text is not isolated, but forms an integral part of a short passage which in Luke immediately follows—and is linked with—Christ's great pronouncement on Christian forgiveness:

27 ...Love your enemies: do well to them which hate you....

31 And as ye would that men should do to you, so do ye to them likewise.

32 For if ye love them which love you, what thank shall ye have: for even the sinners love those that love them. [The Matthew, Bishops, and Great Bibles read: "for sinners also love their lovers."]

33 And if ye do good for them which do good for you, what thank shall ye have? for even the sinners do the same....

35 Wherefore love ye your enemies, and do good, and lend, looking for nothing again, and your reward shall be great, and ye shall be the children of the most High: for he is kind unto the unkind, and to the evil.

36 Be ye therefore merciful, as your Father also is merciful.

37 Judge not, and ye shall not be judged: condemn not, and ye shall not be condemned: forgive, and ye shall be forgiven.

38 Give, and it shall be given unto you: a good measure, pressed down, shaken together, and running over shall men give into your bosom: for with what measure ye mete, with the same shall men mete to you again.

39 And he spake a parable unto them, Can the blind lead the blind? Shall they not both fall into the ditch?

40 The disciple is not above his master: but whosoever will be a perfect disciple, shall be as his master.

41 And why seest thou a mote in thy brother's eye, and considerest not the beam that is in thine own eye?

42 Either how canst thou say to thy brother, Brother, let me pull out the mote that is in thine eye, when thou seest not the beam that is in thine own eye? Hypocrite, cast the beam out of thine own eye first, and then shalt thou see perfectly to pull out the mote that is in thy brother's eye.[3]

Matt. vii, 1–5 corresponds to Luke vi, 36–42, but does not include verses 36, 39 or 40, and does not follow or refer to the command to forgive. Luke vi, 36–42 was evidently considered the more authoritative rendering of the passage: it was the one chosen by the Anglican Church as the gospel for the fourth Sunday after Trinity; as such, it was also the one analysed in the postils (or formal collections of sermons on the assigned readings for the year); and the most famous and popular of the annotated Bibles, the Geneva version, assigns it five explanatory notes as against one to the equivalent texts in Matthew. Doctrinal teaching on the Luke passage, however, differs only slightly from that on the Matthew; and it is this teaching which is of primary importance, since it covers most—if not all—of the major ethical issues that appear in *Measure for Measure*.

To begin with, the authorities argue, the passage shows that it is intolerable when a man "narrowly examineth his brother's manners, and is desirous to bewray his brother's fault", especially if at the same time he neither recognizes nor regrets his own.[4] Critics who are themselves vicious can no more correct others than the blind can lead the blind. The little allegory of the mote and the beam is meant to drive home and reinforce the same lesson. "O how uncomely", cries the author of the *Brief Postil*,

how wicked, how hypocrite like, how uncharitable a thing it is, to judge our neighbours of light matters, whereas we be an hundred time worse ourselves! Why do we not rather gently bear, dissemble, and interpret well the small error and fault of our brethren? Why do we not rather go down to the entrails of our own heart, and see our own stuff?[5]

The forbearance recommended must not of course be carried to the point of condoning or refusing to censure open and serious wrong. As Calvin puts it:

He which judgeth by the rule of charity, always first examining himself, he, I say, keepeth the true and right order of judging. Nevertheless it is not only lawful for us to condemn all sins, but also it is necessary, except we will abrogate the laws of God and overthrow his judgement. For he would have us to be proclaimers of his sentences which he pronounceth as concerning the deeds of men.[6]

William Perkins, in his *Treatise of Christian Equity and Moderation* (Cambridge, 1604), is even more emphatic: courtesy and tolerance, he insists, are proper only so long as

they whom we forbear...do not exceed, nor break out into any outrage, or extremity: for then they are not to be forborne, but to be told, and reproved for them, and man's duty is not to wink at them, but to take notice of them, and to show open dislike of them [p. 41].

But otherwise we are strictly forbidden to judge, condemn, or refuse to forgive our fellows. In the first place, we ought to be merciful, even as God also is merciful:

Because that he hath pardoned and forgiven all our offences and trespasses, of his mere grace, without any deserving, and that through his only son Jesus Christ...according to this example, our heavenly father requireth the same thing of us.[7]

This argument is, as one might expect, used chiefly by writers on Luke, who so pointedly links his version of the passage with the doctrine of Christian forgiveness. Secondly—and on this tenet all the authorities agree—we ought to remember that whatever we do invites retaliation in kind. The good will receive their own back with interest, and. "so in like manner", says Martin Bucer,

they which are malicious against others, seekers of revengement, mindful of wrongs past, straight examiners and judgers of other men's faults, shall find also, by God's justice, such as shall handle them after the like fashion.[8]

The continual use of the passive voice in the Gospels—"ye shall be judged", "ye shall be condemned"—makes it uncertain just who is to exact this reckoning. Becon and Corvinus assume that it is God, but the general consensus seems to be rather that it is other men, for, as Calvin explains, "though this be done by the just vengeance of God, that they should again be punished, which have judged others: yet the Lord doth execute this punishment by men" (p. 210). To back this hypothesis, there is the fact that in Luke (though not in Matthew), Christ declares that "a good measure...shall *men* give into your bosom"; and we must also remember that according to the four English translations most widely used in the sixteenth century—the Matthew, the Great Bible, the Geneva, and the Bishops—the sentence immediately following ought to read: "For with what measure ye mete, with the same shall *men* mete to you again." Here or elsewhere Shakespeare evidently picked up the idea that the verse was to be taken in this sense: Richard of Gloucester uses it in *3 Henry VI* to justify the most savage and literal sort of retaliation in kind:

> From off the gates of York fetch down the head,
> Your father's head, which Clifford placed there;
> Instead whereof let this supply the room.
> Measure for measure must be answered.　　　　　　　(II, vi, 52–5)

But however natural and authorized such an interpretation of the text might have been, it was not quite a satisfactory one when the passage was considered as a whole, especially in the Luke version. For who actually is to return rash judgment for rash judgment, condemnation for condemnation, like for like? Men? The same men who have just been explicitly commanded to forbear judgment and forgive injuries?[9] God, then? The same God whom His Son has just described as "kind to the unkind, and to the evil", the Father according to Whose example we are urged to be merciful? At least one Renaissance theologian, William Perkins, seems to have been so distressed by these alternatives that he feels obliged to explain in his *Exposition* (p. 417) that though God does not will men to return evil for evil, and those who indulge in the practice are miserable sinners, God nevertheless uses their wickedness to punish the other miserable sinners who have done evil in the first place. But the rest of the commentators I have seen hardly appear to recognize the problem at all. It is almost as if they approve of mercy at one level of consciousness, and of retaliation in kind at another: separate concepts which do not interact and remain essentially unfused, like the responsibilities Pooh-Bah attaches to his various offices in *The Mikado*. One is certainly aware of a logical incoherence, a failure to think through the question clearly or completely. We may of course argue that if the professional exponents of the Scriptures did not perceive these difficulties, they would scarcely be likely to worry the Elizabethan layman; but it is at least conceivable that a sensitive reader of the passage, even in the sixteenth century, might have observed them—and been troubled.

One more point of doctrine still remains to be discussed. Since extreme sects like the Anabaptists habitually used Scriptural authority to support their arguments for a community of goods, the abolition of civil government, and the like, Protestant theologians took particular pains to qualify or explain away texts capable of any such dangerous interpretation; and as a result we find Becon, Corvinus, Heminge, Perkins, and the author of the *Brief Postil* going out of their way to make it clear that the commands to be merciful, to forgive, and to abstain from judging are meant to bind only the private individual, not to restrict or abolish the authority of the State. Even the Geneva Bible devotes part of its limited and precious marginal space to a note on Luke, vi, 37, warning the reader that Christ "speaketh not here of civil judgments, and therefore by the words, forgive, is meant that good nature which the Christians use in suffering and pardoning wrongs". "Mark, my friends", says the author of the *Brief Postil*,

that this is only spoken of private judgment and private condemnation, that is to say, I may not be mine own judge, I may not revenge mine own quarrel....It is lawful for rulers, to judge and to condemn, because they do it not in their own name, but as God's ministers and vicars. To this do all the ancient expositors and doctors agree, as Saint Austin, Jerome, Ambrose, Chrysostom, and the rest. Wherefore the wicked Anabaptists are to be banished which condemn temporal or civil judgments.[10]

On the other hand, the civil magistrate was evidently not considered entirely exempt from all the rules Christ lays down in this passage, especially the stipulation that a man should not try to pull the mote from his brother's eye before casting the beam out of his own. "Consider", writes William Perkins in his *Exposition*,

how Christ would have all those which are to give judgment of the offences of others to be themselves without reproof or blame: else they are no fit persons to give censure of those that be under them. And therefore the Magistrate in the town and commonwealth...and every superior in his place must labour to be unblameable [p. 424].

But when the theologians begin arguing in this vein, they are drawing into the discussion the whole question of the rights and obligations of the temporal authority; and it is to the special studies made of this particular subject that we must turn for further light on our problem.

Sermons and treatises defining the status, privileges, and responsibilities of the Christian governor are plentiful enough during the sixteenth century—Antony Guevara's *Dial of Princes*, translated by North in 1557; Geoffrey Fenton's *Forme of Christian Pollicie* (1574); Henry Bullinger's *Fiftie Godlie and Learned Sermons* (1587); James I's *Basilicon Doron* (1599), to name only a few. But in 1603 and 1604, public interest in the question seems to have been especially keen. In those years, King James's *True Lawe of Free Monarchies* was reprinted twice and his *Basilicon Doron* seven times—nine if we count the Welsh translation and William Willymat's digest in Latin and English verse. There also appeared a number of works dealing wholly or in part with the office and duties of the Christian ruler—such as six sermons preached before King James at various times by Thomas Bilson, Richard Eedes, Henry Hooke, Thomas Blague, and Richard Field; reprints of Henry Smith's *Magistrates Scripture* and *Memento for Magistrates*; Andrew Willet's *Ecclesia Triumphans*, a tract showing how James met all the requirements of an ideal ruler; *A Loyal Subiect's Looking-Glasse*, by William Willymat; Ben Jonson's *Panegyre* on the King's first entrance into Parliament; and William Perkins' posthumous *Treatise of Christian Equity and Moderation*. This outburst of concern with the theory of government seems to have been inspired primarily by the accession of James. A certain amount of such preaching and writing would probably have occurred on the arrival of any new monarch, but in this particular case, it must have been greatly stimulated by the fact that the new monarch was himself an authority on the subject, whose work was being eagerly discussed by the public and whose favour the court clergy and *literati* were naturally anxious to gain. It is noticeable how much of the material listed above was originally composed to be delivered before James himself, and how many of the authors manage to include flattering tributes to their royal master and his work in the field, as Thomas Bilson did:

In the Prince's duty I may be shorter, because I speak before a religious and learned King, who both by pen and practice hath witnessed to the world these many years, how well acquainted he is with Christian and godly government.[11]

Now *Measure for Measure* is very largely concerned with the "Prince's duty", particularly in regard to the administration of justice. At no time, perhaps, could Shakespeare have presented such a subject without reckoning to some extent on what his audience would be predisposed to think of his characters and their behaviour. But if he *did* write the play about 1603–4, he had unusually good reason to believe the subject would be popular and to consider it in terms of the contemporary doctrine of rule—even if we do not assume that he, like so many others, was seriously concerned over the problems of Christian and godly government and deliberately trying to catch the eye of the King, at whose court it was acted and to whose well-known dislike of crowds two passages apparently allude (I, i, 67–73; II, iv, 26–9).

According to Renaissance theory, the authority of all civil rulers is derived from God. Hence, they may be called 'gods', as they are in Psalm lxxxii, 6, because they act as God's substitutes, "Ruling, Judging, and Punishing in God's stead, and so deserving God's name here on earth", as Bilson put it in the sermon he preached at King James's coronation.[12] "The Prince", says Henry Smith in his *Magistrates Scripture* (pp. 339–40), "is like a great Image of God, the Magistrates are like little Images of God", though he is careful to point out that they are not indeed divine: the name is given them only to remind them that they are appointed by the Lord "to rule as he would rule, judge as he would judge, correct as he would correct, reward as he would reward". This doctrine may very well explain why the Duke moves through so much of the action of *Measure for Measure* like an embodied Providence; why his character has such curiously allegorical overtones, yet never quite slips over the edge into actual allegory; and finally, why Roy Battenhouse's theory that Shakespeare subconsciously thought of him as the Incarnate Lord is at once so convincing and so unsatisfactory. Any Renaissance audience would have taken it for granted that the Duke did indeed "stand for" God, but only as any good ruler "stood for" Him; and if he behaved "like power divine", it was because that was the way a good ruler was expected to conduct himself.

Furthermore, since the ruler's authority was considered an extension of the same kind of power God delegates to parents, teachers, ministers, masters, shepherds, and husbands, all these terms were frequently used to describe him, especially 'father' and 'shepherd'.[13] So when the Duke compares himself to a fond father who has not disciplined his children for so long that they have run wild (I, iii, 23–8), the image probably meant rather more to a Renaissance audience than it would mean to a modern one. When later, after his discussion with the Provost, he rises at dawn to go about his work with the remark: "Look, th'unfolding star calls up the shepherd" (IV, ii, 219), one wonders if he may not be thinking of himself and his office. God was, moreover, supposed to endow rulers with what was called "sufficiency of spirit" to carry out their duties, though He might withdraw this gift if they disobeyed Him, as He withdrew it from Saul.[14] It is possible that this doctrine has some bearing on the treatment of Angelo in *Measure for Measure*, though there is no reason why Shakespeare should not have been thinking of something much more elementary when he showed him failing to pray successfully after his fall, or lamenting:

> Alack, when once our grace we have forgot,
> Nothing goes right—we would, and we would not. (IV, iv, 31–2)

In their capacity as God's substitutes, rulers have four privileges. The first is sanctity of person, especially in the case of an anointed prince. No man may raise his hand against him, or even disparage him in speech or thought.[15] To abuse a ruler, according to William Willymat, by "evil speaking, mocking, scorning, scoffing, deriding, reviling, cursing", is a thing "most unhonourable, yea worthy of death" (p. 32)—a belief which must have made Lucio's malicious gossip about the Duke appear a much more serious offence than it seems to a modern audience. Secondly, the ruler has sovereignty of power: all men must obey him without question, except when his commands directly contradict God's ordinances. Even then, disobedience must be entirely passive, and any retaliation from the authorities endured with patience—although Roman Catholics held that open rebellion was sometimes permissible when the ruler was a heretic.[16] As the authorities in *Measure for Measure* are not heretics, this particular question does not arise: there is no doubt that the characters are legally bound to reverence and obey them. But this raised a problem which required—and received—very delicate handling. Since to yield to Angelo would mean breaking a law of God, Isabella is fully entitled to resist him; but the measures taken to circumvent him are by no means passive and might even have been considered to savour dangerously of conspiracy against a lawful magistrate if Shakespeare did not slip neatly away from the whole difficulty by making the chief conspirator the highest officer of the State himself. And as if to ensure that no one should miss the point, he brings it out clearly and carefully in IV, ii, where the excellent Provost refuses to join the plot to save Claudio until he is convinced by the Duke's letter that the friar has the necessary secular power to override the deputy.

The third privilege of rulers is the right to enforce the law. In civil matters, the avenging of evil, which God has strictly forbidden to private individuals, is the office and duty of the ruler and his subordinates,[17] to whom the Duke bids Isabella turn when, in her agony at Claudio's supposed death, she momentarily thinks of punishing Angelo herself. The further question of the ruler's title to authority in ecclesiastical as well as civil matters (since, as King James puts it in the *Basilicon Doron*, p. 110, "a King is not *mere laicus*, as both the Papists and Anabaptists would have him; to the which error the Puritans also incline over-far") is not brought up in *Measure for Measure*.

Finally, the ruler has the privilege of using extraordinary means. As Gentillet points out, this certainly does not imply that he is entitled to deceive, betray, and commit perjury in the manner recommended by Machiavelli, but only, in the words of William Willymat, that

Kings, Princes, and governors do use oftentimes to use diverse causes to disguise their purposes with pretences and colours of other matters, so that the end of their drifts and secret purposes are not right seen into nor understood at the first, this to be lawful the word of God doth not deny.

He then cites the examples of Solomon ordering the child divided; Jehu pretending he would serve Baal, when by this subtlety he really intended to destroy the servants of Baal (II Kings x); and the Emperor Constantius threatening to persecute the Christians when all he actually meant to do was by this stratagem to separate the sheep from the goats.[18] Hence, the Duke in *Measure for Measure* is quite justified in using disguise, applying "craft against vice" (III, ii, 291), and secretly watching Angelo much as King James advises his son in the *Basilicon Doron* to watch his own subordinates: "Delight to haunt your Session, and spy carefully their proceedings...to take a sharp account of every man in his office" (pp. 90–2). There would have been no need to apologize for these practices to a Renaissance audience; they would have shrugged them off with the equivalent of Willymat's conclusion to his argument: "Had it not been great lack of wisdom to have interrupted these Christian princes' pretences and commandments tending as afterward proved to so good an end?"

But in the eyes of the Renaissance, the Christian prince had not only authority and privileges, but a clearly defined and inescapable set of duties to perform as well. The first is to remember that he is not really God, but man "dressed in a little brief authority", as Isabella reminds Angelo— mere man, whom his God will in the end call strictly to account, although his subjects may not.[19] He cannot make a single decision at which the Lord is not invisibly present and which He does not weigh and record, as He is said to do in Psalm lxxxii, 1, where, according to Henry Hooke,

the Prophet David reproving the judges and magistrates of his time...rippeth up the secret cause of such supine defect in matter of justice: They understand nothing, saith he, they know not that God standeth as a judge in the middest of their assemblies; therefore, they walk in darkness, the eye of their conscience being hoodwinked, that they could not see to do equity and judgement.[20]

It is to this text (with all its associations) that Angelo is almost certainly referring when he cries at his exposure:

> I perceive your grace, like pow'r divine,
> Hath look'd upon my passes.

(v, i, 374–5)

As ever in his great Taskmaster's eye, therefore, the ruler must labour to be what God would have him. To begin with, he must be sincerely religious [21]—or, as the Duke puts it in his soliloquy at the end of Act III,

> He who the sword of heaven will bear
> Should be as holy as severe. (III, ii, 275–6)

Furthermore, he must know and be able to govern himself; for, says Guevara, "when they asked [Thales] what a prince should do to govern others, he answered: he ought first to govern himself, and then afterwards to govern others"[22]—a principle we have already encountered in the commentaries on the mote and the beam and find again in *Measure for Measure*, where it is most clearly stated when the Duke declares in his soliloquy that the ruler must be a man

> More nor less to others paying
> Than by self-offences weighing.
> Shame to him whose cruel striking
> Kills for faults of his own liking! (III, ii, 279–82)

He should also cultivate all the virtues to the best of his ability, but according to the *Basilicon Doron*,

make one of them, which is Temperance, Queen of all the rest within you. I mean not by the vulgar interpretation of Temperance, which only consists in *gustu & tactu*, by the moderation of these two senses: but I mean of that wise moderation, that first commanding your self, shall as Queen, command all the affections and passions of your mind [p. 84].

Therefore, when Escalus describes the Duke as "one that above all other strifes, contended especially to know himself", and "a gentleman of all temperance" (III, ii, 246–7, 251), what may seem rather faint praise to a modern reader would have been regarded as a very high tribute indeed during the Renaissance. Finally, in all he does, the ruler must remember that his life is the pattern for his subjects, and that, as Richard Eedes explains, "neither are the hearts of the people so easily turned and carried with the dead letter of a written law, as with that life of law, *Justice* living in the life of the prince".[23]

> Pattern in himself to know
> Grace to stand and virtue go, (III, ii, 277–8)

is the way the Duke puts it in his soliloquy.

The more practical and specific duties of the ruler are to get a good education, especially in political theory; to love his subjects and be thoroughly acquainted with them—"O how necessary it is", exclaims Guevara, "for a prince to know and understand all things in his Realm, to the end no man might deceive him, as they do nowadays!" (I, 55^r); to levy no undue taxes, or waste them when collected—the reciprocal duty of the subject being to pay up cheerfully; to keep peace with all nations if possible, but to protect his own against foreign injury or aggression; to make his laws clear and plain; to choose wise subordinates, control them carefully, and according to Gentillet, let them execute any measures so rigorous that the ruler may be suspected of a purely arbitrary use of his power: "to shun that suspicion and blame, it is good that the prince delegate and set over such matters to Judges, which are good men, not suspected or passionate"

(p. 350). It should be noted that this is just what the Duke does in *Measure for Measure*. As he confides to Friar Thomas,

> I have on Angelo impos'd the office,
> Who may in th' ambush of my name strike home,
> And yet my nature never in the fight
> To do it slander.   (I, iii, 40-3)

He also conforms to the Renaissance ideal in loving his subjects and taking steps "to know and understand all things in his Realm, to the end no man might deceive him". His accomplishments in education, taxation, legislation, war, and peace, however, have little bearing on the major issue of the play, and are huddled away under the general statement that "let him be but testimonied in his own bringings-forth, and he shall appear to the envious a scholar, a statesman, and a soldier" (III, ii, 152-5).

But the highest and most important of the ruler's specific duties is to see well to the administration of justice. Here more than anywhere else he and his deputies must act consciously as the substitutes of God; or, in Fenton's words: "the Judges raised by [God] to dispense justice in his place, ought always to have the Majesty of him in their minds, and his judgments in imitation."[24] "They should think", adds Henry Smith, in his *Magistrates Scripture*, "how Christ would judge, before they judge, because God's Law is appointed for their Law" (p. 342). They must not, of course, play favourites, put off decisions, allow their passions to carry them away, accept bribes, give in to fear, be ignorant, listen to slander, or refuse to hear the complaints of the oppressed. But above all, both the chief and the inferior magistrates must cherish the innocent and punish the wicked with all due severity. Bad judges, according to William Perkins' *Treatise on Christian Equity and Moderation*, are of two kinds: the first are

such men, as by a certain foolish kind of pity are so carried away, that would have nothing but *mercy*, *mercy*, and would...have the extremity of the law executed on no man. This is the high way to abolish laws, and consequently to pull down authority, and so in the end to open a door to all confusion, disorder, and to all licentiousness of life. But I need not say much herein, for there are but few that offend in this kind, man's nature being generally inclined rather to cruelty than to mercy.

The second kind are

such men as have nothing in their mouths, but the *law*, the *law*: and *Justice, Justice*: in the meantime forgetting that Justice always shakes hands with her sister mercy, and that all laws allow a mitigation.... These men, therefore, strike so precisely on their points, and the very tricks and trifles of the law, as (so the law be kept, and that in the very extremity of it) they care not, though equity were trodden under foot: and that law may reign on earth, and they by it: they care not, though mercy take her to her wings, and fly to heaven. These men (for all their goodly shews) are the decayers of our estate, and enemies of all good government.

Mercy and justice, he goes on to say,

are the two pillars, that uphold the throne of the Prince: as you cannot hold mercy, where Justice is banished, so cannot you keep Justice where mercy is exiled: and as mercy without Justice, is foolish pity, so Justice, without mercy, is cruelty [pp. 15-18].

The same contrast and conclusions drawn by Perkins can be found in many other authorities;[25] and nobody, as far as I know, quarrels with the general principle that mercy should temper justice. The authorities tend, however, to apply it rather narrowly, and only to cases where, as Gentillet cautiously insists, it can "have a good foundation upon reason and equity" (p. 217), as when a man accidentally kills his friend— the example given by Bullinger (p. 188); or a young boy steals food because of hunger—the one given by Perkins in his *Treatise* (pp. 13–14). No one advocates showing leniency to more serious or hardened criminals. Since, as we know, Christian forgiveness was looked on as something apart from public and civil judgment, it is perhaps hardly surprising to find judicial clemency thus limited in practice to considerations of ordinary common sense and a reasonable regard for the circumstance of a case. But when we remember that ideal rulers were also by definition deeply religious men, who were supposed to "think how Christ would judge, before they judge", we cannot help feeling that the theorists have raised a problem to which they do not give all the attention it deserves. To a lesser degree, this holds true even when they turn to the private individual. He may, they argue, appeal to the law for the redress of injury, since God ordained the civil order for that purpose, though as a Christian he must forgive the malice which accompanied the injury.[26] But as was probably only natural in an age when personal revenge still enjoyed a certain amount of social (though not religious) prestige, the great majority of writers are concerned simply with establishing the tenet that punishment is the proper business of the civil authorities, to whom the private individual must leave it. Whether he has any further practical responsibility for his enemies beyond letting the law take its course is a question they do not go into. Again, however, when we remember how eloquently Erasmus Sarcerius, for instance, can argue (fol. xciv^v) that charity must be extended without reservation to "friends or enemies, Christians or not Christians...according to the example of the heavenly father, as before is said (Math. v, Luc. vi)", we are aware of a certain failure to pull the concepts of mercy and retaliation together—a failure not clearly intentional or obvious, but present, as it is in the commentaries on the measure-for-measure passage we have already discussed.

Allusions to the measure-for-measure passage occasionally crop up in the studies of rule, just as references to the doctrine of rule keep recurring in discussions of the measure-for-measure passage. Guevara, for example, writes that wicked rulers are like the blind leading the blind (I, 50^v), and Fenton, that they are like men with motes or beams in their eyes which prevent them from seeing anything justly (p. 64). Willymat orders the slanderers of princes to stop judging, "lest (as Christ Jesus said) you yourselves be judged" (p. 64), while King James in the *Basilicon Doron* urges his son to give measure for measure, warns him that he must expect to receive it, and advises him to be faultless because what would be "a mote in another's eye, is a beam in yours" (pp. 152, 32, 2). Evidently the passage was one which writers often recalled when working on the doctrine of rule, and frequently brought to the attention of their readers. But Shakespeare would have had special reason to take note of it. The heroine of his play is a private individual wrestling with the very issues raised by the passage: judgment, tolerance, mercy, retaliation in kind, and Christian forgiveness. His hero and his villain are primarily concerned with the same issues as they appear on a different level—to the holder of public office. His villain has, in addition, just those deficiencies of character which form the clearest and most commonly observed link between the doctrine of rule and the commentaries on the passage.

And so, centred as *Measure for Measure* is on the very points at which the two are either parallel or interlocked, it is hardly surprising to find that Shakespeare was apparently influenced to some extent by both.

His treatment of the initial situation seems to have been based in part on the crude but picturesque contrast which the Renaissance theorists so often drew between the two types of bad magistrate. The Duke, at the beginning of the play, would be recognized at once as the type who has failed because he was too merciful to enforce the laws properly. Shakespeare is certainly no Anabaptist—he sees, as clearly as William Perkins himself, the necessity of civil authority, and the terrible picture he paints of Vienna society in decay fully supports Perkins' contention that sentimental pity in a governor merely "opens a door to all confusion, disorder, and to all licentiousness of life". The Duke is essentially a wise and noble man who has erred from an excess of good will; he has put an end to his foolishness before the action proper begins, and so can step gracefully into the role of hero and good ruler; but Shakespeare does not disguise the fact that he has been wrong: he himself frankly describes his laxity as a 'vice' (III, ii, 284), and as such any Renaissance audience would certainly consider it.

Angelo, on the other hand, is a perfect case-study in the opposite weakness. Whatever he afterwards becomes, he is not from the first the ordinary venal judge, who is ignorant or cowardly, refuses to hear complaints (for he listens to Isabella), or takes bribes (for his indignation when she unfortunately uses the word sounds quite real); and as she pleads on his behalf at the end of the play:

> A due sincerity governed his deeds,
> Till he did look on me. (v, i, 451–2)

But he is the epitome of all the men who "have nothing in their mouths but the *law*, the *law*: and *Justice, Justice*, in the meantime forgetting that Justice always shakes hands with her sister mercy". This harshness Shakespeare traces to the personal flaw described in the measure-for-measure passage: the bitter and uncharitable narrowness in judging others that springs from a refusal to recognize or deal with one's own faults. Unlike the Duke, Angelo has not contended especially to know himself; he has no real conception of the potentialities of his own character. As a result, he thinks so well of himself that he neither has any defence against sudden overwhelming temptation nor possesses the humility and comprehension necessary to deal properly with Claudio.

His treatment of Claudio is from the first inexcusable, even by the strict standards of the Renaissance. For clemency in this particular case would certainly have had "a good foundation upon reason and equity": Claudio and Juliet are betrothed; they fully intend to marry; they are penitent; and the law was drowsy and neglected when they broke it. Furthermore, Claudio comes of a good family; and his fault is, after all, a very natural one. Shakespeare wisely leaves these last points to be made by Escalus and the Provost, both kind, sensible men who represent the normal point of view and whose support of Claudio is therefore significant. But Isabella cannot treat the offence lightly without weakening both the dignity of her calling and the force of her horror at Angelo's proposal. So in the first scene where she implores him for her brother's life, she bases her plea chiefly on modulations and variations of the two great Christian arguments we have already encountered in discussions of the measure-for-measure passage, interwoven with appropriate material from the doctrine of rule. The first is most clearly stated when, after pointing out that clemency is considered a virtue in the ruler, she begs him to remember that we must be merciful, as the Father was also merciful in redeeming us:

> Why, all the souls that were were forfeit once,
> And he that might the vantage best have took
> Found out the remedy. How would you be
> If he which is the top of judgement should
> But judge you as you are? O, think on that!
> And mercy then will breathe within your lips
> Like man new-made.   (II, ii, 73–9)

And then, after reminding him that a ruler is only a man dressed in a little brief authority, she urges him to think of his own faults before he condemns Claudio's:

> Go to your bosom,
> Knock there and ask your heart what it doth know
> That's like my brother's fault. If it confess
> A natural guiltiness such as is his,
> Let it not sound a thought upon your tongue
> Against my brother's life.   (II, ii, 136–41)

But it should be noted that she does not threaten him with retaliation in kind for his cruelty. Indeed, in her eagerness to show him that it *is* cruelty and to convince him that he ought to do as he would be done by, she argues rather that she in his place would not be so severe:

> I would to heaven I had your potency
> And you were Isabel! Should it then be thus?
> No! I would tell what 'twere to be a judge,
> And what a prisoner.   (II, ii, 66–9)

Her problem is not, however, to be quite such a simple one. Angelo's next move is not to throw himself on her kindness, but attempt to take advantage of it. If she is truly so merciful, he implies, she should be willing to rescue Claudio even at the expense of breaking what the Renaissance regarded as a most sacred law of God, and one doubly binding upon her because she is not only a virgin but a novice: if she refuses,

> Were you not then as cruel as the sentence
> That you have slandered so?   (II, iv, 109–10)

The modern reader may find it difficult not to echo this question, particularly when Claudio himself breaks down and adds the weight of his own desperate pleading to Angelo's arguments. Why, after all her talk of charity and forbearance, should Isabella not only decline to save her brother's life by an act of generosity, but condemn him so unsparingly for begging her to do so? When, however, we remember the limitations which Renaissance doctrine set on both charity and forbearance, we have no right to assume that Shakespeare is deliberately and cynically implying that his heroine is, in her own way, as narrow and cold as his villain. He seems rather to be trying to emphasize and illustrate the familiar tenet that neither charity nor forbearance must be carried to the point of permitting or condoning outrage. Like the Duke on the public level, Isabella is not entitled to let Angelo and Claudio use her mercy as their bawd; and, as the commentators on the measure-for-measure passage had made clear, her "duty is not to wink at them, but to take notice of them, and to show open dislike of them". Claudio is such a pathetic figure, and his horror of death so dreadfully comprehensible, that it may be fair to wonder if Shakespeare, when writing the prison scene, was not momentarily caught in what Tucker Brooke would call one of his conflicts of "intuitive sympathy with predetermined form";[27] but there is no evidence that he or his audience would not have felt Isabella's conduct was both demanded and justified by the ethical pattern of the play as he had consciously established it.

The conspiracy which follows also has its place in that pattern. It takes the form of a deliberate infliction upon Angelo of like for like, as the Duke is at pains to inform the audience in his soliloquy:

> So disguise shall, by th' disguised
> Pay with falsehood false exacting (III, ii, 294–5)

—offence punishing offence just as it is said to do in the measure-for-measure passage and the commentaries upon it. It should be noted, however, that the responsibility for devising and managing the whole plot rests on the shoulders of the Duke, who has a ruler's right to see to retaliation in kind and a ruler's privilege of using extraordinary means to ensure the success of a worthy cause. The part which Isabella necessarily plays in the conspiracy is as far as possible minimized: we are not allowed actually to see her persuading Mariana, reporting to Angelo, or doing anything but simply agreeing to the scheme because it is presented to her as the only sure way to save Claudio, protect herself, right Mariana, and secure any real evidence against the deputy. Unlike the Duke, she acts from no special desire to pay Angelo back in his own coin; it is only afterwards, when she hears the news of Claudio's death by his treachery, that she breaks down and very understandably cries for personal and immediate revenge: "O, I will to him and pluck out his eyes!" (IV, iii, 124). The calmer Duke then very properly persuades her that she ought instead to turn her cause over to the civil authorities:

> And you shall have your bosom on this wretch,
> Grace of the Duke, revenges to your heart,
> And general honour. (IV, iii, 139–41)

The audience at the first performance of the play probably took this promise at its face-value, as a prediction that Angelo was to suffer full legal punishment for his offences in the trial to come. Nor would they have disapproved. His case is very different from Claudio's. His judge, the Duke, is not, as he was, unfit for his task; and he cannot plead for mercy "with a good foundation upon reason and equity", as Claudio could. Although he has not actually succeeded in doing the worst he intended to do, there is still a heavy count against him: attempted seduction, abuse of his authority, deception of his prince, and treachery of the meanest kind; while if he *had* done what he himself and every character on the stage except the Duke believes that he has, there was nothing to be said against the Duke's sentence:

> The very mercy of the law cries out
> Most audible, even from his proper tongue,

> 'An Angelo for Claudio, death for death.'
> Haste still pays haste, and leisure answers leisure;
> Like doth quit like, and Measure still for Measure....
> We do condemn thee to the very block
> Where Claudio stooped to death, and with like haste.   (v, i, 412–20)

The audience, knowing what they knew, probably did not expect that the execution would really take place; but they can hardly have been prepared for what actually follows. First, Mariana, still pathetically devoted to her husband, begs the Duke for his life; and then, failing, she turns to Isabella—who is not in love with Angelo, who has every good reason to loathe him, who might plead with justice that his punishment is now entirely a matter for the civil authorities —and begs for her help.

The cruelty of the appeal is obvious; and the natural, the instinctive, and (we must remember) the allowed reply to it is implicit in the shocked exclamation of the Duke:

> Against all sense you do importune her.
> Should she kneel down, in mercy of this fact,
> Her brother's ghost his paved bed would break,
> And take her hence in horror.   (v, i, 438–41)

Then Mariana cries out to Isabella again—and she kneels, not in silence, which is all Mariana dares to ask for, but generously to make the best case she can for Angelo. Her act is not natural; it is not (as the Duke has carefully pointed out) even reasonable: it is sheer, reckless forgiveness of the kind Christ advocates in the Sermon on the Mount—the great pronouncement which in Luke immediately precedes and forms part of the measure-for-measure passage. And like Christ, Shakespeare contrasts this sort of forgiveness with another. Mariana is certainly more praiseworthy than the 'sinners' described by the Lord, for Angelo has treated her very badly; but her mercy to him resembles theirs in that it springs primarily from preference and affection: she loves her lover (to quote the common sixteenth-century translation of Luke vi, 32) and she hopes for something again—the renewal of his devotion and a happy marriage with him. Hence, however gracious and commendable her conduct may be, it differs markedly from that of Isabella, who has nothing to sustain her but the conviction that she *must* be merciful and the memory of what she had promised Angelo on the strength of it. And then, almost before the audience at the first performance had time to catch its breath, the Duke, having summoned Claudio and revealed the truth, proceeds not only to pardon him, but to let off Angelo, Lucio, and Barnardine as well, with penalties entirely disproportionate to what their conduct deserved by ordinary Renaissance standards.

We may, if we please, argue that Shakespeare suddenly remembered he was writing a comedy and decided he had better botch up some sort of happy ending to send the audience home contented, regardless of probability and doctrine alike. But all the evidence goes to show that the audience would have left for home equally contented—perhaps even more contented—if Angelo, Lucio, and Barnardine had been punished, like Shylock, or remanded for judgment at some future date, like Don John in *Much Ado about Nothing*. And when we recall the special difficulties and defects of Renaissance doctrine, it seems at least possible that the conclusion of

Measure for Measure may rather represent a deliberate effort—perhaps a little clumsy, certainly romantic—to "do something" about that disturbing discrepancy between the concepts of religious mercy and secular justice which we find in the commentaries on the measure-for-measure passage and again in the studies of rule. Like the theorists, Shakespeare was apparently prepared to concede that the private Christian should not (in the name of mercy) weakly condone every form of injustice and oppression, and may, if necessary, invoke secular authority to defend what he knows to be right. But it is not enough merely to wash his hands of personal revenge, and—let the secular authority do the dirty work for him. Nor should the secular authority himself forget that "judging as Christ would judge" means something more than weighing each case according to common sense and ordinary good will. He need not make a scarecrow of the law: he must be vigilant to suppress or prevent disorder and evil; and he should see to it that the innocent are properly protected—that Isabella's name is cleared by her traducer; that Barnardine is committed to the friar instead of being turned loose on society; that Claudio makes amends to Juliet, Angelo to Mariana, Lucio to the girl he has wronged. He may even, to a certain extent, use retaliation in kind, or the threat of retaliation in kind, to bring malefactors to their senses: it is no accident that Angelo is paid with falsehood false exacting, or finds himself sentenced to the very block where Claudio stooped to death, and with like haste. But his primary duty is, like God, to show mercy whenever he possibly can, even when the fault is disgusting and the criminal despicable: to remember that Lucio's slanders hurt chiefly the Duke's own personal feelings; that Barnardine is a mere animal,

> A creature unprepared, unmeet for death;
> And to transport him in the mind he is
> Were damnable; (IV, iii, 71–3)

that Angelo has been blasted and shamed out of his appalling complacency, and may, as Mariana pleads: "become much more the better / For being a little bad" (v, i, 445–6). It is the difference between the "Like doth quit like" with which the Duke begins his sentence on his deputy and the "Well, Angelo, your evil quits you well", with which he concludes it.

In all this, Shakespeare is not so much rejecting the ordinary Christian doctrine of the Renaissance as clarifying it, strengthening it, and holding it true to its own deepest implications. Just how or when he formed his own opinions on the question there is no telling. We do not know what books he read or what sermons he attended, although we should note that he could have picked up practically all the necessary doctrinal instruction from reading two books or hearing two sermons that interested him, while the agreement between the various authorities makes it certain that the theories he was taught would not differ drastically from the ones we have already summed up and discussed. The investigation, however, sheds no light on his own denominational preferences; he touches in this play only on such elements of traditional theology as were shared by Anglican, Puritan, and Roman Catholic alike. Nor, since to dramatize a doctrine is not necessarily to believe in it, are we entitled to use *Measure for Measure* as evidence that he himself was even a Christian. All that can be said with safety is that when he put his mind to it, he could produce a more coherent, a more independent, and in the last analysis, a more Christian piece of thinking on the subject than nine out of ten professional Renaissance theologians.

NOTES

1. This article is based on material gathered when the writer was holder of a research fellowship at the Folger Shakespeare Library.

2. R. W. Battenhouse, "*Measure for Measure* and Christian Doctrine of the Atonement", *P.M.L.A.* LXI (1946), 1029–59; C. J. Sisson, *The Mythical Sorrows of Shakespeare* (Annual Shakespeare Lecture of the British Academy, 1934), p. 17; R. W. Chambers, *The Jacobean Shakespeare and 'Measure for Measure'* (Annual Shakespeare Lecture of the British Academy, 1937), p. 54.

3. Luke vi, 27–42. Geneva version (London, 1599). The spelling of this and all subsequent citations from Renaissance sources has been modernized for the convenience of the reader.

4. John Calvin, quoted by Augustine Marlorate, in his *Catholike and Ecclesiasticall Exposition of...S. Mathewe*, trans. Thomas Tymme (London, 1570), p. 136. See also J. Calvin, *A Harmonie vpon...Matthewe, Marke, and Luke*, trans. E. P. (London, 1584), p. 209; *The Epistles and Gospelles with a Brief Postil* [ed. R. Taverner], (n.p., 1540), sig. Bb. 1ʳ; Desiderius Erasmus, *The First Tome...of the Paraphrase...vpon the Newe Testament* (London, 1548), fol. lxxviiᵛ; [Antonius Corvinus], *A Postill...vpon Euery Gospell through the Yeare* (n.p., 1550), sigs. Piiᵛ–Piiiiᵛ; Nicholas Heminge [Niel Hemmingsen], *A Postill or Exposition of the Gospels*, trans. Arthur Golding (London, 1569), fol. 208ʳ; William Perkins, *Exposition of Christs Sermon in the Mount* (Cambridge, 1608), pp. 408–13; the Rheims note on Matt. vii, 1 in William Fulke's *Text of the Newe Testament...translated out of the vulgar Latine by the Papists of the Traiterous Seminarie at Rhemes* (London, 1589), sig. F1ᵛ.

5. *Brief Postil*, sig. Bb. 1ʳ. See also Calvin, p. 211; Musculus and Bullinger, quoted by Marlorate, *Exposition of Matthew*, p. 137; Thomas Becon, *A New Postil* (London, 1566), sigs. Eeiʳ–Eeiiᵛ; note on Luke vi, 42 in Geneva Bible; Perkins, *Exposition*, pp. 419–31; Corvinus, sig. Piiiiᵛ; Erasmus, fol. lxxviiiʳ; Heminge, fol. 210ᵛ.

6. Calvin, p. 209. See also Marlorate, *Exposition of Matthew*, p. 136; *Brief Postil*, sig. Bb. 1ʳ; Rheims note on Matt. vii, 1; Geneva note on Luke vi, 37; Perkins, *Exposition*, pp. 408, 424–5; Erasmus, fol. lxxviiᵛ.

7. Corvinus, sig. Piiiiᵛ. See also Becon, sigs. Ddiʳ–Ddiiiiʳ; Ddvᵛ–Ddviʳ; *Brief Postil*, sigs. Aa. iijʳ–Aa. iijᵛ; Erasmus, fol. lxxviiʳ; Heminge, fols. 208ᵛ and 209ᵛ.

8. Quoted by Marlorate in *A Catholike and Ecclesiastical Exposition of...S. Mark and S. Luke*, trans. Thomas Tymme (London, 1583), p. 160. See also Calvin, pp. 209–10; Perkins, *Exposition*, p. 415; *Brief Postil*, sig. Aa. ivᵛ; Corvinus, sigs. Pvʳ–Pvᵛ; Becon, sig. Eeiʳ; Erasmus, fol. lxxviiʳ; Heminge, fol. 210ʳ.

9. It should also be noted that in Matt. v, 38 ff., the passage which corresponds to the pronouncement on Christian forgiveness in Luke (vi, 27–35) begins with a specific repudiation of the *lex talionis*.

10. *Brief Postil*, sigs. Aa. iijᵛ–Aa. ivʳ. See also Becon, sigs. Ddiiiʳ–Ddiiiᵛ; Corvinus, sig. Piiiiʳ; Heminge, fols. 207ᵛ, 208ʳ, 209ʳ; Perkins, *Exposition*, pp. 407–8.

11. Thomas Bilson, *A Sermon Preached at Westminister before the King and Queenes Maiesties, at their Coronations* (London, 1603), sigs. C3ʳ–C3ᵛ. See also Andrew Willet, *Ecclesia Triumphans* [1603], (Cambridge, 1614), p. 33 and sigs. A3ʳ–A4ʳ, A4ᵛ–A5ʳ; William Willymat, *A Loyal Subiects Looking-Glasse* (London, [1604]), sig. A1ʳ, pp. 10, 39, 46; Richard Eedes, "The Dutie of a King", two sermons preached before James (9 and 30 August, 1603), printed in *Six Learned and Godly Sermons* (London, 1604), sigs. Fijᵛ–Fiijʳ.

12. Bilson, sigs. A6ᵛ–A7ᵛ. See also Perkins, *Treatise*, p. 6; Willymat, pp. 3–4, 5–6; Willet, p. 3; Richard Field, *A Learned Sermon Preached Before the King* (London, 1604), sigs. A3ᵛ–A4ʳ; Henry Smith, *The Magistrates Scripture* [1590], printed in *Sermons* (London, 1631), p. 344; Ben Jonson, *King James His Royall and Magnificent Entertainment* (London, 1604), sig. A4ᵛ; Erasmus Sarcerius, *Commonplaces of Scripture*, trans. R. Taverner (n.p., 1538), fol. lxxi; H. Bullinger, *Fiftie Godlie and Learned Sermons*, trans. H. I. (London, 1587), pp. 152, 219; Geoffrey Fenton, *A Forme of Christian Pollicie* (London, 1574), p. 61; G. Gifford, *A Dialogue Betweene a Papist and Protestant* (London, 1599), pp. 101–2; James I, *True Lawe of Free Monarchies* (London, 1604), sig. B3ʳ.

13. The reason for applying such terms to rulers is given by Bilson, sigs. B5ʳ–B5ᵛ, C3ʳ; [*Homilies*] *Certaine Sermons Appointed by the Queenes Maiestie* (London, 1595), sig. 13ʳ; Bullinger, pp. 145–6; J. Dod and R. Cleaver, *Exposition of the Ten Commandments* (London, 1604), p. 181; R. Bellarmine, *An Ample Declaration of the Christian Doctrine* (Roane, n.d.), p. 182; Henry Smith, *A Memento for Magistrates*, printed in *Sermons* (London, 1604), pp. 534–5. The ruler is also called, or compared to, a 'parent', or 'shepherd', or 'teacher', etc. by Willet, sig. A2ʳ;

Jonson, *Panegyre*, in *Entertainment*, sig. F1ʳ; Fenton, p. 310; Antony Guevara, *The Dial of Princes*, trans. T. North (n.p., 1568), I, 53ᵛ; Laurentius Grimaldus Goslicius, *The Counsellor*, trans. anon. (London, 1598), p. 74; James I, *True Lawe*, sigs. B4ʳ, B4ᵛ–B5ʳ, D2ᵛ–D3ᵛ, and *Basilicon Doron* (London, 1603), p. 25. See also commentaries on measure-for-measure passage: Becon, sig. Ddiiiʳ; Perkins, *Exposition*, p. 424.

14. Bilson sigs. A7ᵛ–A8ʳ; Eedes, sigs. Evᵛ–Eviʳ; Smith, *Magistrates Scripture*, pp. 341–3, 337, and *Memento for Magistrates*, p. 530.

15. Bilson, sigs. B1ʳ–B1ᵛ; *Homilies*, sigs. I8ᵛ–K2ʳ; Mm4ᵛ–Nn1ᵛ; Nn7ʳ–Nn7ᵛ; Bullinger, p. 219; Dod and Cleaver, pp. 235–6.

16. Bilson, sigs. B6ʳ–B6ᵛ; Willymat, pp. 4–5, 26–7, 44–5; *Homilies*, sigs. I5ᵛ–I8ᵛ; Bullinger, pp. 173–5; Dod and Cleaver, p. 236; Nicholas Gibbens, *Questions and Disputations Concerning the Holy Scriptures* (n.p., 1601), p. 377; James I, *True Lawe*, sigs. B7ᵛ–C5ᵛff.; Gifford, pp. 145–51.

17. Bilson, sigs. B3ᵛ–B4ᵛ; Perkins, *Treatise*, pp. 6–7; *Two Guides to a Good Life* (London, 1604), sig. G2ᵛ; Willymat, pp. 48–9; Sarcerius, fols. lxxiiᵛ, ccvʳ, ccviiiʳ; Innocent Gentillet, *A Discovrse vpon the Meanes of Wel Governing*, trans. Simon Patericke (London, 1602), pp. 109–10; *Homilies*, sigs. F2ᵛ–F3ᵛ, I4ʳ–I5ᵛ; Bullinger, pp. 168, 196–8; Fenton, pp. 75–6; Gibbens, pp. 376–7; Bellarmine, pp. 153–4; James I, *True Lawe*, sigs. D5ᵛ–D6ʳ. See also commentaries on the measure-for-measure passage: listed under note 10, above.

18. Willymat, pp. 58–9. For other arguments in favour of the ruler's right to use extraordinary means, see Bilson, sig. B4ᵛ; Gentillet, pp. 246–51; Goslicius, pp. 90, 119–20; James I, *True Lawe*, sigs. D1ᵛ–D2ʳ.

19. Bilson, sigs. C3ᵛ–C4ʳ; James Godskall, *The Kings Medicine for this Present Yeere* (London, 1604), sig. K1ʳ; Smith, *Magistrates Scripture*, pp. 336–7; Jonson, *Panegyre*, sigs. E4ʳ and F1ᵛ; Bullinger, p. 172; Fenton, pp. 57–8, 65–8; James I, *Basilicon Doron*, pp. 17, 95, and *True Lawe*, sigs. B4ʳ, E3ᵛ.

20. Henry Hooke, *Sermon Preached Before the King* (London, 1604), sig. Bviʳ. See also Bilson, sig. C7ʳ; Perkins, *Treatise*, pp. 86–7; Bullinger, p. 172; Smith, *Memento for Magistrates*, p. 532; Fenton, pp. 66–7; Goslicius, p. 105.

21. Bilson, sigs. C3ᵛ–C4ʳ; Willet, sig. A4ʳ; Godskall, sigs. N2ᵛ–N3ʳ, G7ᵛ–G8ʳ, K1ʳ; Eedes, sigs. D1ᵛ–Diiʳ; Smith, *Magistrates Scripture*, pp. 339–41, 337, and *Memento for Magistrates*, p. 527; Jonson, *Entertainment*, sig. A3ʳ; Sarcerius, fol. ccviᵛ; Gentillet, pp. 97, 357; *Homilies*, sigs. I4ʳ, I5ʳ–I5ᵛ, Pp5ᵛ; Bullinger, pp. 175–6, 184, 187–8; Fenton, pp. 7, 69–71; Goslicius, pp. 100, 104, 107; James I, *Basilicon Doron*, pp. 1–21. See also commentaries on the measure-for-measure passage: Becon, sig. Ddiiiᵛ; Perkins, *Exposition*, p. 424.

22. Guevara, I, 51ᵛ. See also *ibid.* 52ʳ; James I, *Basilicon Doron*, pp. 1–2; Goslicius, p. 106. See also commentaries on the measure-for-measure passage: Erasmus, fol. lxxviiiʳ; Perkins, *Exposition*, p. 424.

23. Eedes, sigs. Dviiiʳ–Dviiiᵛ. See also Willet, sig. A3ᵛ; Godskall, sig. K1ʳ; Jonson, *Panegyre*, sig. F1ʳ; Gentillet, pp. 99, 279; Smith, *Memento for Magistrates*, p. 532; Fenton, p. 13; Guevara, I, 50ᵛ; Goslicius, p. 104; James I, *Basilicon Doron*, pp. 3, 23–4, 60–61, and *True Lawe*, sigs. D1ᵛ–D2ʳ.

24. Fenton, p. 64. See also *ibid.* pp. 58–9; Bilson, sig. C7ʳ; Smith, *Magistrates Scripture*, pp. 337, 339–40; Jonson, *Panegyre*, sig. E4ʳ; Bullinger, pp. 152, 194; Guevara, I, 4ʳ–4ᵛ; James I, *Basilicon Doron*, pp. 35, 91, and *True Lawe*, sigs. B3ʳ–B3ᵛ.

25. Eedes, sigs. Eijʳ–Eiiijʳ, Eiᵛ–Eiiʳ; Guevara, III, 3ᵛ; Goslicius, pp. 106–10; James I, *Basilicon Doron*, pp. 29–31; Thomas Blague, *A Sermon...Before the Kings Maiestie* (London, 1603), sig. B4ᵛ. The following writers condemn the over-merciful judge, but not the over-severe one: Gentillet, p. 189; *Homilies*, sig. F3ᵛ; Bullinger, pp. 168, 197–8; Fenton, pp. 81–2; and in the commentaries on the measure-for-measure passage: Becon, sigs. Ddiiiᵛ–Ddvʳ. The following writers condemn the over-severe judge, but not the over-merciful one: *Two Guides*, sigs. K2ʳ–K3ᵛ; Bellarmine, pp. 234–5. The general principle that mercy should temper justice is approved by Bilson, sigs. C2ʳ–C2ᵛ; Gentillet, p. 276; Bullinger, pp. 118, 199; Bellarmine, p. 234; Willet, p. 22; Jonson, *Panegyre*, sig. F1ʳ; Hooke, sigs. Diiiᵛ–Divʳ; and in the commentaries on the measure-for-measure passage: Becon, sig. Ddiiiᵛ.

26. Perkins, *Treatise*, pp. 55–6; Fenton, p. 355; Godskall, sig. K7ʳ.

27. Tucker Brooke, "The Renaissance", in *A Literary History of England*, ed. A. C. Baugh (New York, 1948), p. 527.

THE INDIVIDUALIZATION OF SHAKESPEARE'S CHARACTERS THROUGH IMAGERY

BY

MIKHAIL M. MOROZOV

The degree to which and the means by which Shakespeare individualized the style of speech used by his various characters are still unsettled.[1] This question is of practical as well as theoretical interest—especially for actors of Shakespearian roles and for translators of Shakespeare. This is particularly true of the Soviet theatre which, as I have noted elsewhere,[2] strives for the maximum individualization of Shakespeare's characters.

Rowe, Shakespeare's first biographer (1709), and Alexander Pope maintained that even if Shakespeare had not indicated the names of the characters speaking in the text, we would have been able to recognize them. Although the great dramatist's English has since been covered with "the dust of ages", many modern readers 'instinctively' feel that Hamlet, for instance, speaks differently from Ophelia, that Othello's style of speech is different from Iago's. Wherein, exactly, does this difference lie? Strange as it may seem, this question has not been thoroughly studied to this day.

Shakespeare's language, as everyone knows, is exceptionally rich in imagery. "Every word with him is a picture", Thomas Gray wrote of Shakespeare. This suggests the hypothesis that the 'natures' of the characters may in some measure be reflected in these pictures. In real life, in our every-day speech, we quite probably usually compare the things we talk about with that which is particularly near and comprehensible to each of us. In literature the case is evidently often different, for in inventing a metaphor the poet or writer may disregard his personal inclinations in favour of the aesthetic canons of some definite 'school' or 'tradition'. In plays the characters frequently speak in the language, and hence the images, of the author. Hypotheses alone, like 'instinctive' feelings, are far from sufficient.

In discussing the distinctively individual features of Shakespeare's characters in his book *Shakespeare's Language and Style*,[3] the author of these lines wrote: "The range of the predominating image met with in the speeches of a character is of tremendous significance." This assertion, however, was not bolstered up at that time by an analysis of the facts. Most probably, in the vast literature on Shakespeare, quite a number of such similar assertions are to be found. However, there is a no lesser abundance of denials of any definitely defined individuality in the speech styles of his characters. True, the overwhelming majority of books on Shakespeare do not touch on this question at all, although it is of paramount importance to a study of Shakespeare's poetics.

The most fundamental investigation of Shakespeare's imagery is Caroline Spurgeon's well-known book *Shakespeare's Imagery*.[4] In this book, however, his imagery is considered only in respect to all his work as a whole, or in respect to some one play. Spurgeon does not touch on the part imagery plays in revealing character. Only in the appendix of her book does she make any mention of the other interesting functions of imagery. Listing these functions, she speaks of the assistance a study of imagery can be in revealing the temperament and nature of the character who uses this imagery. This is a very interesting theme, she says, and is worth investigating. To prove her point she cites Falstaff's imagery in the two parts of *Henry IV* as offering clear indication of the change which takes place in the stout knight.[5]

Spurgeon touched on this rich theme only briefly and in passing. As we have already said, most Shakespeare studies do not deal with this theme at all, while many of them deny or minimize the distinct individuality of the style of speech used by each of Shakespeare's characters.

About twenty years ago, thanks to the studies of Dover Wilson and Granville-Barker,[6] it was the fashion among English students of Shakespeare to regard Shakespeare chiefly as a dramatist. Of recent years, however, Shakespeare is coming more and more to be regarded chiefly as a 'dramatic poet'. The realism of Shakespeare's characters, their specific psychological traits, and hence distinctive styles of speech, are often being thrown into obscurity.[7]

We are obliged to erect the edifice of our investigation on an unexplored site. If, as a result of our investigation, we should find definite laws governing the imagery of the individual characters we shall thereby, first, again confirm the fact that Shakespeare's characters do not speak for the author but, so to say, 'for themselves', i.e. are independent individuals (in other words we shall obtain new confirmation of Shakespeare's *realism*); secondly, we shall record *one* of the means by which Shakespeare (probably subconsciously) individualized the speech of his characters; and, finally, the particular figures of speech predominating in the role of any given character will provide us with a valuable key to that character's psychological make-up.

1. *OTHELLO*

OTHELLO

The images to be found in Othello's speeches fall into two sharply contrasting groups. First—and chiefly—there is what may be called *lofty* and *poetic* imagery. Instead of saying "for the greatest fortune" Othello says "for the sea's worth" (I, ii, 28). He says that Desdemona "was false as water" (V, ii, 132). Instead of "always be suspecting" Othello says "to follow still the changes of the moon with fresh suspicions" (III, iii, 178).

It is a noteworthy fact that the image of the moon occurs four more times in Othello's speeches: instead of "nine months" he has "nine moons" (I, iii, 84); "the moon winks" (IV, ii, 76) to hide Desdemona's supposed adultery from its eyes; after murdering Desdemona Othello compares the catastrophe to "a huge eclipse of sun and moon" (V, ii, 99) and states that the moon "makes men mad" (V, ii, 107). In this repetition of the word 'moon' we divine something peculiar to the man, something of Oriental origin, the 'atmosphere' Pushkin felt:

> Why does young Desdemona
> Love her Moor
> As the moon loves the dark of night....

This first impression is confirmed by others of Othello's florid and grandiose figures of speech. He does not say that the sybil who sewed the handkerchief he presented to Desdemona was two hundred years old, but that she "had number'd in the world the sun to course two hundred compasses" (III, iv, 72). He invokes the "chaste stars" (v, ii, 2). To kill Desdemona means "to put out the light" (v, ii, 7). The lamp he holds in his hand is a "flaming minister" (v, ii, 8). To kill Desdemona is to pluck the rose (v, ii, 13), to kiss her as she sleeps is to smell the rose on the tree (v, ii, 18). Had Desdemona been true to him he would not have sold her for a world made "of one entire and perfect chrysolite" (v, ii, 143). Desdemona's skin is whiter "than snow, and smooth as monumental alabaster" (v, ii, 4). Instead of saying that he is a man already advanced in years, Othello says that he is "declined into the vale of years" (III, iii, 266). He compares Desdemona to a hawk (III, iii, 265) and to the fountain from which his current runs (IV, ii, 58). Instead of simply vowing "by heaven", he says much more picturesquely "by yond marble heaven", with marble probably used as a synonym for enduring, constant, inviolable. He calls patience a "young and rose-lipt cherubin" (IV, ii, 62). Learning, after her death, that Desdemona was innocent, Othello weeps tears of joy and compares his tears with the "medicinable gum" of "the Arabian trees" (v, ii, 349). After Desdemona's death he compares himself with "the base Indian", who "threw a pearl away richer than all his tribe" (v, ii, 346). Contemplating death he speaks of the "very sea-mark of my utmost sail" (v, ii, 267). The following images, too, it seems, should be classed as poetic. Othello compares his heart to a stone: he strikes his breast and it hurts his hand (IV, i, 181). The image of a heart turned to stone recurs in Othello's speeches: "thou dost stone my heart", he tells Desdemona (v, ii, 63). Othello tells the Senators that custom "hath made the flinty and steel couch of war my thrice-driven bed of down" (I, iii, 231).

Thus, lofty and poetic images are abundant in Othello's speech. The epithet *poetic* is particularly appropriate to them. Some of them are full of Oriental atmosphere: the moon, the "two hundred compasses" of the sun, the fragrance of roses, a world of chrysolite, skin as white as alabaster. The gum of Arabian trees and the Indian with his pearl are frankly exotic. Investigators who refuse to admit exotic colour in Othello's role are therefore in the wrong.

The numerous classical images he uses are also of the lofty and poetic type. He speaks, for instance, of the "light-wing'd toys of feather'd Cupid" (I, iii, 268). Waves are "hills of seas Olympus-high" (II, i, 191). Thunder is "th' Immortal Jove's dread clamours" (III, iii, 356). Desdemona's name was, according to Othello, "as fresh as Dian's visage" (III, iii, 388). He compares his feelings with the Pontic (Black) sea which flows ever forward (III, iii, 453). He calls life "Promethean heat" (v, ii, 12). The image of chaos in the famous phrase "when I love thee not, Chaos is come again" (III, iii, 92) is also to be regarded as classical. Finally, the image of a personified justice evoked by the words: "O balmy breath, that dost almost persuade Justice to break her sword" (v, ii, 16), may also be included here. Justice is allegorically pictured as a feminine figure carrying a sword.

Lofty, poetic and solemn imagery is so abundant and so essential in Othello's role that we are quite justified in calling it the dominant theme in his world of images. However, it is not the only theme. In sharp contrast to it there is another theme represented by a whole group of images which may be called low.

Othello calls a suspicious, jealous man a 'goat' (III, iii, 180). "Goats and monkeys!" he exclaims in a fit of jealousy (IV, i, 264).[8] He says he "had rather be a toad, and live upon the vapour of a dungeon" than be cuckolded (III, iii, 270). He compares Desdemona to "a cistern for foul toads to knot and gender in" (IV, ii, 60). He commands his bosom to swell with its "fraught, for 'tis of aspics' tongues" (III, iii, 451). Desdemona's singing, he says, is capable of taming a bear, thereby comparing himself with a savage bear (IV, i, 188). "If that the earth could teem with woman's tears, each drop she [Desdemona] falls would prove a crocodile" he says (IV, i, 256). He declares that Desdemona is 'honest' as "summer flies are in the shambles that quicken even with blowing" (IV, ii, 65). He calls the infidelity of wives a "forked plague" (III, iii, 276). It is remarkable that this theme—the theme of the menagerie—goats, monkeys, toads, aspics, wild bears, crocodiles, flies—is absolutely identical, as we shall see, with the dominant theme of Iago's imagery.

Othello's famous comparison of his thoughts about Desdemona's handkerchief with a raven over an infected house (IV, i, 20) is pervaded with bleak gloom. And his comparison of Desdemona herself with a lovely, fair, sweet-smelling weed (IV, ii, 66) is an image in which, side by side with its poetic quality, there is something akin to Iago's dominant theme.

Othello says that Iago has "set me on the rack" (III, iii, 336). He compares his cheeks, ready to burn with shame, with a forge (IV, ii, 73). He says that had all Cassio's hairs "been lives, my great revenge had stomach for them all" (V, ii, 75).

The image of a monster appears twice in Othello's speeches. He says of Iago "there were some monster in his thought too hideous to be shown" (III, iii, 106). "A horned man's a monster and a beast", he declares (IV, i, 62). As we shall see the image of jealousy as a monster recurs in the speeches of Iago, Desdemona and Emilia.

Thus, besides the lofty, poetic and bright images, which predominate in Othello's world of images, we also find mean images (goats, monkeys, toads, etc.) and gloomy images which sometimes have a suggestion of the demonic (the raven over an infected house). This contrast is strikingly conveyed in one of Othello's images: "And let the labouring bark climb hills of seas Olympus-high, and duck again as low as hell's from heaven" (II, i, 190). The first, poetic, theme is properly Othello's; the second, low, theme is, as we shall see later, borrowed.

It is noteworthy that the low and gloomy images are not scattered haphazardly through Othello's speeches. They invade his speeches, violating the bright dominant theme, at a logical point—following the words "and when I love thee not, Chaos is come again" (III, iii, 92). This is the point at which Iago gains the ascendancy over Othello's soul, so that the latter begins to think in Iago's images, to see the world with Iago's eyes.

It is also a fact worthy of note that Othello returns to his own dominant theme not after he learns of Desdemona's innocence, but much earlier. In the scene of Desdemona's death there is only one low and coarse image: Othello says that had all Cassio's hairs been lives, his great revenge had had stomach for them all (V, ii, 75). This is merely a reflection, a reminiscence of a past mood, as is the coarse word 'whore' which escapes him twice in this same scene. On the whole, Othello's part in the scene of Desdemona's death abounds in lofty and poetic imagery. The monologue he pronounces over the sleeping Desdemona at the beginning of the second scene of Act V is particularly rich in such imagery, for Othello kills Desdemona loving her.

In his monologue in Act III, Scene 3, Othello speaks of "plumed troops", of the "spirit-stirring drum", of the "royal banner", of the "rude throats" of "mortal engines", etc. For the rest there are no military motifs in Othello's imagery, with the exception, perhaps, that, when meeting Desdemona at Cyprus, he calls her "my fair warrior" (II, i, 185). It is interesting to note that his classical images likewise do not deal with military motifs: neither Mars nor Caesar is mentioned.

We shall not touch on the scattered, incidental images in Othello's speech which do not constitute integral groups. For instance, early in the play we meet a metaphor very typical of Shakespeare in general, a metaphor of the theatre. "Were it my cue to fight, I should have known it without a prompter" (I, ii, 82). Or, to take another example, there is an image from Biblical legend. Othello says that Emilia has an office opposite to that of Saint Peter; i.e. that she keeps the gates of hell (IV, ii, 90). All these scattered themes are not of importance to us.

Thus we find a definite order in Othello's world of images. The lofty-poetic dominant is over-powered by the low theme stemming from Iago, only to triumph again at the last. The point at which the second theme makes its invasion is the image: "Chaos is come again." It is our opinion that this image has an objective rather than a subjective meaning, i.e. that chaos has come again in the universe, that the cosmos, the universe, has been upset; in other words, that the world has changed in Othello's eyes. Were we to take this image as subjective, i.e. as meaning that chaos had returned to Othello's soul, we should have to assume that chaos had already been resident there at some former time, an assumption for which there are no grounds in the text. Othello's story of his life (his monologue in the Senate) confirms that the lofty-poetic theme, connected with the cosmos, is 'native' to Othello, that he is a highly *harmonic* man and that, consequently, the low theme, connected with chaos, comes wholly from Iago.

IAGO

The low images prove predominant in Iago's role. The prevailing images are of beasts, represented as embodiments of foolishness, lechery and all kinds of loathsome vices. Iago sees the surrounding world as a stable or malodorous menagerie. A faithful servant is like an ass (I, i, 46). Othello is trustful and can be led by the nose like an ass (I, iii, 407). Iago says that Othello will yet reward him for making him an ass (II, i, 321). He does not want to "wear my heart upon my sleeve for daws to peck at" (I, i, 64). "Plague him [Othello] with flies", i.e. with petty annoyances, Iago counsels Roderigo (I, i, 71). Othello is "an old black ram" tupping a "white ewe" (I, i, 88). The carousing warriors of Cyprus are a "*flock* of drunkards" (II, iii, 62). Othello is "a Barbary horse", Brabantio's grandchildren will neigh, and Brabantio will have coursers and gennets for relatives (I, i, 112 f.). When in each other's arms, Othello and Desdemona make "the beast with two backs" (I, i, 117). Iago calls Desdemona a prostitute, choosing the jargon word 'guinea-hen' as a synonym; he dissuades Roderigo from drowning himself for love of a 'guinea-hen' (I, iii, 318). He says that sooner than do that he would "change my humanity with a baboon" (I, iii, 319). "Drown cats and blind puppies", he tells Roderigo (I, iii, 341). Women in their kitchens are 'wild-cats' (II, i, 110). In Iago's words one man differs from another as "the cod's head" from "the salmon's tail" (II, i, 155). "With as little a web as this will I ensnare as great a fly as Cassio" (II, i, 169) says Iago, comparing himself to a spider. He compares Roderigo to a hunting dog which he sets upon Cassio (II, i, 316). When Cassio has drunk some wine, he will become as quarrelsome as Desdemona's dog (II, iii, 54). He assures Cassio that Othello has punished him for the sake of policy, in order to put fear into the hearts of the people of Cyprus, "as one would beat his offenceless dog to affright an imperious lion" (II, iii, 278). Cassio and Desdemona are, in his words, as lecherous as goats, monkeys and wolves (III, iii, 404). He compares a married man to a yoked ox (IV, i, 67). This 'menagerie' of Iago's is reflected, as we have seen, in Othello's speeches, forming the second theme (goats, monkeys, toads) in the latter's world of images. Iago does indeed succeed in poisoning Othello's soul for a time.

Other low images fit in with the 'menagerie'. "The food", says Iago, "that to him now is as luscious as locusts shall be to him shortly as bitter as coloquintida" (I, iii, 354). Iago compares Cassio's slender fingers to 'clysterpipes' (II, i, 179). When Roderigo speaks of Desdemona's "blest condition", Iago mocks him, saying "blest fig's end" (II, i, 260). He calls Roderigo a "young quat" he has rubbed "almost to the sense" (V, i, 11).

His images are generally concrete and substantial. He compares the human body with a garden, will with gardeners: what we plant in this garden depends upon ourselves. Idleness he compares with sterility, industry with manure, love is the scion of lust (I, iii, 324 f.). "My invention", he says of himself, "comes from my pate as birdlime does from frize" (II, i, 126). He calls Cassio, the military theoretician, a 'counter-caster' (I, i, 31). In his opinion Cassio understands no "more than a spinster" in the tactics of battle (I, i, 24). He ironically calls his slander 'medicine': "Work on, my medicine, work!" (IV, i, 46). The suspicion that Othello has lived with Emilia gnaws his vitals "like a poisonous mineral" (II, i, 309). "Dangerous conceits", he reflects, "are, in their natures, poisons" (III, iii, 326).

Iago frequently repeats the word 'devil'. Usually he employs it merely as a swear word. He calls black Othello a 'devil' (I, i, 91). "You are one of those", he tells Brabantio, "that will not serve God, if the devil bid you" (I, i, 109). Offended women, Iago says, are 'devils' in their anger (II, i, 111).

However, besides this form of swearing, Iago's imagery also contains demonic motifs. "Hell and night", he says, "must bring this monstrous birth to the world's light" (I, iii, 409). "I do hate him [Othello] as I do hell-pains", says Iago (I, i, 155). "There are many events", he declares, "in the womb of time, which will be deliver'd" (I, iii, 378). The following image also has a suggestion of the demonic. In the scene before Brabantio's house Iago tells Roderigo to shout "with like timorous accent and dire yell as when by night and negligence, the fire is spied in populous cities" (I, i, 76). The demonic motif in Iago's role receives its most striking expression in the image of jealousy as a monster, an image we have already met in Othello's role. Iago, however, gives fuller expression to this image. He calls jealousy "the green-eyed monster which doth mock the meat it feeds on" (III, iii, 166).

Lofty-poetic images, which, as we have seen, constitute the dominant theme in Othello's imagery, are totally lacking in Iago's role. True, in a dialogue with Othello, he calls a good name "the immediate jewel" of the soul (III, iii, 156), but he is here obviously imitating Othello's 'style'. He also says that Desdemona has been "framed as fruitful as the free elements" (II, iii, 350), and terms the soldiers of Cyprus "the very elements of this warlike isle" (II, iii, 60). If these are exceptions, they prove the rule. It is much more likely that we are here dealing with *exclusions*. We introduce this term to denote those passages in Shakespeare where a character seems to exclude himself (switch over) from his proper role and assume the function of a chorus, explaining the events taking place, describing other characters, etc., quite regardless of his own individuality. It is common knowledge that such passages are to be found quite frequently in Shakespeare. In any case, whether this is exception or 'exclusion', we have, on the whole, every right to say that Iago's role is devoid of lofty-poetic imagery.

We do find a few classical images in his speeches. He swears by Janus (I, ii, 33). It is characteristic, by the way, that he swears by a two-faced God! He says that Cassio's military abilities are such as make him fit to stand with Caesar (II, iii, 128). He tells Cassio that Desdemona would have been "sport for Jove" (II, iii, 17). In contrast to the peaceful classical images in Othello's role (Cupid, Diana) Iago's are of a warlike nature (Janus, the god of war, and Caesar). Iago is a professional soldier, a soldier by trade, and it is therefore not to be wondered at that he himself speaks of "the trade of War" (I, ii, 1).

There is one other group of images in Iago's role which is evidently not accidental, for it is quite a large and distinct group. These are typically naval images. Iago says that Cassio "be-lee'd and calm'd" him, i.e. won promotion over his head (I, i, 30). Instead of saying that the Senate had no other man of such abilities as Othello, as we would say to-day, Iago says that "another of his fathom they have none" (I, i, 153).

Iago says that he must put out "a flag and sign of love, which is indeed but sign" (I, i, 157). Brabantio, in Iago's words, will pursue Othello, in so far as "the law…will give him cable" (I, ii, 17). Iago assures Roderigo that he is knit to him with "cables of perdurable toughness" (I, iii, 343). Iago expresses it that in marrying Desdemona Othello "hath boarded a land carack" (I, ii, 50), which in sailor's slang of that time meant a prostitute. Iago doubts whether it will prove a "lawful prize", an expression typical of freebooters. "My boat sails freely, both with wind and stream", says Iago (II, iii, 66). All this seems to indicate that Iago was probably once a sailor. In any case, he had been in England (II, iii, 79), and had also observed Danes, Germans and Hollanders drinking themselves drunk.

DESDEMONA

Desdemona's role is poor in imagery, but whatever there is of it is characteristic. First there are poetic motifs: Desdemona accompanies her husband to the wars because she does not want to sit at home and be "a moth of peace" (I, iii, 258). She sings about the willow tree (IV, iii, 41), privately comparing herself to it, for the willow used to be the symbol of a girl or woman abandoned by her lover (Ophelia drowns under a weeping willow). "Her salt tears fell from her", sings Desdemona, "and soften'd the stones" (IV, iii, 47)—an image echoing the image of the stony heart which occurs twice in Othello's role. Desdemona cannot understand why Othello should have changed toward her and says that evidently something "hath puddled his clear spirit" (III, iv, 142), and this, too, echoes Othello's expression, cited above, that Desdemona is his 'fountain'. Desdemona's statement that "I'll watch him tame" (III, iii, 23) implies a comparison of Othello to a hawk, and these words again echo Othello, who, as we have seen, likens Desdemona to a hawk. Thus, many of the images used by Desdemona echo Othello's images.

Desdemona's role also includes images of everyday domestic things. She says that she will tirelessly persuade Othello to reinstate Cassio: "His bed shall seem a school, his board a shrift" (III, iii, 24). She says that her request to reinstate Cassio is as if she were asking Othello to "wear gloves, or feed on nourishing dishes, or keep you warm" (III, iii, 77). The following is closely related to the same group of domestic, intimate images: when a finger aches all the other members of the body seem to share the pain (III, iv, 145).

There is also a militant-heroic note in Desdemona's imagery. "That I did love the Moor to live with him, My downright violence and storm of fortunes May trumpet to the world!" she declares in the Senate (I, iii, 250). Paraphrasing Othello, who called her a "fair warrior", she calls herself an "unhandsome warrior" (III, iv, 150).

Finally, in Desdemona's speeches, as in Othello's, Iago's and Emilia's, there occurs the image of jealousy as a monster. When Emilia calls jealousy a monster "begot upon itself, born on itself", Desdemona exclaims: "Heaven keep that monster from Othello's mind!" (III, iv, 162).

The combination of poetic with domestic images, the presence of a militant, heroic note, and echoes or reflections of the images used by Othello who rules her being—this is the world of Desdemona's imagery.

Thus, we have found that each of the three leading characters in this tragedy has his own world of images. This is, of course, much more strikingly and sharply evident in the roles of Othello and Iago. Desdemona's images are much paler.

2. *MACBETH*

MACBETH

A large part of Macbeth's imagery is distinctly magniloquent. "Two truths are told", he declares, "as happy prologues to the swelling act of the imperial theme" (I, iii, 128). "Why", he asks, "do you dress me in borrow'd robes?" (I, iii, 108). Here the very word 'robes' has an 'imperial' ring. Banquo, likewise speaking metaphorically, says simply 'garments' (I, iv, 145). Macbeth says that justice "commends th' ingredients of our poison'd chalice to our own lips" (I, vii, 11). He speaks of "the vessel of my peace" (III, i, 67). These images carry us either to some imperial palace or some medieval Gothic cathedral. The following image harmonizes with the above. Macbeth calls his soul "mine eternal jewel" (III, i, 68). He is a remarkable artist. His figures of speech are extremely colourful. He does not say "good opinion" but "golden opinion" (I, vii, 33), not "white-livered" but "lily-liver'd" (V, iii, 15), not "red-cheeked" but "the natural ruby of your cheeks" (III, iv, 115). "Here lay Duncan", says Macbeth, "his silver skin laced with his golden blood" (II, iii, 119). Gold, lilies, rubies, silver, golden lace—again we have before us either some richly decorated palace or the splendours of a Gothic cathedral.

Macbeth compares Duncan's virtues with angels with voices like trumpets (I, vii, 19); pity is "like a naked new-born babe, striding the blast, or heaven's cherubin, horsed upon the sightless couriers of the air" (I, vii, 22). These images seem to present huge frescoes to our eyes. Macbeth also makes use of powerful allegorical images. Murder is pictured as a sinister old man: "wither'd murder, alarum'd by his sentinel, the wolf, whose howl's his watch" (II, i, 52).

Realistic details sometimes stand out in these fantastic frescoes picturing allegorical figures: "the innocent sleep, sleep that knits up the ravell'd sleave of care; the death of each day's life, sore labour's bath, balm of hurt minds, great nature's second course, chief nourisher in life's feast" (II, ii, 37). Addressing the fall of night, Macbeth says: "Scarf up the tender eye of pitiful day; and with thy bloody and invisible hand cancel and tear to pieces that great bond which keeps me pale" (III, ii, 46). On another fresco we see innumerable to-morrows as creatures slowly and relentlessly creeping forward (V, v, 19).

Winds fight churches, frothy waves swallow ships, the corn is lodged to the ground, trees are blown down, castles topple on their warders' heads, palaces and pyramids 'slope' their heads to their foundations (IV, i, 52). All this is echoed by Ross when he tells about Duncan's horses having eaten each other (II, iv, 19). Macbeth's images are often full of mystery. The "wither'd murder" mentioned above "towards his design moves like a ghost" (II, i, 55). Life is "a walking shadow" (V, v, 24). The fantastic Gothic cathedral of Macbeth's imagination is peopled by chimeras, gorgons and monsters. "O, full of scorpions is my mind", says Macbeth (III, ii, 36). He refers to "the rugged Russian bear," the rhinoceros, and "the Hyrcan tiger" (III, iv, 100), animals which Englishmen of Shakespeare's day pictured as strange and fantastic. Enumerating various breeds of dogs, he mentions the 'demi-wolf' among them (III, i, 94). He likewise mentions bats (III, ii, 40) and twice speaks of snakes (III, ii, 13; III, iv, 92). It is against the background of all these 'Gothic' monsters that we see Macbeth himself, who compares himself, in the last moments of his life, with a man being burnt at the stake (V, vii, 1) and with a bear (V, vii, 2).

Phantasmagoria is the dominant theme in Macbeth's world of images. Let us cite two more images here, probably the most grandiose of all his fantastic images. One of them is striking for its vivid colourfulness—suggestive of dreams under the influence of narcotics: "Will all great Neptune's ocean wash this blood clean from my hand? No; this my hand will rather the multitudinous seas incarnadine, making the green one red" (II, ii, 61). The following symbolic image is likewise fantastic. Macbeth calls the present the "shoal of time" (I, vii, 6), thereby comparing eternity to a boundless ocean.

As we see, Macbeth is a man of imagination. Indeed, at the very beginning of the tragedy he anticipates the future (cf. I, iii, 134 f.). After murdering Duncan he is distracted by committing his crime over and over again in his mind. Imagination is more real to him than reality. "Nothing is but what is not" (I, iii, 141). The full value of these words as a key to Macbeth's character becomes clear only after studying his figures of speech.

We likewise find the theme of nature in Macbeth's imagery: his life "is fall'n into the sear, the yellow leaf" (V, iii, 22). But these images of nature, too, are constantly given fantastic colouring. He fears that the very stone will betray his whereabouts (II, i, 58). Pity is so strong in his breast that his tears are like to "drown the wind" (I, vii, 25). He feels as though he were wading in blood (III, iv, 136).

There is a small group of images in Macbeth's role which are associated with the castle of a knight and with medieval modes. "I have no spur", says Macbeth, "to prick the sides of my intent, but only vaulting ambition which o'erleaps itself, and falls on th'other" (I, vii, 26). In the next image we see the vaults of a medieval castle, whose most precious treasure and pride were its barrels of old wine. "The wine of life is drawn", says Macbeth, "and the mere lees is left this vault to brag of" (II, iii, 102). Telling about the murderers stained with blood, Macbeth says that they are "steept in the colours of their trade" (II, iii, 113). Spurs, vaulting, the owner of a castle who boasts of the wine preserved in his vaults, the guilds with the "colours of their trades"—all this is suggestive of a knight's castle of the Middle Ages.

It is possible that those of Macbeth's images that have to do with the theatre are there by more than chance. As we have mentioned in discussing Othello's imagery, theatrical figures are frequent in all Shakespeare's plays, regardless of the character speaking. With Macbeth, however, they may quite probably be definitely intended to reflect his acting in real life: "We must... make our faces vizards to our hearts", says Macbeth (III, ii, 34). If the enemy could cure Scotland, he says, he "would applaud thee to the very echo, that should applaud again" (V, iii, 53). He compares man's life with the performance of a poor player "that struts and frets his hour upon the stage, and then is heard no more" (V, v, 24).

Among classical images, we have already mentioned "great Neptune's ocean" (II, ii, 61). Macbeth compares his steps to "Tarquin's ravishing strides" (II, i, 54). He makes mention of Hecate twice: "pale Hecate" (II, i, 52) and "black Hecate" (III, ii, 41). He compares himself to Mark Antony (III, i, 57). Besides, towards the end of the tragedy, while refusing to surrender and fighting on to the end, he says: "Why should I play the Roman fool, and die on mine own sword?" (V, vii, 29). Quite possibly, he is thinking of Antony here, too. This comparison to Antony is quite deliberate. Antony, the gallant general, dies because of his passionate love; Macbeth dies because of his ambitious dream of the "imperial theme".

The path of crime leaves Macbeth spiritually devastated. The "Gothic cathedral" (as we have termed it), built by his imagination, topples, and there appears in its place an image horrifyingly bare: "Life", says Macbeth, is "a tale told by an idiot, full of sound and fury, signifying nothing" (V, v, 26).

Finally, the demonic theme is also to be found in Macbeth's imagery, lending darkness to his character. "The bell invites me", says Macbeth. "Hear it not, Duncan; for it is a knell that summons thee to heaven or to hell" (II, i, 63).

LADY MACBETH

Let us now proceed to Lady Macbeth. Here too the dark, demonic theme is strong. "Come, thick night, and pall thee in the dunnest smoke of hell, that my keen knife see not the wound it makes" (I, v, 51). Some of her images echo Macbeth's 'Gothic' imagery. "The raven himself is hoarse that croaks the fatal entrance of Duncan under my battlements" (I, v, 39). The idea of murdering Duncan was first conceived by Macbeth. Lady Macbeth reminds him of this: "What beast was't, then, that made you break this enterprise to me?" (I, vii, 47). The thick smoke of hell, the raven, the beast—all this is closely related to Macbeth's 'Gothic' theme, but with Lady Macbeth it has less of colourful fantasy and assumes a grimmer tone.

Certain of Lady Macbeth's images are connected with knighthood. She calls memory "the warder of the brain" (I, vii, 65). "A hideous trumpet calls to parley the sleepers of the house", says Lady Macbeth (II, iii, 79). These images are full of courageous militancy, a quality much more weakly developed in Macbeth.

Most of Lady Macbeth's images are much more concrete and substantial than Macbeth's. What Macbeth calls the "imperial theme" she calls "the golden round" (I, v, 29), referring, naturally, to a crown, i.e. to a substantial *thing*. She bewails the fact that there is too much of "the milk of human kindness" in her husband's nature (I, v, 17). She prays to the spirits to "take my milk for gall" (I, v, 49). She begs her husband to "screw your courage to the sticking place" (I, vii, 60). She compares the brain of a drunken man to the vessel wherein the alchemists distilled substances into fumes (I, vii, 67), i.e. again with a solid object. Being so realistically minded she could, conversely, have compared the dreams of the alchemists, and in fact all dreams in general, to drunkenness. Macbeth's 'hope', i.e. his dream of the "imperial theme", which remains only a dream and is not translated into action, she ironically calls 'drunk' (I, vii, 36). Macbeth reminds her of "the poor cat i' th'adage" (I, vii, 45). She calls the slumbers of a drunken man "swinish sleep" (I, vii, 68). What is not sober is abhorrent to her. Dreams are non-existent as far as she is concerned. She compares sleeping men and dead men to 'pictures' (II, ii, 55). In contrast to Macbeth, she has no inclination for fantasy and inventions. "Consider it not so deeply", she tells Macbeth (II, ii, 29); and in another passage: "you must leave this" (III, ii, 35).

Only towards the end, when, broken by all that has happened, she walks in her sleep, she gives voice to an image which contrasts with her previous severity and strikes us because of its unexpected tenderness and sadness. "All the perfumes of Arabia will not sweeten this little hand. Oh, oh!" (V, i, 46). This is a most unexpected picture to come from the lips of a woman who seemed so courageous, grim and sober and who did violence to her nature and exchanged "milk for gall".

BANQUO

Banquo's imagery is of an altogether different type. Here everything is peaceful, placid, idyllic. "If you can look into the *seeds* of time", he tells the witches, "and say which *grain* will *grow* and which will not..." (I, iii, 58). "There [in Duncan's heart] if I grow, the *harvest* is your own", Banquo tells Duncan (I, iv, 33). He calls the bird which has made its nest in the wall of the castle "this guest of summer" and compares its nest to a *bed* and a *cradle* (I, vi, 3 f.). When he steps out into the courtyard of the castle on a dark night, he says: "There's husbandry in heaven, their candles are all out" (II, i, 5).

Yet the heroic motif is not wanting in his imagery. After Duncan's murder he says in a lofty, chivalric style that he stands "in the great hand of God" and is ready to fight treason (II, iii, 125). Banquo is a virtuous hero. Let us note, in conclusion, that classical imagery is absent from Banquo's speeches. Such images are evidently unnecessary to his idyllic, tranquil and modest picture of the world.

Thus in *Macbeth*, too, the imagery used by the three leading characters is suited to their 'natures'. The study of imagery facilitates, as we see, a closer knowledge of the characters.

3. *HAMLET*

HAMLET

One would expect Hamlet's role to be full of lofty, poetic comparisons and metaphors. In reality we find that his role is almost totally devoid of this type of imagery. On the contrary, simple and extremely prosaic images predominate. Hamlet tends towards substantial, concrete comparisons and metaphors. The actor who gesticulates excessively while declaiming is, in Hamlet's words, "sawing the air" (III, ii, 4). "O, it offends me to the soul", says Hamlet in the same monologue, "to hear a robustious periwig-pated fellow tear a passion to *tatters*, to very *rags*, to *split the ears of the groundlings*." The verb *split* suggests a very concrete image here: by shouting an actor seems to chop at the ears of an audience with an axe. Poor actors, he says, make him think that "nature's journeymen had made men" (III, ii, 38).

Hamlet speaks of the perfect man with enthusiasm. Yet he expresses this dream of his in concrete, substantial words. He does not say "what a miracle of nature is man" or "what a marvellous creation is man", as his words are usually translated into Russian, but: "what a piece of work is a man!" (II, ii, 323).

Construction images occur several times in Hamlet's role. He calls the earth a "goodly frame" (II, ii, 317), the sky "this majestical roof fretted with golden fire" (in the same monologue): precisely a *roof*, and not a *vault*. Other images of this class are as follows. Hamlet regrets that he is not made of pure *metal* (II, ii, 602). When Gertrude asks him to sit beside her he replies, indicating Ophelia: "Here's *metal* more attractive" (III, ii, 117), i.e. a magnet. He tells Gertrude that his words will wring her heart "if it be made of penetrable stuff; if damned custom have not *brazed* it" (III, iv, 36).

Images which may be termed 'technical' are also to be found in Hamlet's role. "Adieu. Thine evermore, most dear lady, whilst this machine is to him, Hamlet", he writes to Ophelia (II, ii, 124). It is characteristic also that he calls the laws of thinking "the pales and forts of reason" (I, iv, 28). "For 'tis the sport", he says, referring to his enemies Rosencrantz and Guildenstern, "to have the engineer hoist with his own petar" (III, iv, 206), adding that he "will delve one yard below their mines." We repeat: Hamlet's imagery is for the most part substantially concrete. He compares virtue with wax that melts in the fire of "flaming youth" (III, iv, 84). He calls his own head a "distracted globe" (I, v, 97). He compares the cracked voice of a boy actor playing female roles to a cracked gold piece unfit for circulation (II, ii, 446). According to him, if he had killed Claudius while the latter was praying it would have been "hire and salary, not revenge" (III, iii, 79). He does not say "who would bear life's adversities", but "who would fardels bear, to grunt and sweat under a weary life" (III, i, 76). He does not say that art ought to copy nature, but that art should "hold, as 'twere, the *mirror* up to nature" (III, ii, 26), i.e. again makes use of a definite object to give expression to his thoughts. Hamlet tells Gertrude that he will "set you up a glass" (III, iv, 19). He compares the air and the sky to a canopy (III, ii, 298). In his words, Fortinbras' soldiers are ready to "go to their graves like beds" (IV, iv, 62). He does not say "the external expressions of woe", but "the trappings and the suits of woe" (I, ii, 86). He resorts to definite objects even to express his most hidden and complex feelings and ideas. He could have been, he says, "bounded in a *nut-shell*, and count myself a king of infinite space" (II, ii, 264). He likens his soul to a *pipe* which Rosencrantz and Guildenstern try to play with clumsy fingers (III, ii, 354). He calls death "the undiscover'd country, from whose bourn no traveller returns" (III, i, 79), an image typical of an age of geographical discoveries, when many set out across the seas in ships in search of new lands and treasures and frequently failed to return. Dying, Hamlet declares that "this fell sergeant, death, is strict in his arrest" (V, ii, 325). All these images are concrete, substantial. Typical of the tangible substantiality of Hamlet's style is the fact that looking at Yorick's skull, he does not say "here is where the lips were", but "here hung those lips" (V, i, 177).

Among Hamlet's images is a definite set relating to nature and to gardening and agriculture. "O, that this too, too solid flesh would melt, thaw, and resolve itself into a dew!" he cries (I, ii, 129). The world is "an unweeded garden that grows to seed" (I, ii, 135). He compares the earth to "a sterile promontory" (II, ii, 297), again a realistic image. His father died unshriven, "his crimes broad blown as flush as May" (III, iii, 81). He asks his mother not to "spread the compost on the weeds to make them ranker" (III, iv, 150). He compares Claudius to "a mildew'd ear" (III, iv, 64).

Hamlet also makes use of images relating to food and the process of digestion. He says that his mother "would hang" on his father "as if increase of appetite had grown by what it fed on" (I, ii, 144). Gertrude's marriage followed close upon the funeral of her first husband: "the funeral baked meats did coldly furnish forth the marriage tables" (I, ii, 180). Hamlet avers that some people have the bad habit "that too much o'er-leavens the form of plausive manners" (I, iv, 29), i.e. that some people overdo their attempts to please. He calls a play that has not pleased the populace "caviare to the general" (II, ii, 425), i.e. too refined a delicacy. He speaks of putting the king "to his purgation" (III, ii, 293). In another passage he says that kings, like common people, are eaten in the grave by worms; the worm is eaten by a fish, the fish by a beggar, and thus, says Hamlet, a king "may go a progress through the guts of a beggar" (IV, iii, 34).

Hamlet also uses images having to do with the human body. He likens a moral defect in a man to a mole (I, iv, 24). Self-deception is like a film forming over an ulcer "whilst rank corruption, mining all within, infects unseen" (III, iv, 147). Wars, he says, are caused by inner abscesses (IV, iv, 27).

Most of Hamlet's comparisons and metaphors are simple, lucid, comprehensible and concretely substantial. He has no use for euphuism. No wonder he mocks Osric's flowery style (v, ii). He dislikes all showy externals, "the trappings and suits". "Seems, madam! nay, it is; I know not 'seems'", he tells Gertrude (I, ii, 76). He strives to understand life to the end, to approach it directly and face to face. All his thoughts are concentrated on man's earthly existence. It is therefore no wonder that his speeches abound, as we have seen, in the names of real objects and phenomena. Hamlet has a clear view of reality and things; they wear no "romantic veil" for him.

Hamlet is very observant. He sees right through people. He divined Claudius' criminal nature even before the apparition of the Ghost ("O my prophetic soul!" he exclaims upon learning from the Ghost who killed his father—I, v, 40). He immediately realized that Rosencrantz and Guildenstern were concealing something from him. Ophelia's embarrassment when Claudius and Polonius are listening behind the arras does not escape his keen eyes. He recognizes Horatio's disinterested honesty. Hamlet is an observant man, a man of realistic mentality. At the same time, however, Hamlet is a dreamer. Comparison of Hamlet with the author of *Utopia* naturally suggests itself. We may note here that Thomas More was also a realist. One had to see all the ugliness and imperfection of real life to hate injustice as Thomas More and Hamlet hated it, to refuse to accept this injustice and create *a dream*. Hamlet dreamt of the perfect man as passionately as did the author of *Utopia* of the perfect human society. The gulf between dream and reality, the impossibility, at that time, of bridging this gulf plunged both of them into deep sorrow. Hamlet admired man, the nobility of his reason, his infinite faculty, but in the same breath he said that "man delights me not" (II, ii, 309). He called death felicity and said it was hard to breathe "in this harsh world" (v, ii, 361–2).

Hamlet's images are often rather coarse. He compares Claudius to a toad, bat, and gib (III, iv, 190). He says that he should long since "have fatted all the region kites with this slave's offal" (II, ii, 614). His ironic question "How now! a rat?" (III, iv, 23) suggests a comparison of Claudius to a rat (he had thought that it was Claudius behind the arras, and not Polonius). The play he has the actors put on he figuratively (as he himself says—'tropically') calls "The Mouse Trap" (III, ii, 250): Claudius is the mouse that Hamlet traps. In another passage he compares Claudius to a peacock (III, ii, 300). Judging by the rhyme, he had meant at first to compare him to an ass, but thought better of it and said peacock (thus spoiling the rhyme, for which meticulous Horatio reproves him): Claudius was not a fool and the comparison to the ornate, proud bird was the more appropriate. In another place Hamlet calls Claudius "a cutpurse" (III, iv, 99). He says that Claudius 'whored' his mother (V, ii, 53). Hamlet compares Osric to a 'water-fly' (V, ii, 84). He calls people who look for security in property and forget that they too cannot escape death "sheep and calves" (V, i, 124). The rich man who acquires land, or 'dirt' (V, ii, 91), becomes the lord of other people and is admitted to the king's table: "let a beast be lord of beasts", says Hamlet, "and his crib shall stand at the king's mess" (V, ii, 88). In other words, Hamlet likens the rich to cattle. In his anger Hamlet compares Gertrude to a sheep: "Could you on this fair mountain leave to feed, and batten on this moor?" (III, iv, 66). Hamlet calls the wedding bed of Claudius and Gertrude a "nasty sty" (III, iv, 94). He speaks of "the rank sweat of an enseamed bed" (III, iv, 93). "I'll lug the guts into the neighbour room", he says in reference to Polonius' corpse (III, iv, 212), whom when he was alive he called a 'calf' (III, ii, 112). Rosencrantz and Guildenstern are "fang'd adders" (III, iv, 203). He compares the king's courtiers with sponges: they soak in the wealth of the people and then the king squeezes them dry (IV, ii, 12 and 22). The king does not hurry to swallow them (such officers), but "keeps them, like an ape, in the corner of his jaw" (IV, ii, 19). Angry with himself for procrastinating, Hamlet berates himself as a 'whore' and a 'scullion' (II, ii, 622 f.).

The reader has probably already been struck by the resemblance between these motifs and the dominant theme in Iago's imagery. This resemblance, however, is confined to the fact that both Hamlet and Iago are realists in their imagery, and that each of them has his own 'menagerie'. However, whereas Iago's 'menagerie' extended to all mankind, all men in general, including Othello ('ass'), Desdemona ('guinea-hen'), and Cassio ('a great fly'), Hamlet's menagerie is confined to his enemies. Therefore, only the following resemblance can be constituted: Hamlet hates his enemies just as Iago hates all mankind, Iago's 'menagerie' is an expression of cynicism, Hamlet's of wrath against his enemy. One reflects predatory nature, the other proves, in the final analysis, to be a component part of the humanistic theme. Hamlet praises man highly, admires him greatly, comparing him with an angel and with a god, calling him "the beauty of the world", "the paragon of animals" (II, ii, 323), and for this reason Claudius' courtiers, whom he observes daily, seem more like animals to him than men. His mother married Claudius immediately after her first husband's death. "O God!" exclaims Hamlet, "a beast, that wants discourse of reason, would have mourn'd longer" (I, ii, 150). (This, of course, does not mean that Hamlet was hostile towards Gertrude in general, but at that particular moment he spoke of her as of an enemy.) "What is a man", asks Hamlet in another passage, "if his chief good and market of his time be but to sleep and feed? a beast, no more" (IV, iv, 34). (Let us note, by the way, as typical of Hamlet's realistic style, the image of "chief good and market".) In that bestial world in which Hamlet lives even the beautiful may engender evil. Hamlet had proof of this subsequently when Ophelia unconsciously became the accomplice of Claudius and Polonius. "If the sun breed maggots in a dead dog," said Hamlet, "being a god kissing carrion" (II, ii, 183), i.e. even the most beautiful engenders something loathsome when it has to do with loathsome things.

The biting severity of those of Hamlet's images directed against his enemies and everything foreign to his nature must certainly have endeared Hamlet to the popular audience: the common people have never been chary of sharp expressions in speaking about their enemies. The general nature of his metaphors and comparisons, the majority of which are realistic, must also have enhanced Hamlet's popularity. Let us recall to the reader's mind some of the images cited above: a saw, an axe, journeyman, "sheep and calves", sheep pasturing on mountains and moors, pigsties, compost, mildew'd ear of grain, beggar eating fish, loads under the weight of which the bearer sweats and grunts, the fell sergeant—all these are images reflecting the life of the lower depths.

The riddle images to be found in Hamlet's speeches were also close to "the heart of the common element". "Yourself, sir, shall grow old as I am, if, like a crab, you could go backward", Hamlet says to Polonius (II, ii, 209), i.e. if Polonius could grow younger he would in time reach Hamlet's age. The following reply is also in the nature of a riddle: "Now, Hamlet, where's Polonius?" asks Claudius. "At supper", replies Hamlet (IV, iii, 18). Hamlet then explains that at this supper Polonius is not eating, but is himself being eaten by worms. We know that this type of riddle used to be very popular among the people in Shakespeare's day.

Games, too, figure among Hamlet's images—and always the most popular kind. "Ay' there's the rub", he says in his "To be, or not to be" monologue. Bowling was very popular among the people. Dicing was also very popular in England and eager groups gambling away with dice were to be seen on all the corners and cross roads of London. The game attracted numerous sharpers. Hamlet tells Gertrude that she has made "marriage vows as false as dicers' oaths" (III, iv, 45). "What devil was't that thus hath cozen'd you at hoodmanblind?" he asks Gertrude (III, iv, 76). "Hide fox, and all after!" Hamlet cries to Rosencrantz and Guildenstern (IV, ii, 32), repeating the words of a children's game. Hamlet shudders at the thought that human bones, dug out of a grave, can be used for playing "at loggats" (V, i, 89). Similarly comprehensible to the popular audience were metaphors of the medieval theatre and medieval popular revels occurring in Hamlet's role. Hamlet terms exaggerated declamation and gesticulation on the stage "out-heroding Herod" (III, ii, 16), referring to a character in a miracle play. He compares Claudius to "a Vice" (III, iv, 98), a character in a morality play. He likewise calls Claudius "a king of shreds and patches" (III, iv, 102): for him the ranting of an actor is worse than the mouthings of a town-crier (III, ii, 4). Fireworks, all kinds of "fiery showers", formed part of the programme of court festivals, and these not only amused the crowd but often frightened it as well. Hamlet's remark in the 'mouse-trap' scene: "What, frighted with false fire!" (III, ii, 282) when Claudius hastily leaves the hall was comprehensible and peculiarly comical to the groundlings in the yard. It is easy to imagine how the groundlings exulted when Hamlet says: "the toe of the peasant comes so near the heel of the courtier, he galls his kibe" (V, i, 149). The affected mannerisms of the courtiers were always ridiculous in the eyes of the common people. And how must the groundlings have enjoyed Hamlet's saying that even as an infant Osric was ceremonious with his mother's breast before he sucked it (V, ii, 193). For Sir John Falstaff, knight, the host of an inn would carry sack to his room on a tray, but in the common ale-houses small beer was poured directly from the barrel, the mouth of which was stopped with a plug. This plug, as Hamlet says, might be made of the dust of Alexander (V, i, 234). Caesar's clay, he says, might be used for patching a wall in winter to keep the wind away (V, i, 238). This evokes the image of a thin-walled house—a picture of the life of the poor.

Hamlet's speeches often contain popular sayings and proverbs. "Let the gall'd jade wince", he tells Claudius, "our withers are unwrung" (III, ii, 257), i.e. the matter does not concern us. "While the grass grows...", says Hamlet (III, ii, 359). This is equivalent to the Ukrainian proverb: "While the sun rises the dew can eat your eyes out." He calls himself 'John-a-dreams' (II, ii, 603), which is something like our saying "Oh, Vanka, you loafer!" Good handwriting did him "yeoman's service" (V, ii, 36) when he tampered with Claudius' letter to the King of England (the English infantry, the most reliable part of the army, was made up of yeomen). Hamlet calls his hands "these pickers and stealers" (III, ii, 349). "If the rest of my fortunes turn Turk with me", says Hamlet, i.e. if fate robs him and turns him into a beggar (III, ii, 292). "If thou knews't our purposes", says Claudius, to which Hamlet replies "I see a cherub that sees them" (IV, iii, 51), i.e. I do know somewhat. Paraphrasing the Bible, Hamlet says: "man and wife is one flesh" (IV, iii, 55). All these were evidently current expressions among the people, well known to the groundlings.

Hamlet called the important official Polonius a 'fishmonger' (II, ii, 174), which, in the rough language of the taverns, evidently meant a procurer (Hamlet insinuates that Polonius is selling Ophelia). The following expressions are unquestionably like sayings and proverbs in tone. "Would I had met my dearest foe in heaven" (I, ii, 182). "Nay, then, let the devil wear black, for I'll have a suit of sables" (III, ii, 138). "A knavish speech sleeps in a foolish ear" (IV, ii, 25). "A man's life's no more than to say 'one'" (V, ii, 74). Hamlet's text is full of the simplest, most prosaic and, if we may say so, banal figures of speech. "I do not set my life at a pin's fee" (I, iv, 65), which is equivalent to the Russian "I value my life at less than a grosh". Hamlet says that his thanks are "too dear a halfpenny" (II, ii, 288). "Why, what an ass am I!" he exclaims (II, ii, 619).

"Two thousand souls and twenty thousand ducats will not debate the question of this straw" (IV, iv, 26), Hamlet says of the war started by Fortinbras. And, in the same scene: "to find quarrel in a straw" (IV, iv, 52), i.e. in trifles. In Hamlet's words, Fortinbras' army risks all "for an egg-shell" (IV, iv, 53), i.e., for the sake of that which is not worth a penny. He compares people like Osric to foam; "do but blow them to their trial, the bubbles are out" (V, ii, 202).

There are many allegorical figures in Hamlet's speeches, as in all Shakespeare's work, in regard to which we hardly have the right to apply the term 'poetic' in the sense of individual poetic invention. We are dealing here with a whole people's manner of thinking at a definite period in its development, with a style that has found reflection in folklore and in popular riddles. Hamlet does not say "O, women, nonentity is your name!" as Polevoy translated, modernizing Hamlet's language; what he says is "Frailty, thy name is woman!" (I, ii, 146). This suggests an allegorical figure of inconstancy who is called Woman. The following images are of the same type. "Murder, though it have no tongue, will speak with most miraculous organ" (II, ii, 630). "Let the candied tongue lick absurd pomp" (III, ii, 65). "If his occulted guilt do not itself unkennel in one speech" (III, ii, 85). "For in the fatness of these pursy times virtue itself of vice must pardon beg, yea, curb and woo for leave to do him good" (III, iv, 155). When Hamlet calls imagination the "mind's eye" (I, ii, 185), we see an image of the 'Soul', with a face and eyes, as it used to be depicted in medieval 'icons'. Iconographic images also suggest themselves when Hamlet says that "heaven's face doth glow; Yea, this solidity and compound mass, with tristful visage, as against the doom, is thought-sick at the act" (III, iv, 48). "While memory holds a seat in this distracted globe", says Hamlet, indicating his head (I, v, 96). The phrase "holds a seat" implies comparison of man's psychological function to a king's council in which each function, memory included, "holds a seat", i.e. is a member. Comparison of man to a state, so widespread in the Middle Ages, was very familiar to Shakespeare (cf. *Coriolanus*, I, i, 101), just as was comparison of the state with the cosmos (*Troilus and Cressida*, I, iii, 85). All this use of allegory, typical of medieval thinking, is reflected in Shakespeare's language, and, consequently, in Hamlet's. The latter grieves over the death of the May-Day hobby-horse, over the disappearance of the old medieval revels. In the language of the common people, in Shakespeare's language, in Hamlet's language, these 'hobby-horses' were still alive. If Hamlet speaks of these things more often, perhaps, than do Shakespeare's other characters, the reason lies in Hamlet's closeness to the common people.

Hamlet's letter to Ophelia—"To the celestial and my soul's idol, the most beautified Ophelia" (II, ii, 109)—which Polonius reads to the King and Queen, is astonishing for its artless simplicity, as is the image "stars are fire" occurring in Hamlet's halting love verses. Hamlet himself admits, in this same letter, that "I am ill at these numbers; I have not art to reckon my groans". In the milieu to which Hamlet belonged, the court, this was something of an exception, which likewise sets Hamlet negatively, so to say, apart from this milieu. It must be remembered that his was the period of the cult of the sonnet. Hamlet's letter to Horatio (IV, vi, 13) is striking for the same artless simplicity—in an age of the cult of epistolary style and high-flown prose.

Hamlet's poetic fantasy may be illustrated by his comparison of a cloud to a camel, a weasel and a whale (III, ii, 400), the artless simplicity of which brings to mind folk-tales for children. The following image likewise echoes folk-lore: "Be thou as chaste as ice, as pure as snow", Hamlet tells Ophelia (III, i, 142). This carries us away to the world of images connected with the English popular ballad. The metaphor "the rose of innocent love" is also of this type. It is characteristic that Hamlet combines this metaphor with one purely realistic: he tells Gertrude that her act "takes off the rose from the fair forehead of an innocent love, and sets a blister there" (III, iv, 42), hinting at a prostitute branded on the forehead. The following image also echoes the ballad: before his duel with Laertes Hamlet asks him to believe that "I have shot mine arrow o'er the house, and hurt my brother" (v, ii, 257), i.e. accidentally committed a grave crime—a plot which might have served as the material, and perhaps did serve as such before Shakespeare's time, for a popular ballad. The poetic vein in Hamlet's imagery is close to the popular ballad.

At first glance some of Hamlet's images seem stilted, but in reality they are so common that they may safely be classed as 'fossilized' images, in other words, as stock sayings. "In the very torrent, tempest, and, as I may say, the whirlwind of passion, you must acquire and beget a temperance", Hamlet tells the actors (III, ii, 6). This "as I may say" is very characteristic here. "Wings as swift as meditation or the thoughts of love" (I, v, 29) also belongs to this class.

Possible exceptions are "the slings and arrows of outrageous fortune" (III, i, 58) and "to take arms against a sea of troubles" (III, i, 59) from the "To be, or not to be" monologue. Quite probably, however, they too belong to the 'fossilized' images. In that case "slings and arrows" simply means 'blows', while "sea of troubles" is identical with "many troubles". This is all the more probable in the case of "sea of troubles", since only by regarding it as a 'fossilized' image can we eliminate the sharp violation of metaphoric unity which caused some commentators to suggest changing "sea of troubles" to "siege of troubles" or "seat of troubles", i.e. an allusion to Claudius' throne.

In all Hamlet's imagery we have found only two incontrovertible exceptions. First, "sepulchre ...hath oped his ponderous and marble jaws" (I, iv, 50), which calls to mind Macbeth's fantastic 'Gothic' imagery; secondly, "heaven-kissing hill" (III, iv, 59), which not only resembles the lofty poetical style of Othello's imagery in general, but directly echoes Othello's "hills whose heads touch heaven" (*Othello*, I, iii, 144). However, we are not concerned here with individual exceptions.

Of course, Hamlet can speak pompously on occasion. For example, upon encountering Laertes in the cemetery: "And if thou prate of mountains, let them throw millions of acres on us, till our ground, singeing his pate against the burning zone, make Ossa like a wart!" (v, i, 302). But Hamlet was here parodying Laertes, ridiculing the 'stilted' style then fashionable. In his dialogue with Osric, Hamlet satirizes euphuism: "I know, to divide him inventorially would dizzy the arithmetic of memory", he parodies (v, ii, 120). This whole scene, in which Osric, the lover of the euphuistic, ornate style of speech in vogue at the court, is presented as a contrast to Hamlet, is the best confirmation of our conclusions. Hamlet himself, by the way, confirms these conclusions when, telling Horatio about Claudius' letter to the King of England, he makes sport of the bombastic and pretentious comparisons used in this letter. Punning, Hamlet calls them "as-es of great charge" (v, ii, 43), "burdened as", or "burdened comparisons", and also "burdened asses". Hamlet terms a flowery style 'ass-like' nonsense.

The tragic tale of *Hamlet, Prince of Denmark* "came home to the vulgars' element", to quote a contemporary of Shakespeare. But we must not forget that *Hamlet* was also performed in the Universities of Cambridge and Oxford, as stated on the title-page of the First Quarto. Hamlet, himself a student and the friend of the student Horatio, could not but evoke a response in the universities, especially, of course, among the progressive, humanistic youth of that age.

We see Hamlet with a book in his hands when Polonius asks him: "What do you read, my lord?" It is characteristic that Hamlet does not speak of his 'black' cloak, but of his 'inky' cloak (I, ii, 77). He talks of "the table of my memory" (I, v, 98), and "the book and volume of my brain" (I, v, 103).

Hamlet's erudition is particularly manifest in his classical metaphors. These are bookish metaphors and they reveal a well-read man, a scholar. We have seen that Othello, Iago and Macbeth have each their own classical images characteristic of their natures: Othello's poetic, Iago's warlike, Macbeth's rather phantasmagoric (Hecate, for instance). Lady Macbeth and Desdemona do not use classical metaphors at all, nor does the artless and even rather simple-minded Banquo. Hamlet's speeches, on the contrary, abound in them, and they testify to the encyclopaedic nature of his classical education. He compares his father with Jove (III, ii, 299; III, iv, 56), Apollo (I, ii, 140; III, iv, 56), a satyr (I, ii, 140); weeping Gertrude with Niobe (I, ii, 143); his faithful friend Horatio with Damon (III, ii, 297). He mentions Hercules twice (I, ii, 153; v, i, 313), speaks of the Nemean lion (I, iv, 83), Vulcan (III, ii, 89), Quintus Roscius, an actor of ancient Rome (II, ii, 419), the Emperor Nero (III, ii, 419), the mountain of Ossa (v, i, 305). It is characteristic that this learned humanist asks the actor to recite a monologue on a classical theme—Aeneas' tale to Dido (II, ii, 477). We can readily believe Ophelia's statement that Hamlet had a "scholar's tongue" (III, i, 151).

Another group of images found in Hamlet's speeches relates to hunting. "Why do you go about to recover the wind of me," he asks Rosencrantz and Guildenstern, "as if you would drive me into a toil?" (III, ii, 361). In the rhymed verses which Hamlet exultingly recites after he has sprung his "mouse trap", he likens himself to a hart at play and Claudius to a stricken deer (III, ii, 287). Some of these hunting metaphors may be classed as proverbs and sayings. "When the wind is southerly", he tells Rosencrantz and Guildenstern, "I know a hawk from a handsaw" (II, ii, 397). "We'll e'en to't like French falconers, fly at any thing we see" (II, ii, 450), says Hamlet. Hunting metaphors, however, are liberally sprinkled all through Shakespeare's texts, and we hardly have the right to take them as 'characteristic'.

Our remarks, of course, by no means exclude the inner complexity of Hamlet's nature, his spiritual conflicts, his deep and often contradictory feelings. Nor do they exclude his tragedy. "I loved Ophelia: forty thousand brothers could not, with all their quantity of love, make up my sum!" he exclaims (V, i, 293). Let us note, however, that even here 'quantity' and 'sum' are characteristic of his concrete way of thinking.

From all the foregoing we may draw the following conclusions. Hamlet is not "a delicate and tender prince". These words (IV, iv, 48) relate not to Hamlet, but to Fortinbras, Hamlet's antipode. Judging by his imagery, there is nothing delicate about Hamlet, just as there is nothing external, no adornments. He sees life itself without embellishments. He is a man of a realistic turn of mind. He is very observant and can 'tell' a hawk from a 'hand-saw'. He is not overly trusting like Othello, a man of a lofty poetic cast, and not overly suspicious like Macbeth, a man of imagination. He is close to the common people and at the same time is distinguished for his scholarship. This humanist thinker in the garb of a Danish prince looks at life with open eyes.

OPHELIA

Ophelia's imagery is very simple and clear, as is she herself and her attitude towards life. "I do not know, my lord, what I should think" (I, iii, 104). "I shall obey, my lord" (I, iii, 136). "I think nothing, my lord" (III, ii, 125). On the other hand, her world is wonderfully harmonious and complete. We see the room of a young maiden in a castle. There are her mirror and her casket in which she keeps cherished objects and letters. The maiden goes to church on Sundays. She is particularly fond of picking flowers and loves their fragrance. As was the custom in Shakespeare's time, the girl takes music and drawing lessons and sings ballads. The monotony of life in the castle, guarded at the gate by a sentry, is sometimes broken by the visit of some merry young neighbour, stout beyond his years, who is fond of food and drink. Here you have the whole life of this girl, who obeys her father implicitly and loves her brother. It is a remarkable fact that the whole range of Ophelia's metaphors fits into this description patly. Ophelia calls Hamlet "the glass of fashion" (III, i, 162). She assures Laertes that his advice will be locked in her memory (as in a casket) and he himself will keep the key (I, iii, 86). She begs Laertes not to be like the "ungracious pastors" who preach "the steep and thorny way", but do not practise what they preach (I, iii, 47 f.). Hamlet's mind, which she calls "noble and most sovereign" but considers affected by disease, she compares to church bells jangling out of tune (III, i, 167). We know from Gertrude's words that Ophelia was gathering flowers and perished because she wanted to hang the garland she had woven on a willow branch suspended over the river.

Gertrude compares Ophelia to a flower: "Sweets to the sweet", she says when throwing flowers into Ophelia's grave (v, i, 265). Flowers hold an important place among Ophelia's metaphors. The "ungracious pastor...the primrose path of dalliance treads" (I, iii, 50). She calls Hamlet the "rose of the fair state" (III, i, 161). She "suck't the honey" of his confessions of love (III, i, 165), comparing herself to a bee sucking honey from flowers. Hamlet's vows of love have now, she says, "their perfume lost" (III, i, 99). When she goes mad (IV, vii) she appears either with real or, more probably, imaginary flowers, since no mention of flowers is made in the remarks to the Quarto and Folio editions. Each of these flowers represents an image: rosemary stands for remembrance, pansies for thoughts. The phrase "sweet flowers" occurs in one of the ballads Ophelia sings (IV, v, 38). She compares Hamlet's vows of love to music (III, i, 155). When Hamlet came to her, she says, he studied her face so intently "as he would draw it" (II, i, 91). In the scene of her madness Ophelia sings ballads and folk songs full of the imagery typical of them (e.g. "His beard was as white as snow, all flaxen was his poll"—IV, v, 194). Among the images borrowed from popular legend we should include that of the baker's daughter who was turned into an owl (IV, v, 42). Ophelia tells Laertes that his advice will be "as watchman to my heart" (I, iii, 46). She begs Laertes not to be "like a puft [from excess of food and wine] and reckless libertine" (I, iii, 49).

Thus, every word of our description has found confirmation in Ophelia's imagery. On the other hand, her world of images was wholly exhausted in our brief description. As was to be expected, Ophelia uses no classical metaphors. The images used by each of Shakespeare's characters are logically suited to each one, individually.

LAERTES

Laertes' world of images is likewise small, but also characteristic in its own way. In the first place, he mentions flowers several times. True, these images always relate to Ophelia or are connected with her. Remember that flowers are one of Ophelia's leading motifs and that Gertrude compares Ophelia herself to a flower. Laertes calls Hamlet's love for Ophelia "a violet in the youth of primy nature" (I, iii, 7), "the perfume of a minute" (I, iii, 9). "And from her fair and unpolluted flesh may violets spring!" says Laertes over Ophelia's grave (v, i, 261). He calls Ophelia a "rose of May" (IV, v, 156). "The canker galls the infants of the spring too oft before their buttons be disclosed", he warns Ophelia (I, iii, 39). To these images we may also add the comparison of youth to morning dew (I, iii, 41). These images, as we can see, relate to Ophelia. Nevertheless, they harmonize well with Laertes' other images in which beauty, or rather prettiness, predominates. This may be said to be Ophelia's world of images turned towards us with its artificial side. To say "infants of the spring" instead of simply 'flowers'—is that not stilted? Laertes calls the skilful horseman Lamond "the brooch, indeed, and gem of all the nation" (IV, vii, 93). No wonder that, falling in with Laertes' tone, Claudius compares the art of fencing with a "riband in the cap of youth" (IV, vii, 77).

This young gallant expresses himself in very refined language, as was the fashion of the time. He does not say 'chastity', but "chaste treasure" (I, iii, 31). "The chariest maid", he teaches Ophelia, "is prodigal enough, if she unmask her beauty to the moon" (I, iii, 36). He compares man's body to a temple in which mind and soul do service (I, iii, 12). When he resorts to military images he still remains true to his flowery style: "And keep you in the rear of your affection, out of the shot and danger of desire", he teaches Ophelia (I, iii, 35). Even at moments of extreme agitation his images remain over-refined, as, "That drop of blood that's calm proclaims me bastard", etc. (IV, v, 117). Or take the following heavy, euphuistic image: "Too much of water hast thou, poor Ophelia, and therefore I forbid my tears" (IV, vii, 186).

This young noble has evidently read widely of the fashionable euphuistic literature and is probably well acquainted with Sidney's *Arcadia* (and, of course, he writes love letters and verses much more skilfully than Hamlet). He speaks in metaphors patterned after these books. Thanks to their perfection, Ophelia's virtues stood "on mount of all the age" (IV, vii, 28). He says that he has "a speech of fire, that fain would blaze" (IV, vii, 191). He compares himself to a pelican because he is ready to repast Polonius' friends with his own blood (IV, v, 145). And, of course, he uses classical metaphors. He makes mention of "old Pelion or the skyish head of blue Olympus" (V, i, 275). "Blue Olympus" is a typically refined epithet. Only at the very end of the tragedy, when he is mortally wounded, does Laertes cast aside this glittering tinsel and, addressing himself to Osric, express his thought in a simple, realistic comparison: "As a wood-cock to mine own springe, Osric; I am justly killed with mine own treachery" (V, ii, 320).

Such is *artificial* Laertes, whom Shakespeare contrasts to *natural* Hamlet.

HORATIO

In Horatio's speeches we find a number of concretely substantial images reminiscent of the dominant motif in Hamlet's imagery. Remembering the Ghost troubles him like a mote in his "mind's eye" (I, i, 112). We may note, in passing, that this same image of "the mind's eye" is to be found in Hamlet's speeches. Young Fortinbras, Horatio says, is "of unimproved mettle hot and full" (I, i, 96). In Horatio's words, if Claudius succeeds in concealing his crime it will be tantamount to theft (III, ii, 94). Osric's store of euphuisms gives out and Horatio says that "His purse is empty already: all's golden words are spent" (V, ii, 127). We also find, in Horatio's speeches, several of the most 'banal', if we may call them so, idiomatic turns of speech which verge upon 'slang'. Fortinbras, Horatio says, "hath in the skirts of Norway, here and there, sharkt up a list of lawless resolutes" (I, i, 98). Horatio relates how Marcellus and Bernardo were "distill'd almost to jelly" with fear when they saw the Ghost (I, ii, 205). To Bernardo's astonished query (at the beginning of the tragedy): "What, is Horatio there?" he jestingly replies: "A piece of him" (I, i, 19), a phrase which is variously interpreted by commentators and which has nonplussed many translators, but which I believe to be merely a jesting idiomatic turn of speech denoting "he himself", or "I answer for him".

Horatio compares the courtier Osric, who wears a big hat, to a lapwing, just hatched, running away with his shell still on his head (V, ii, 193). Folk legend in that day had it that the lapwing was already able to run as soon as it was hatched from the shell. All this brings Hamlet to mind. Horatio's images, like Hamlet's, show scholarship. It goes without saying that Horatio uses many classical metaphors: he recalls "the most high and palmy state of Rome" and "the mightiest Julius" (I, i, 113). His description of the events which took place at the time of the assassination of Caesar is full of images steeped in the spirit of the classical world: there is "the moist star, upon whose influence Neptune's empire stands" (I, i, 118), and dread portents which he calls "harbingers preceding still the fates" and "prologue to the omen coming on" (I, i, 122–3). At the end of the tragedy he compares himself to "an antique Roman" (v, ii, 354). We think the following image is likewise classical in nature: Horatio calls the cock "the trumpet to the morn" that "doth...awake the god of day", i.e. the sun (I, i, 150).

In his book *Shakespeare and the Popular Dramatic Tradition*, the English investigator Bethell, mentioned above,[9] uses all possible means to prove that Shakespeare did not individualize his characters, and, consequently, the style of speech of his characters. He contends that it was a matter of indifference to Shakespeare which of his characters pronounced descriptive speeches. We find matter-of-fact Horatio exclaiming lyrically about the sunrise: "But, look, the morn, in russet mantle clad, walks o'er the dew of yon high eastern hill" (I, i, 166).[10]

Had Bethell glanced more attentively at matter-of-fact Horatio's world of images, he would have found more than one poetic image there. Besides the above splendid picture of the morning dressed in a russet mantle, and the no less vivid image: "the trumpet to the morn" that "doth...awake the god of day", we can mention his description of the colour of the old Hamlet's beard as "sable silver'd" (I, ii, 241), or Horatio's exclamation at the end of the tragedy: "And flights of angels sing thee to thy rest" (v, ii, 374), which brings to mind the pictures of the Italian Renaissance painters. Horatio, the poor student, who is like Hamlet in the realism of his metaphors and his knowledge of ancient Roman literature, is not an artificial poet like Laertes, but he is a genuine poet.

It is, of course, impossible to speak of any "world of images" in regard to the minor, episodic roles in Shakespeare. But even in regard to them we can draw characteristic conclusions, although these are rather more of a negative nature, so to say, than positive. For example, the three soldiers who stand on guard on the platform before the castle—Marcellus, Bernardo and Francisco—use no classical or 'scholarly' images. In general, the few images we do find in their speeches are far from 'bookish'. "Something is rotten in the state of Denmark", says Marcellus (I, iv, 90). The image used by the "honest soldier" Francisco is also coarse: "Not a mouse stirring" (I, i, 9)—probably a stock expression at the time, approximating the Russian: "Not even a fly flew past." Bernardo borrows a metaphor from military life: "Sit down awhile; and let us once again assail your ears that are so fortified against our story" (I, i, 31). Such is this modest, primitive world, which, however, does have its own individuality.

POLONIUS

Polonius' world of images is expressive in its own way. He is indeed a very sober man, and, despite his cunning, a very primitive, limited character. "And it must follow, as the night the day" (I, iii, 79). The unquestionable, primitive logic of this metaphor evidently pleases Polonius, for in another passage he uses it again, varying it as follows: "To expostulate...why day is day, night, night, and time is time, were nothing but to waste night, day, and time" (II, ii, 85). Metaphysics is evidently not to his taste, although he does like to use high-flown phrases.

"Take this from this if this be otherwise", says Polonius (II, ii, 156). Most of his images are similarly straightforward. The word 'tether' is frequently used idiomatically in modern English as a fossilized image in the sense of limit, sphere. In Shakespeare's time it evidently still had the quality of a coloured image in analogous phrases. Polonius says that as a prince Hamlet has a longer tether than Ophelia (I, iii, 125). Comparing Hamlet and his own daughter to cattle is quite in the spirit of Polonius.

Polonius tells the King that if he, Polonius, errs in considering love the cause of Hamlet's insanity, "let me be no assistant for a state, but keep a farm and carters" (II, ii, 166). Polonius, the King's chamberlain, here appears to us as the proprietor of a manure farm, which, evidently, just suits his character. It is no wonder that a few lines later Hamlet calls him a 'fishmonger' (II, ii, 174), adding, immediately, that he wishes he were as honest. London's fish-dealers evidently were not famed for their honesty, yet in Hamlet's opinion they were more honest than was the courtier Polonius. The term 'fishmonger', by the way, also meant a procurer, the proprietor of a brothel, which, of course, was likewise a suitable vocation for Polonius. The latter is fond of indecencies. "He's for a jig or a tale of bawdry, or he sleeps", Hamlet says of him (II, ii, 530). Polonius himself makes mention of a brothel, calling it "a house of sale" (II, i, 60). Polonius calls Hamlet's vows to Ophelia "sanctified and pious bawds" (I, iii, 130).

As was to be expected, Polonius' images are simple and concrete for the most part. Friends should be 'grappled' to the soul "with hoops of steel" (I, iii, 63). A newly acquired and still untried friend is a "new hatcht, unfledged comrade" (I, iii, 65). Vows of love are "blazes... giving more light than heat" (I, iii, 117). Reynaldo has the right to 'sully' Laertes a little "as 'twere a thing a little soil'd i' th' working" (II, i, 40). Polonius says that he did not want to "play the desk or table-book" (II, ii, 136). He likens his artful tricks to the game of bowling (II, i, 66). Good news at the end of a story is like "fruit to" a "great feast" (II, ii, 52). "With devotion's visage and pious action", says Polonius, "we do sugar o'er the devil himself" (III, i, 48). He uses fishing metaphors: wise people, he says, take the "carp of truth" with a "bait of falsehood" (II, i, 63); and hunting metaphors: he knows how to hunt "the trail of policy" (II, ii, 47), and in speaking with Ophelia he calls Hamlet's vows of love "springes to catch woodcocks" (I, iii, 115). The latter image echoes one of Laertes' that we mentioned above (V, ii, 320), when, as we have seen, at the end of the tragedy Laertes casts off, as it were, the brilliantly embroidered cloak of euphuisms.

All this points to Polonius' quite realistic turn of mind. We should look in vain for poetic images in his speeches. Even what seems so 'pretty' an image in the eyes of the modern reader— "the wind sits in the shoulder of your sail" (I, iii, 56)—was probably merely a stock phrase and simply meant that there was a fair wind blowing.

Polonius, as we have already mentioned, likes to talk 'eloquently'. Remember how he shows off with his figures of speech in the presence of the King and Queen (II, ii, 86 f.). "In his young days", Belinski[11] writes about Polonius, "he was a feather-brained, mischievous rake; then, having sown his wild oats, he turned staid, as is the general way, and became:

> An old man, jesting as of old,
> exquisitely, adroitly and cleverly,
> which is now rather ridiculous. (PUSHKIN)

Polonius was a great admirer of the theatre. In his student days he took part in plays and "was accounted a good actor". "I did enact Julius Caesar. I was kill'd i' th' Capitol, Brutus kill'd me" (III, ii, 109), he relates. Enumerating all kinds of plays, he makes mention of Seneca and

Plautus (II, ii, 428). Thus, the classical names met with in his role are connected with the theatre. Polonius himself, who adores puns, rather 'play-acts' in real life.

"Polonius", writes Belinski, "is a man with a faculty for administrative work, or, rather, one able to seem capable of it." In any case, he spent his life in administrative posts. This affected his phraseology. In his dialogue with Reynaldo he speaks of "the prenominate crimes" (II, i, 43) instead of simply saying "the little sins I mentioned". He likens Hamlet's vows of love to "implorators of unholy suits" (I, iii, 129).

There is one other theme in Polonius' imagery which reveals a hidden trait which we can only guess at. He is indignant with Ophelia for having "ta'en these tenders for true pay" (I, iii, 106), i.e. believed Hamlet's vows. Ophelia is to be "somewhat scanter of your maiden presence, set your entreatments at a higher rate than a command to parley" (I, iii, 123). He likens Hamlet's vows to 'brokers' (I, iii, 127). This hidden trait in Polonius, which is not directly mentioned anywhere in the text, is love of money. He probably had a good deal to do with it.

Thus we have found that definite laws govern the images of the characters we have considered. As has been said above, we have thereby confirmed the fact that these characters speak in their own words and not in the words of the author. The metaphors used by each of them have certain definite themes. We have therefore ascertained one of the means by which Shakespeare individualized the language of his characters. And in these metaphors we have found valuable and graphic material for the psychological characterization of Shakespeare's dramatis personae.

NOTES

1. The present paper is a fragment of an investigation of Shakespeare's poetics.

2. Cf. "Shakespeare on the Soviet Stage", *Theatre Almanac* (All-Union Theatre Society, no. 6, 1947).

3. Cf. *From the History of English Realism* (U.S.S.R. Academy of Sciences Press, 1941).

4. Caroline F. E. Spurgeon, *Shakespeare's Imagery* (Cambridge, 1935).

5. Spurgeon, *ibid.* pp. 379–80.

6. Cf. Dover Wilson, *What Happens in Hamlet* (Cambridge, 1937); Granville-Barker, *Prefaces to Shakespeare* (1927).

7. For instance, see Bethell, *Shakespeare and the Popular Dramatic Tradition* (1944).

8. The usual interpretation: Othello recalls Iago's words, comparing Cassio and Desdemona to lecherous goats and monkeys. But N. Mordvinov in the role of Othello (as produced by Yuri Zavadsky in the Mossoviet Theatre in Moscow, 1942) addressed the words to all the characters present on the stage: at that moment the whole world seemed to Othello to be a menagerie. As the reader sees, both interpretations are possible: all people begin to seem beasts to Othello; on the other hand, this is the result of Iago's influence, an echo of his theme.

9. See p. 84.

10. Bethell, *op. cit.* p. 72.

11. Belinski, "Hamlet, Shakespeare's Drama, and Mochalov in the Rôle of Hamlet".

TREND OF SHAKESPEARE SCHOLARSHIP

BY

HARDIN CRAIG

In the year 1636 René Descartes published his *Discourse on Method*, and thereby succeeded in dividing the new world from the old.

Shakespeare lived in a Pre-Cartesian world, that is, a world which had in it little uncertainty as to the nature of things and little idea as to the importance of research. Descartes began with universal doubt, and it is the presence of doubt that chiefly distinguishes our world from that of Shakespeare. Descartes discarded tradition (doubted its truth), and he and his followers have subjected all moral, religious, and intellectual ideas and beliefs to scientific investigation. Modern science has, however, made only a partial conquest of the world, partly because many people have continued to accept tradition and authority, and, partly, because there seem to be some regions into which science cannot enter or can enter only in an unconvincing way. Nevertheless there is no doubt that the scientific method and attitude have deeply affected all the life of the mind. The Pre-Cartesian world is thus in some measure a lost world to modern learned culture. Fragments of it, even large fragments, are continually being found by scholars, but they seem usually to remain fragments. The spirit and temper, the essence, of that world before the age of reason and science apparently make themselves known only to a few wise, patient and imaginative scholars and critics. The difficult quest for the spirit of Shakespeare and his age goes on, but with varying success, and most intellectuals are perhaps the dupes of literature as well as of science. Clearly, if we are to escape into the Pre-Cartesian world, we must not, although we carry our present with us, make over that past into the likeness of our present. We are tempted to do this very thing by the circumstance that human nature, although affected and no doubt in some measure controlled by the characteristics and consequential ideas of each particular time, is proverbially always the same.

When, however, we behold our shortcomings as Post-Cartesians, we cannot justly declare war against ourselves, for it must be admitted that the age of science rediscovered Shakespeare and has been busy for generations in making his greatness manifest.

When the learned world saw, mainly in the Age of Reason, that Shakespeare without the patronage of learning continued to live, continued to afford pleasure to his readers and his spectators and to explain and illuminate the world in which we live, they began to construct a long series of Cartesian 'intuitions' or as we say hypotheses about Shakespeare and by means of investigation found out the truth about them, so that Shakespeare's pre-eminent greatness became a by-word. Shakespeare in drama was seen to have been right, and the Aristotelians with their decorum and their three unities were put in their proper place. This process has continued, and some modern scholars, not all of them, actually see that Shakespeare was a creator of drama, developed his own special form of it, and did this quite independently of all the teachings of Renaissance classicism. Ordered scientific study of Shakespeare has yielded enormous results and continues year by year to yield more and more truth.

But the inherent defects of scientific rationalism in the investigation of Shakespeare stay with us. In its hands Shakespeare became a specimen, and in some measure he still is. Whether Shakespeare likes it or not, he must be compelled to mean something, must be subjected to research, explained by hypotheses, and demonstrated to the last detail. But there is nothing else to be done, and we must go forward, but with added care. One has only to remember the laborious good sense of Malone, the intuitions of Coleridge, the insight of Kreyssig and Rümelin, the interpretative excellence of Dowden and Bradley, and the patient scholarship of W. W. Greg, of Granville-Barker and of other workers of our own day in order to realize the greatness of Shakespeare scholarship. The current activities of eminent scholars like J. Dover Wilson, E. E. Stoll, T. W. Baldwin, L. B. Campbell, O. J. Campbell, E. M. W. Tillyard, Theodore Spencer, L. L. Schücking, and dozens of others show that Shakespeare is still subject to scientific investigation. However, that an essential Shakespeare is being revealed, except in single aspects after approaches from chosen points of view, cannot be definitely stated. To deprecate modern Shakespeare scholarship and criticism would be absurd, and I am ready to admit that my attempt to investigate the investigators is as Cartesian as any of the tasks to which I have alluded.

My problem must rest on a determination of limits, and we might make the situation clearer by a sort of imaginary diagram. Let us suppose the existence of three concentric circles, or better still, three concentric globes. Let us imagine ourselves at the centre and as mainly concerned with the innermost circle or globe, yet so situated that we are constantly influenced by the larger areas outside our own. All three regions act upon us and are constantly within our ken. The partition is meant to indicate degrees of scientific investigability. The innermost circle we will suppose is the circle of the individual as such, the individual with his personal and racial inheritance, his needs, his instincts, his affections, his morals (in so far as they pertain to his duty to himself), his conscience, and his religion. Into it enter his immediate relations as a member of a family, a neighbourhood, and a clan. But as we go outward and leave the region of the individual human heart, we enter more and more into the intermediate circle, or the field of what we call the social sciences. Relations in that intermediate area have so widened that emphases are no longer individual but social. The outermost circle is that of more or less complete objectivity, or perhaps it would be better to say that to a greater or less degree this outermost area is capable of controlled manipulation. It is the field of the natural sciences. This outermost area is the region in which the followers of Bacon and Descartes have scored their greatest successes. Into the innermost circle the scientific method has so far not been able to enter with any convincing certitude. The life of individual man is not without truth; it is not without guidance, but it must content itself with probability rather than proof or mathematical certainty. In the intermediate circle the social sciences, by means of often costly trial and error and by the use of the statistical method, hope to arrive at greater and greater certainty, but the difficulties are very great. There seem to be limits to the application of the scientific method in that field, and so far science has not been able to pry very deeply into the actual centres of social life. Social science has usually to content itself with probabilities. The scientific method has exploited and continues to exploit material and manipulable matters, it meets with varying success in the intermediate region, but so far has been baffled by the centre, which refuses to make way even for determinism.

A very simple approach to the problem may be found in the critical dicta of Francis Bacon. It is not my intention, however, to apply to Shakespeare study the whole body of errors and vanities and peccant humours against which Bacon gives warning. In the *Advancement of Learning* and more fully in the doctrine of Idols in *Novum Organum* Bacon suggests that any scholarly enterprise may be subject to three kinds of errors: first, vain affectations or the limitations imposed by the intellectual environment of particular periods in history; secondly, vain altercations or the errors committed and fostered by the professional interests and techniques of literary and historical scholarship; thirdly, vain imaginations or the ineptitude of individual minds to comprehend or appreciate fully the wealth of human experience and the depth of human understanding recorded and set forth in great literature. In this instance we are dealing with Shakespeare's works.

Of the first class we might find illustrations in the neo-classic rejection of Shakespearian drama from the Restoration until the middle of the eighteenth century; the early fallacies of textual criticism, such as Pope's censure of the Folio of 1623 on the ground that it came from common players and a vulgar theatre; Theobald's pedantry in the emendation of Shakespeare's texts on classical principles; Farmer's theory that Shakespeare was unlearned and a constant plagiarist (a very harmful error); and even Malone's suspicion of all quartos as surreptitious. Note, too, the moralistic interpretations of characters and situations by Richardson, Whately, Morgann, McKenzie, Francis Gentleman, Mrs Griffith, and others. Remember that Johnson's highest ultimate judgment of Shakespeare was that he was a sound moral teacher. Recall also the excessive idolatry of Shakespeare in the age of Coleridge and Hazlitt, which, especially when robbed of the style of those worthies, was patently extravagant. Consider also the results of the too narrowly based treatment during the nineteenth century of the plays of Shakespeare as closet drama without connection with the stage. Victorian propriety is thought to have gone to too great lengths in deciding what Shakespeare did or did not write in his plays. Note also the thesis-ridden contributions of German scholars and of scholars strongly under German influence throughout the nineteenth century, ending, let us hope, in the exaltation of Shakespeare as a typically Nordic genius. Finally, consider the surrealistic conclusions about Shakespeare of the Freudians in our own day.

The pursuit of vain contentions may be profusely illustrated in contemporary Shakespeare scholarship, which not infrequently shows the extremes to which scholarly machinery and specialized research may be carried. There is, for example, the attempt to bind Shakespeare by a rigidly systematized faculty psychology, which for the Elizabethans themselves, as it is for us to this day, was mainly a method of expression. There are also modern cosmological studies which would have us believe in an Elizabethan uniformity of mind greater than the farthest dreams of a totalitarian state. There are also the many anachronistic applications to Shakespeare of modern dogma derived from psychology, psychiatry and medicine.

There are finally, and perhaps in this age especially, what Bacon called vain imaginings, "delight in deceiving and aptness to be deceived; both imposture and credulity". We see this illustrated in the six or seven claimants to the authorship of Shakespeare's plays, in the varied romances of the Dark Lady of the *Sonnets*, in strange stories of undivulged paternities, and of social and political intrigue. But vain imaginings have many entrances into the most highly respected scholarly circles. It is doubtful if the badness of all bad quartos is to be accounted for by even so ingenious a theory as that of the pirate actor. There may be cases to which the theory applies, but the unwillingness of a very great scholar, in spite of his own distrust of the theory, to refrain from applying it to the 1602 edition of *The Merry Wives of Windsor* is a case in point. Another is the persistent attempt of many German scholars and of at least two most eminent English-speaking scholars to prove the stenographic origin of various Shakespearian quartos including the Pide Bull Quarto of *King Lear*. The authority of great scholars is such that they pass on erroneous or doubtful traditional opinion as truth and meantime create new erroneous dogmas of their own. The formula for "memorial reconstruction" of which we have heard so much and which may perhaps have special applications, when applied as a general principle by minds lacking in caution or penetration, becomes the source of much error. We must substitute a sober policy of weighing probabilities for self-indulgence, contentiousness and mere theory.

If we are to play the scientific game, it must be played according to the rules and with the caution of the scientific method. Modern scholarship continually falls into the trap which Bacon describes when he says that the fact that the parts of a given system agree with each other is no proof that the system as a whole is in accordance with truth. Given a theory and a determination to prove it, a scholar by hunting widely for fact and opinion which agree with his contention and by ignoring those cases which are non-committal or which disagree with it may prove almost anything. A cypher weighted ever so slightly on the side of higher frequency may unearth wonders and prove impossibilities. Thus in Shakespeare scholarship Cartesian intuitions continually entrap us. They are aided in that operation by those scholars who deny probability to all hypotheses except their own. We cannot as children of this age reject the scientific method, nor is it desirable that we should. We must continue to build our building, but we must build it solidly and in accordance with the dictates of truth and reason.

The initial contention of this paper, however, is that scholarship, like all scientific investigation, is inadequate when it approaches the region where Shakespeare's greatest greatness lies. We know a great deal more about Shakespeare than we did. Our ideas as to his environment and his activities are far saner and more adequate than they used to be. We understand his art much better than it was once understood, and, although erroneous opinions still flourish, there is no cause for discouragement. Our underlying idea, seldom expressed, is also sound. We have the idea that we as scholars will open the way, remove all obstacles to understanding and let Shakespeare speak, both on the stage and in the study. But the question is, can we get still closer to the centre of his being? In this attempt we shall not need to demonstrate anything, since it is a matter of policy rather than of execution. The operation is Pre-Cartesian and is nothing less than seeing as Shakespeare saw and feeling as Shakespeare felt. I have some suggestions for embarking on this great adventure.

My principal suggestion is, and here I fall in line with Dilthey as well as Croce, that we make ourselves at home in the Renaissance. The important step, it seems to me, has to do with the range of knowledge and the attitude that men of the Renaissance assumed toward knowledge. The attempt may well turn out to be factitious; without the kindling of imagination it is sure to be so. We are also doomed to fail unless we are able to sympathize with Renaissance men on such subjects as birth and death, love and friendship, poverty and riches, and man and God. In the realm of mind alone we may, however, find a door ajar which will admit us to the parks and grounds of the Pre-Cartesian world. Indeed, we may find the beginnings of a solution in the fact that Renaissance men knew everything, or thought they did, so that they did not, with all their ranging curiosity, regard knowledge as an end in itself. Bacon took all knowledge as his province, not, as ordinarily thought, as a province to be explored in the future, but as a province of which he was definitely assuming command. Burton vindicates the claim that Pre-Cartesian men knew everything, or at least had all knowledge at hand.

When, however, we begin to think of ourselves in this connection, we begin to tremble. Our sense of the vast extent of human learning is so great that we give up the fight, and yet our reason for doing so is specious. The effect of three hundred years of science has been to make the world much simpler than it was. Indeed, relative omniscience is within our grasp. Our ordinary school books of physics and chemistry tell us more in less space than was known by all the scientists from Albertus Magnus to Rutherford. We are frightened by technology; the stuff itself is very simple. Man's chances to understand his physical environment are far greater than they ever were before. But we, who have a chance to be comprehensive in our knowledge, insist on specializing our studies and attainments; whereas the Elizabethans, surrounded and beset by error, obscurity and difficulty, calmly mastered the entire system and regarded specialization as an evidence of weakness. It is the attitude of inclusiveness that matters. The ideal of the all-round scholar still has validity, still works, but I do not know anything more repugnant to modern man and his offspring than is the ideal of breadth and versatility.

J. E. Spingarn, writer on the history of criticism, discusses Benedetto Croce's doctrine of critical immediacy, according to which a critic of earlier literature, confronted by a work of an earlier time, restores within himself the thought and feeling of the author of that work, repeats the process of creation, and comprehends immediately the work before him. Spingarn infers from this that Croce would dispense with all intermediate processes, such as textual criticism, biographical knowledge, history, the temper of the age that produced the book in question, philology, languages, rhetoric, poetics, and the principles of art. It is doubtful, however, whether Croce demands such wholesale denudation of the critic, since he or any sensible man would regard these things as indispensable parts of the knowledge and culture of the critic. He seems to mean that these scholarly processes are not themselves part and parcel of the critical act, not precisely ends in themselves, although they offer such difficulty and are so important that they may properly occupy the lives and efforts of the best minds. Spingarn was wrong in setting up a ground of opposition between scholarship and literary criticism. He and others who have misunderstood Croce have helped to fill the world with ignorant, ill-equipped, and anachronistic critics. A critic equipped, as no doubt Croce is, with abundant knowledge of ancient and modern literature, history, and all branches of philosophy, and endowed besides with sympathy, imagination, and insight, may well practise immediacy; but his work depends for its truth on the extent as well as the quality of his comprehension. This would be particularly true of the literature of the Renaissance, with its inclusive scope.

Three hundred years of science, the latter part of which is technological and materialistic, have raised a barrier between us and the age of Shakespeare, a barrier which has to be crossed again and again by every man who would know and understand Shakespeare. In considering how that barrier may be crossed I have suggested that universality of knowledge and catholicity of mind offer, particularly to Shakespeare scholars, a practical and ready pathway.

In order that we may understand why it is important to cross this great divide between Shakespeare and modern man, let me read a short paragraph from Bertrand Russell's *Principles of Social Reconstruction*:

If life is to be fully human it must serve some end which seems, in some sense, outside human life, some end which is impersonal and above mankind, such as God or truth or beauty. Those who most promote life do not have life for their purpose. They aim rather at what seems to be a gradual incarnation, a bringing into our human existence of something eternal, something that appears to imagination to live in a heaven remote from strife and failure and the devouring jaws of Time. Contact with this eternal world—even if it be only a world of our imagining—brings a strength and a fundamental peace which cannot be wholly destroyed by the struggles and apparent failures of our temporal life. It is this happy contemplation of what is eternal that Spinoza calls the intellectual love of God. To those who have once known it, it is the key to wisdom.

Shakespeare is the storehouse of these things, and Shakespeare and his age, with all its faults, do offer us some freedom from the shackles with which we have bound ourselves. That freedom lies in the first instance, I suggest, in the assumption of a more catholic point of view and a more inclusive and a broader mind, particularly on the part of scholars, and in a refusal to over-specialize. Scholars are sometimes more shut away from Shakespeare than are ordinary people. To ordinary people Shakespeare continues to speak directly. They have greater difficulties in understanding what Shakespeare says than scholars do, but their inclination is to take immediately to their hearts what they do understand. Vulgar errors about Shakespeare are numerous and are almost ineradicable, and yet much true Shakespeare lives on in the popular mind. There is still an open road, not a very straight or easy one, to the Pre-Cartesian world of Shakespeare through the minds and hearts of simple people. From this fact we may derive a suggestion and an illustration.

The suggestion is that scholars might be less concerned with pointing out errors and limitations in particular pieces of Shakespeare scholarship and more concerned with finding out and making manifest what Shakespeare really means. Whatever interesting things may be read into Shakespeare by imaginative critics and stage directors, there is no doubt, in the minds of scholars at least, that Shakespeare's own meaning is the greatest of meanings and is the one the world needs. It does the world little good to see *The Tempest* as a mere modern spectacle, *A Midsummer Night's Dream* as an orgy of colour and dance, or *The Taming of the Shrew* as a vulgar farce; or, let us say, to see the solemn consultation of the greatest ecclesiastics of the realm by King Henry V as slap-stick comedy. It is a disservice to Shakespeare and to the modern world to misinterpret his plays, and it is my hope that the Shakespeare Memorial Theatre will more and more take upon itself the task of achieving correctness in the interpretation of Shakespeare's plays. It would by its authority confer upon the world a great blessing if it should do so.

Our way as scholars is the way of the intellect, and I have suggested that we broaden and increase our knowledge until we are able to think and feel in terms of a complete and balanced authoritarian world, a world in which knowledge, much sought after, was nevertheless not an end in itself, and, finally, a world which knew better than we do how to put things in their proper places, because its values were less transitory than ours. No other method of procedure is so likely to meet with success as the bringing of this breadth of comprehension to bear on the problem of Shakespeare scholarship. Scholars by their thoroughness can seek and maintain a minor omniscience, and the most successful efforts always show the validity of this method and approach. What great scholars do and have always done is to study Shakespeare so carefully and from so many sides and angles that he has to reveal his meaning; the lapse of time and the great alteration in the philosophy of intellectual life fail to obscure his meaning and dim his glory. Such scholarship will deprecate both unjustified conservatism and the needless creation of new dogma.

I should like to illustrate the painstaking labour I have recommended from the last complete essay of the late Harley Granville-Barker. I refer to his study of *Coriolanus*. The play has always been a puzzle. Its greatness has usually been admitted, but no critic has quite known how Shakespeare conceived of the principal character and action of that play. When Granville-Barker sought to solve the mystery, he studied the play from every possible point of view, let nothing escape him. The action, the source, the characters, the staging, the versification, the stage-directions, the text itself came in for the most detailed and patient scrutiny. One felt in reading the essay that Shakespeare could not escape from such thoroughness and such competency, so that the reading of the essay itself became an occasion for dramatic suspense. Granville-Barker's interpretation, arrived at by these honest means, I think may be described as triumphant, as the best study of *Coriolanus* ever achieved by a critic, and as all the greater because it releases Shakespeare from the necessity of having some one definable purpose in mind. *Coriolanus* seems to be a drama that satisfies not one but many ends and is seen to satisfy the multiple art of the Renaissance.

Whenever Shakespeare study is sufficiently broad, detailed and objective, whenever it refuses to resort to the use of pigeon-holes, general characteristics and values tend to emerge. It is so in the textual studies of J. Dover Wilson, W. W. Greg, and, of course, of the late R. B. McKerrow. The same effect of thoroughness is seen in the field of interpretation in work of the kind I have just described as pursued by Granville-Barker in his study of *Coriolanus*. There has been much work of that kind, but not enough.

I should like to suggest that breadth and thoroughness tend to reveal a general characteristic of primary importance, which has to do with the achievement of unity. The prevailing type of unity observable in medieval art was unity in variety, and this multiple art lived on through the Renaissance. It is seen, for example, in tapestries. I recall a tapestry of the Trojan War I saw long ago, I think in Brussels. In it there were selected scenes from the tale of Troy, from the sacrifice of Iphigenia to the burning of Ilium. They were presented without reference to sequence, size or chronology, indeed, with no one major emphasis; and yet the whole effect was that of a vivid representation of the Trojan War. Chinese pictorial art seems to have the same multiple quality. Medieval drama is unified only in episodes and, as it were, accidentally. The stage itself was often, perhaps usually, a stage of many places. The use of this old, conventional multiple stage is plainly to be seen in *Richard III*, and there are traces of it elsewhere in Shakespeare. Even when there is a single unifying character as in Marlowe's *Tamburlaine*, the art is still in some measure the particularized art of the Middle Ages. Unity achieved by omission or subordination of unimportant particulars was still a long way in the future.

Shakespeare's art is large, multifarious, and relatively indefinite. It would follow that theses, to which our scientific method makes us habitually resort, do not normally arrive at these large effects and are not always conscious of them. They are not likely to do so as long as we pre-suppose or demand a modern kind of unity in Shakespeare. Can it be that Shakespeare had no one clearly definable thing to say about humanity when he put Hamlet on the stage, or that he did not mean some one thing by Coriolanus? Did he mean to say: "A representative human being did once, when so situated and so confronted, act and speak in such and such a way"? If so, that is a very different thing from saying: "Human beings, if greatly perplexed or if beset by inordinate pride, will in the presence of such issues always behave in these ways." There is more here than a mere matter of emphasis. In the first supposition, which in my judgment is the true one, we see that Shakespeare in the spirit of his age refused to fetter mankind. Perhaps this is suggestive of an important difference between our age and the Pre-Cartesian world and between Shakespeare and many of his interpreters. It may suggest that our modern scientific scholarship, important, indispensable, and inevitable as it is, does not always lead us directly into Shakespeare's world. To carry over the features of a particularized multiple art, whose emphases depend on events in their full setting, into the field of interpretation is no easy thing, since to do so lays upon the interpreter the necessity of comprehending far more than the principles of unity and proportion. It puts the Renaissance conception of character in a new light, since it uses a pattern of life rather than of art, enmeshes character in environment and distributes dramatic interest over groups of characters.

We have inherited a realistic outlook, but it happens that in maturing thought toward realism there lay the doom of the dogmatic age. I would not recommend a return to it in any vital particular, but I would say that Shakespeare lived and thought in conformity to an older authoritarian system and that his breadth as well as his sweetness reveal themselves in this ancient order. When scientific acumen reaches a certain height (beyond mere fact-finding) and imagination has been disciplined into real skill and ingenuity, then the normal growth of scholarly interest should lead us into a type of historical thinking in which Pre-Cartesian dogma ceases to be restrictive. The most insistent facts of existence have always been respected, else we should not be here.

As we bring, in greater and greater measure, the power of knowledge to bear on the study of Shakespeare, it would be well also if we could bring along with our knowledge certain other qualities which the Elizabethans had in abundance and we have in smaller measure. Might we not bring a sharpened curiosity? We might be encouraged to try this by the thought that, in spite of all the scientists have done, the greater and more important part of the world, the region where we live, the part that concerns us most as living men, is still unexplored and is as full of wonders as the Elizabethans thought the physical world might be. Might we not restore our faith and stock ourselves with it even as the Elizabethans did? Such a thing would give us a courage like theirs. They believed that this is a world in which something can be done. They believed that this is God's world, and they accepted the experience of mankind with reference to sin and its consequences and virtue and its rewards. They were not so disposed as we are to let themselves be the playthings of a hypothetical determinism. It is easy and sometimes amusing to designate the faults of the Elizabethans, but this one can say, they were the children of God and they knew it.

SHAKESPEARE IN FRANCE: 1900–1948

BY

HENRI FLUCHÈRE

I do not propose to write a scholarly article on the subject of Shakespeare in France during the last fifty years, such as would offer an exhaustive survey of criticism, translations and productions since the beginning of the century. I am here limiting myself to the taking stock of the ever-increasing interest Shakespeare has raised in my country and of the manifold attempts which bear witness, with various degrees of success, to the fact that Shakespeare belongs to our literary tradition as much as any of our own classics—that he has, indeed, become part and parcel of our literary consciousness. We may not have arrived at a right estimate or appreciation of his works as works of art, but, after all, it is of the essence of genius to offer a wide range of interpretation and influence, and Shakespeare less than any other great writer can escape the common fate.

To make the present position of Shakespeare in France clear, I should like to remind the reader of a few well-known facts of literary history. Shakespeare's real fame in France started in the latter part of the eighteenth century, when Voltaire, the 'discoverer' and introducer of Shakespeare,[1] went blind with fury against Letourneur's admirable translation. True it is Voltaire's brilliant though fragile supremacy in the theatre was then being seriously threatened. He had sought to identify his own drama with the great productions of the classical school, which, he thought, he had renewed and rejuvenated with precisely what he had learnt and borrowed from Shakespeare's strange pieces. Letourneur's unrestrained encomium of Shakespeare's comedies and tragedies he violently denounced as an insult to the genius of France, and he trembled with fear and rage at the thought that this 'monster' (Letourneur) already had "a party in France".[2] Voltaire's wounded vanity carried more than a personal resentment: in fact, two radically opposed aesthetic conceptions and artistic achievements were then for the first time openly facing one another. The French classical doctrine of what a successful dramatic work of art should be, and, consequently, the whole French classical conception of the universe, were being baffled by the stupendous revelations implied in Letourneur's enterprise. Shakespeare was here being looked upon as a rising star which threatened the virtual extinction of the steady luminaries of the past; and with them, according to Voltaire, order and beauty—orderly beauty and beautiful order—would be destroyed. The time, indeed, was not far off when a new consciousness would awake and when the Romantics would frantically cry: *Shakespeare avec nous!* The fierce romantic battle which broke out at the beginning of the nineteenth century, culminating with *La préface de Cromwell* and *La bataille d'Hernani* could hardly bring out a reasonably valuable estimate of Shakespeare's genius. What mattered *was* the genius, was what it stood for, as against the antiquated and jejune classical standpoint. The very fury with which Shakespeare's flag was hoisted and brandished against the 'old beards', accounts for the superficial and biased view which prevailed far into the century. It was enough for the romantics that Shakespeare could serve their cause and could be produced as a powerful ally. His name meant liberty of expression, repudiation of the unities, *mélange des genres* and poetry. No serious investigation was made into his technique or means of expression, no effort to replace him into his own Elizabethan setting, not even an adequate analysis of his characters. He rose strangely alone, depersonalized as it were by the power of his genius, *un phénomène de la nature*, justifying all excesses of praise by his existence alone, protean and unreal, imaginative and sensational, a profound thinker, an intense lyrical poet, a philosopher, a moralist and what not. Through being thus launched into fame by his fanatic eulogists of the romantic movement, Shakespeare has badly suffered in France from a lack of real critical interest—of the kind, for example, he received in Germany. The list of French books or articles on Shakespeare in the nineteenth century is surprisingly thin if one compares it with the work done by German critics. Apart from a vivid chapter in Taine [3] and the perfunctory, yet pleasant, survey of A. Mézières,[4] one would look in vain for a single valuable work of criticism in the whole century worthy of any serious consideration. The dithyrambic volume of Victor Hugo, the pale comments of Lamartine or Philarète Chasles, can hardly be said to be criticism at all. Victor Hugo's famous book is a wonderful jumble of epithets and inspired oratorical effects about *le génie, Shakespeare et moi—merveilleux et effrayant, la bouche d'ombre* and so on. Exciting and misleading, it fixed for a long time the French attitude to Shakespeare, it somehow isolated him, and allowed any amount of sentimentalizing and idolatry. However wrong the approach and false the conception, Shakespeare's vogue in France has known no ebbing since then.

Meanwhile, translators and adapters had been busily at work. No less than seven or eight complete translations of the plays had been undertaken before 1900, the most famous being that of François Victor Hugo, son of the poet. In turn, Antoine Bruguière, the baron de Sorsum, Duport, Guizot, Francisque Michel, Benjamin Laroche, Emile Montégut and Georges Duval tried to emulate Letourneur [5]—to say nothing of the numerous translations or adaptations of separate pieces, for the stage, for some *édition de luxe*, or for the private satisfaction of some obscure admirer in love with Venetian romance, disporting in fairyland or the tragedy of love. Thus *Romeo and Juliet, Macbeth, Hamlet, Othello, Julius Caesar* had been turned into French about thirty times each in the course of the century, sometimes by renowned writers. Alfred de Vigny tried his hand at *Othello* and *The Merchant of Venice*, George Sand preferred the pastoral *As You Like It*, while Alexandre Dumas collaborated in turning *Hamlet* into a drama *de cape et d'épée*, for the greater glory of Sarah Bernhardt.

The mention of Sarah Bernhardt compels me to say how incredible it is to think that in nineteenth-century France Hamlet's part was carried to the apex of its popularity by an actress— and in Dumas's versified translation at that! What a fine figure she must have been, in her black tights and 'inky cloak', a skull in her hand, with her deep, 'golden' voice: thus was the silhouette of Hamlet fixed for generations: theatre-goers of the nineties could not think of Hamlet but in terms of Sarah Bernhardt.[6] Thus the conflict between classical tragedy and romantic drama had been resolved in an absorption of the one by the other, but at the expense of Shakespeare. Hamlet became the romantic figure *par excellence*, but he spoke in French the classical idiom, and his behaviour, his gestures, his voice, had been toned down to something which could be admired without too much open-mouthed bewilderment, yet remained puzzling enough to cater to the public's romantic imagination. The noble and the pathetic were finely blended together, all the inconsistencies of incident and character disappeared, the tragedy went smoothly to its denouement, and the 'philosophical' reflections with which the chief character's soliloquies were interspersed gave the play a seriousness and profundity which raised it far above the somewhat discredited romantic drama proper. The famous "To be or not to be" monologue, the churchyard scene, Ophelia's madness and death, Hamlet's final utterance—"The rest is silence", all stood out as unforgettable examples of that bitterly disillusioned awareness which was admired in the Shakespearian hero. Hamlet's outlook on life, however vague and uncertain, once disentangled from the circumstances which only can explain it in the modern critic's eye, became the symbol of man's tragedy—the themes of revenge and love and death, the pettiness of man in front of the universe, the sarcastic despair which leaves so much unexpressed and yet seems to take in all human experience, and the poetry of it! Here was a character wholly steeped in a poetical atmosphere, in as much as poetry meant a blurred something which could nourish the "inexpressible aspirations of the soul".

In the same way, I believe, were all the great 'classical' figures of Shakespeare romanticized and poeticized. The abstract notions of love, jealousy, ambition, revenge, death and madness, with which Shakespeare's tragic heroes have been identified (and it would be easy to put a name to each one) thus became wrapped in a poetical aura which enhanced their dramatic interest and their glamour. Shakespeare's imagery, of course, his innumerable metaphors—the unsurpassed sweetness of some, the unexpected abruptness of others—and his masterful rhetoric contributed to the development of the poetical fallacy which led to so much confusion between dramatic construction, characterization and poetry itself. As a rule, however, the hero or the heroine was regarded as much more important than any other element of the play, and the interest of the reader or the spectator was focused upon the 'psychology' of the characters. What could not be explained in terms of our classical dramatic psychology was given to the credit of genius. In general, Taine's point of view had prevailed, not only because of the inability of French critics to get rid of the inveterate habit of forcing Shakespeare to lie on the Procrustean bed of classical order, not only because of the romantic trend of thought and feeling, but also because of their lack of accurate information (and fruitful curiosity) regarding the conditions of the Elizabethan drama in general. It is only fair to add that, after all, if Taine's pioneering work proved unsatisfactory, and even sterile, the fault lies perhaps in part with the very confusing condition of English criticism as well. The only way to a sound appreciation of Shakespeare's plays and 'genius' would have been to exploit Taine's theory, if not of la race, at least of le milieu and le moment, but this was something that could come only at a later date.

It is thus necessary to lay stress on the 'romantic' and 'psychological' outlook on Shakespeare in order to understand the general aspect of French twentieth-century Shakespeare studies. The phase of criticism I have thus very briefly and, I am afraid, superficially expounded did not belong solely to the preceding century. When we look back to the early decades of the present century, we realize that some entirely new attitude was badly needed, which could have been brought about only if critics had been bold enough to abandon the beaten tracks and the polished ruts of an age-old, conventional critical habit, devoid of imagination, wanting in insight and equally poor in first-hand knowledge of primary facts. The field of 'psychology' was soon to prove unsatisfactory, since the overwhelming richness of Shakespeare's characters could not be cast into the mould of a single personality, however comprehensive it might be. So many keys could be fitted in Shakespeare's heart that it was a hopeless job to open it. And yet the strength of the stock theories was so great that one of the most striking features of twentieth-century Shakespeare criticism in France is its incredible lack of boldness. The course of this criticism is one long timid attempt to escape from the false position thus created by the preceding age, and for years a rather unsuccessful one. The bogy of psychology had assumed the dignity of an academic vested interest. And the party from which one should reasonably have expected some enlightenment, namely the body of university teachers, was lost in the sands of erudite research, or preoccupied merely with the explanation of the text itself, or concerned with the adventurous task of besieging Shakespeare's personality. Attempts were made to explain Shakespeare by the 'psychology' of his characters, and the personality thus revealed, if not found conforming to the rules of a credible psychology, had to be justified—so that it would not be too much to describe a great deal of this critical effort as "A justification of Shakespeare for being Shakespeare".

There was, of course, as hinted above, the uncompromising battlefield of erudition. But this was nothing more, on the whole, than a form of escapism—escape from the main problems, which are, and always have been, aesthetic or artistic problems. Proving that Shakespeare is not Shakespeare amounts to confessing one's incapacity to prove (and justify) that Shakespeare is Shakespeare. Given the 'extraordinary' quality of the mind of the author of the plays, and given the apparently insuperable difficulty of assigning such bewildering masterpieces to the vulgar mind of a vulgar denizen of Stratford-upon-Avon, some critics sought to find a masterful personality to whom these astounding masterpieces might be attributed. These escapists, even when they laboured unwearyingly in unearthing new information, were ultimately guilty of begging the question. For, after all, if Shakespeare is not Shakespeare but is, for instance, Derby (as Abel Lefranc would have it), how could that knowledge help us to explain the difference in style or in the outlook on life between, say, *A Midsummer Night's Dream* and *King Lear*? Nevertheless, it must be confessed that such French critics had a rather lively time of it. While Général Cartier (an outsider) attempted to bring forward new proofs of Bacon's authorship, Albert Feuillerat's rejoinder destroyed the effect, Guy de Pourtalès could conclude "N'y aurait-il plus d'affaire Shakespeare?", and the Countess Longworth Chambrun could spend a lifetime in patient and loving research in order to keep intact from any foreign pollution the legitimate object of her unreserved admiration. The Stratfordian stronghold has not, of course, ever been in danger of being carried, and the controversy, even though it has been revived by Abel Lefranc's recent book[7] and even though it has induced Georges Connes to produce his ironical display of erudition, *Le mystère Shakespearien*, if it has amused public opinion much as the Loch Ness monster did, has not affected the main position nor the major problem.

Another form of escapism (though this may be considered as a misuse of the term) is what may be called the impressionistic criticism of Shakespeare. The unsurpassed model in this field is, and always will be, Victor Hugo's delirious essay. Here we get a variety of themes—the adventures of my soul carried away by Shakespeare, or Shakespeare's personality as a compound of the hundreds of personalities which fret and strut on his stage, or again, Shakespeare's political, moral, philosophical views, such as can be found or interpreted in the various utterances of his heroes. Here are collections of trite phrases—how true, how profound, how sublime—how lovely, how deeply poetical, how ravishingly subtle. This kind of criticism is always highly sentimental, and it is worth precisely what the author's personality is worth. If Léon Daudet's *Le voyage de Shakespeare* can be read as a novel and does not deserve any other attention, the inspired lyricism of André Suarès[8] is quite a different matter. This important book has not been paid the attention it deserves, for nothing which André Suarès has written is indifferent. While it is not criticism but merely the relation of the far-reaching emotions stirred in him by Shakespeare's plays and characters, it contains a rich crop of varied remarks and formulas each of which can be an endless source of pleasurable meditation on some dark wintry night, and might furnish a university examiner with innumerable subjects for a set paper. Beside it, the book of Fagus (*Essai sur Shakespeare*) seems dull and compares very poorly. It is dry, insignificant, and utterly uninspired. Louis Gillet's *Shakespeare*, on the other hand, has the elegance, the distinction, which that versatile and by no means ill-informed writer could impart to any subject he dealt with. The book is a labour of love and shows the author's wide knowledge of the plays. The refined sensibility of Louis Gillet delights in following the meandering paths of Shakespeare's woods and dales, plays with the graceful figures of his heroines, escapes towards wider horizons with his fateful heroes, philosophizes with them as a cultured humanist, endowed with a sober imagination and no mean artistic sense, can do. Despite the tribute paid in the preface to such different classes of critics as Barrett Wendell, Bradley, Middleton Murry and Schücking, the volume does not become anything else than the most distinguished and, I must say, useful attempt to draw a picture of "un Shakespeare 1930" for a cultured French public.

I must return now for a moment to academic criticism. The magnificent advance of English studies in France since the pioneer work of Alexandre Beljame, Auguste Angellier, Emile Legouis and others, is well known and appreciated in this country, and therefore does not need to be stressed. As early as the first decade of this century French scholars could compete with the very best in any part of the world, and since then they have produced many admirable works. Their teaching, too, has covered many fields and been deeply influential. I, for one, was attracted to English studies by the urbane erudition of Emile Legouis and by the masterly analytical achievement of a course of lectures by Louis Cazamian. The learned and subtle disquisitions of Legouis, ranging widely over the Elizabethan field, were so exciting and inspiring that the student might well have thought himself a regular attendant at the Boar's Head Tavern or at the Swan Theatre, and a zealous courtier of Queen Elizabeth. When he spoke, his supple fingers kneaded the paste out of which the colourful figures of Elizabethan characters emerged and danced their way back to life before our eyes. He was mostly concerned with this period, and through his influence a Shakespearian drama or comedy is now always included in the list of the *agrégation* set books. One thing, however, is strange: in spite of so many years passed in the companionship of Shakespeare, none of the distinguished scholars mentioned above has written any outstanding book on the subject. Nor in the impressive list of our doctorate theses do we find any devoted to Shakespeare, except for a few *doctorats d'Université*, mainly undertaken by foreign students upon some point of comparative literature. It seems as if our university teachers had been shy of tackling the major subject, as if Shakespeare were forbidden ground upon which it would be mere folly to risk a venture. Most of the time we were told to follow tamely in the steps of English criticism and to hold fast by the great classics. The knowledge of Shakespeare's works which our teachers had acquired through a lifelong familiarity with them might well have entitled them to more boldness, but they were equally averse to digging up and accumulating material for a monument of erudition, and to launching a new theory of interpretation in the light of recent discoveries. No French scholar ever put his pen to the task of writing a general study of the language or of the prosody of Shakespeare, and apart from a few essays or articles published in periodicals very little can be mentioned relating to special aspects of Shakespeare's literary style or dramatic technique. The absence of such studies is rendered the more puzzling by the fact that much has been done in the field of Shakespeare's contemporaries: we have, for instance, excellent books on Ben Jonson (Maurice Castelain), Peele (P. H. Cheffaud), Greene (René Pruvost), Lyly (A. Feuillerat) and Massinger (M. Chelli). Perhaps the best pieces of French criticism on Shakespeare are to be found in the prefaces to separate plays published in the two collections of translations which have succeeded each other since the First World War, and of which a few words will be said later in this article. These prefaces are generally elaborate and comprehensive, and study the main interesting points of the play. Great attention is paid to the sources, to the construction of the plot, to the psychology of the characters (an inclination which French critics will never forsake), to the poetic style, and, by way of conclusion, to the human problems raised by the situations and the characters. Even these, however, although useful to the student and sometimes truly illuminating, are, to my mind, too much concerned with the obvious and too little concerned with the new attitude to Shakespeare brought about by the patient investigations of English and American criticism in the last twenty years—investigations which are, I believe, seriously shaking the foundations of the old theories.

A change, however, may be coming. During the past few years there seems to have been a renewal of interest in Shakespeare studies, and in 1947-9 for instance, no less than three important books were published. Before these, it is only fair to mention that June 1940 (the cruellest month!) saw the reprint of the special number of *Les Cahiers du Sud* on *Le théâtre élizabéthain*, published seven years earlier. The book is a miscellany of non-scholarly essays designed for the general public, dealing with the main figures of the Elizabethan age and not seldom interspersed with boldly personal views. The success of this volume (it was rapidly sold out) is indicative of the keen interest shown by a large public (even in abnormal circumstances) in that supremely individualistic period of English literary history. Perhaps the present generation finds in the cares and worries and pangs of the past a pathetic echo to its own.

Three years later, there appeared a new biography of Shakespeare by Léon Lemonnier, based chiefly on the previous work of the Countess de Chambrun, but differing from it on minor points. The book is well written and is free from any cumbrous erudition—but it cannot be said to bring anything new. In 1945 Abel Lefranc carried more grist to his Derbyian mill, with his *A la découverte de Shakespeare*, while M. Petit Dutaillis examined the historical environment of *Le Roi Jean*.

Far more interesting, however, is Cazamian's penetrating study of *L'humour de Shakespeare*. Here, the psychological bent of French criticism (of which too much has already been said in the course of this essay) takes a new shape, and the subtle intelligence of that master of analysis, following Shakespeare's character by the bias of humour, so succeeds in weaving together the elusive threads of their implicit responses to a significant situation as to compose a coherent portrait of Shakespeare's inner and wiser self: "Le plus haut humour de Shakespeare n'est ni joyeux ni triste; c'est une attitude pensive et souriante qui embrasse le domaine de l'homme, et absout ses caprices innombrables les uns par les autres, dans un émerveillement toujours nouveau devant leur variété infinie."[9] Louis Cazamian's brilliant essay was written during the war, and ends with a subdued appeal to the higher wisdom of Prospero. This was not a mere coincidence, any more than the interest taken by Floris Delattre in Shakespeare's attitude to war. Delattre's essay (*Shakespeare et la guerre*) draws a parallel between Jean Giraudoux' and Shakespeare's ways of dealing with the Trojan War. One feels throughout the essay how near to the writer's heart is the subject of his study and what comforting lesson of hope and humanity he strives to bring out of Shakespeare's dubious problem play. This is the point of view of the moralist more than that of the aesthetic critic. The essay was perhaps the fruit of particular circumstance, yet that very fact serves to demonstrate how vitally Shakespeare has come to live in the French mind.

Compared with this attitude, Paul Reyher's impressive volume (*Essai sur les idées dans l'œuvre de Shakespeare*) seems to be wholly detached in time and space. This is an important book, the substance of which cannot be absorbed at one superficial reading. It is indeed the work of a lifetime. The author, a retired professor, sets out to study the ideas contained in Shakespeare's works, "their sources, their nature, their development, their relations and their general unity"—a formidable task. It is the first time, in France, that so many points of view, carefully documented, have been put together in a single book. The result may well frighten the specialist student as well as the casual reader. So much scholarship, such minute endeavour to track, explain and analyse the shifting shades of Shakespeare's 'thought' from scene to scene and play to play seems at first rather disconcerting—for we may never forget that Shakespeare, after all, is an artist and not a thinker, that it is not the thought in itself which is important but the way in which the thought is expressed and given life, or, in other terms, how the thought informed the poetic expression through the sensibility of the poet and how the poet's experience passed into his work of art. Nevertheless, I repeat, the book is an important one, particularly since it shows signs of the disappearance of that hesitation of which I spoke earlier in this essay. Here at last we have an attempt at a comprehensive synthesis, the fruit of an unbiased and careful study of the plays.

The diverse critical activities I have thus briefly reviewed have, of course, been accompanied by the still more numerous and impressive activities of translators, adapters, and producers. A complete inventory of translations and productions is utterly impossible, so large is the number of professionals and amateurs who have essayed this field. But the mass itself witnesses to the ever-growing interest the French public at large takes in Shakespeare's works. Four, and even five, complete translations have been either launched or completed since the late thirties.[10] The most popular (*La Pléiade*, 2 vols.), prefaced by André Gide, contains the works of several translators. Several of the more famous plays have here been newly rendered by writers whose names carry authority in the world of letters (Supervielle, Marcel Schwob, Guy de Pourtalès, Pierre Leyris, Maeterlinck, Jacques Copeau and Suzanne Bing, André Gide), while for the rest François Victor Hugo's translation has been kept unrevised. The total effect is rather confusing for the unsophisticated reader, since the differences in style belong more to the personalities of the translators than to Shakespeare himself. The dry limpidity of André Gide's beautiful French changes the sensuousness of *Antony and Cleopatra* into something which carries us far from Alexandria, while the charming resilience of Supervielle's rhythms gives to *As You Like It* an air *d'avant le Déluge*. Messiaen's complete translation, on the other hand, has the merit of coherence and unity. It is a good piece of work, reliable, accurate, and pleasant to read. Each play is accompanied by a preface from the translator's pen, which, being a Roman Catholic pen, finds many occasions (not infrequently indiscriminate) to draw Shakespeare into St Peter's fold. Here too, should be mentioned the enterprise of René Lalou, who is revising François Victor Hugo's translation: a few volumes only have appeared up to the present date.

Special note must be made of the recent work of university specialists. Struck by the some-times shocking incompetence of the enthusiastic lay translator, several distinguished scholars, under the leadership, I believe, of Emile Legouis and André Koszul, started, in the twenties, a complete translation of Shakespeare's plays on the same lines as the Greek and Latin Classics in the Budé Collection. Both the English and the French versions were given, facing each other page by page (which makes the volume handy and helpful). The aim in the French version was to provide a perfect mirror of the English text: rhymed verse was to be rendered in rhymed verse, blank verse in unrhymed French lines, and prose in prose. The principle is an ideal one, but the achievement falls far below its aim. For one thing, Shakespeare's five-beat line, whether blank or rhymed, is not reducible to a French alexandrine. The imperative rhythm is destroyed, and the wonderful suppleness of the later blank verse is reduced to the invertebrate commonplaceness of bad French *vers libre*. Then (and this is a still more serious reproach), the scrupulous care with which the translators have tried to copy to a nicety the Shakespearian idiom has thwarted their efforts to produce fluency and naturalness. The result is something which is cramped and rugged, awkward in syntax, obsolete in words and turns of phrases—a pure product of sheer erudition, praiseworthy in itself but remote from life, and utterly useless for an actor. The first requirement of a good translation is that it should flow fluently from the lips. Shakespeare's style is not an old curiosity shop style. It was written to fit the mouths of the actors impersonating the characters. The vocabulary, the rhythms, the syntax, the imagery were such as would express, in the best possible way, the emotional experience of the hero in a given situation. And even if one argues that Shakespeare's idiom in many places departs from modern spoken English, I am sure it should not be turned into the speech of Montaigne.

The shortcomings of that first experiment were so obvious that another collection has been started, ostensibly on the same lines but with much more vigour. The bilingual *Collection Aubier*, apart from the fact that it contains the excellent introductions I have alluded to, has not fallen into the same trap. The translations, though of varying merit, are reliable and readable. Some are very good. The collection is in progress and it is to be hoped that it will reach completion. If it does, it will then constitute an indispensable instrument for the student and be a source of pleasure for the general reader.

As the specialists have seldom been able to write a good stage version, producers have fre-quently applied to some writer of renown or have themselves prepared a theatre text. Translations of this kind are numerous, and many have not found their way into print. The French stage is also "a monster of ingratitudes" and a great devourer of translations. The demand has steadily increased since the dawn of the century, and particularly so since the remarkable success of Jacques Copeau's productions. That was just before the First World War, when he staged *Twelfth Night* and *The Winter's Tale* at the Vieux Colombier. His production of *Twelfth Night* in particular was a revelation and a revolution. Here was the authentic Shakespeare spirit, its grace and its movement. When the production was restaged in 1919, it drew immense crowds into the austere, exiguous, chapel-like house that Copeau had made his own. Such a production needed intelligence, sensibility and taste: Copeau had all three. He was careful to avoid all pomposity, maudlin sentimentality and extravagance. Never had Shakespeare been put on the stage in France with such simplicity, liveliness and freshness. Almost without a *décor*, but with costumes very carefully studied, the poetical atmosphere was created by the sheer play of the actors, the sprightliness of the dialogue, the gracefulness of the tempo. It was Shakespeare rediscovered.

Almost at the same time, Firmin Gémier, who was in charge of the Odéon (the sister theatre to the Comédie Française, but a bit musty and dusty at that time), produced *The Merchant of Venice* with different means, but equal success. Some time later, Charles Dullin, who, like Jouvet, had been a pupil of Copeau, began his career as producer at L'Atelier, where, for over twenty years, he indefatigably fought against all odds for his theatre. His greatest success was a Jonson play, *Volpone*, but he also produced a very impressive *Richard III* and a *Julius Caesar*. His production of *King Lear*, staged two or three years ago in the too spacious Théâtre de la Cité, was not, I am told, of the same quality. Gaston Baty and Georges Pitoëff should also be mentioned for their Shakespearian productions. Gaston Baty can boast of a certain amount of Elizabethan scholarship. He was the man to stage the first version of *Hamlet*, which he finds more dramatic than the second, and he was also responsible for a weird *Macbeth*. As for Pitoëff, his production of the complete version of *Hamlet* was an act of courage, which perhaps decided the Comédie Française to resort to another translator than Alexandre Dumas. He also produced a very moving *Romeo and Juliet*, and an *Othello*.

Among the plays inscribed in the repertory of the Comédie Française about 1920, one finds, naturally enough, *Hamlet*, but also *The Taming of the Shrew*, which was the favourite part of the famous Cécile Sorel—an actress who was so boisterously carried away by her part that one night she fell into the orchestra pit! The performance of *Coriolanus* at the Comédie Française in 1934 should also be mentioned, not because of any particular originality or theatrical excellence, but because the political situation of the time (remember the famous 6 *Février* riot in Paris) seemed to be mirrored in the play. The invectives of Coriolanus against the tribunes were then relished by all the anti-democratic cliques, and the atmosphere of more than one performance was strongly reminiscent of a political public meeting stirred up to abuse and shouting by professional agitators. But the breaking with old production methods at the Comédie was effected only a few years before the war under the influence of the producers of what was called *Le Cartel*, namely Copeau, Jouvet, Dullin and Gaston Baty. Its work was completed under the brief reign of Jean Louis Barrault, who produced *Hamlet* (Schwob's version, not Gide's) and *Antony and Cleopatra* in Gide's version, just after the Liberation. Jean Louis Barrault's productions have a particular character: they partake of the masque as well as of tragedy. He requires a great luxury of costumes, scenery, lighting and the sumptuousness of the *mise-en-scène* leaves far behind all that has been done before him, except perhaps by Jouvet, whose love for elegance and harmony has never been equalled. Barrault's *Antony and Cleopatra* is a magnificent show, perhaps too magnificent. It seems as if the producer's aim is to redeem the cold classicality of Gide's style by a rich display of colours and shapes and movement. His galley scene, perfect as it is in balance and grouping, introduces an element of *grand spectacle* which diverts the attention, and (as I think) breaks the spell. As to the pantomime of the sea-fight, it is frankly extraneous to Shakespeare's play and badly spoils the tragedy.

After having left the Comédie Française, Barrault retired to the Théâtre Marigny, a successful Aventin, where Gide's *Hamlet* has confirmed his reputation. The production is too much stylized for my taste, yet its creator remains what he always has been—a very intelligent and original actor.

It would be unfair to close this all too rapid survey without saying a word about Louis Ducreux, the founder of *Le Rideau Gris* in Marseilles, whom I have assisted in producing some Elizabethan plays. I remember the delightful performance he gave of Peele's *Old Wives' Tale*, shortly before he attempted *The Tempest* and *Macbeth*. Ducreux has since then established a reputation as a producer and as an author in Paris, where in 1937 he produced my adaptation of *The Duchess of Malfi*. The success of *Le Rideau Gris* associates the 'provinces' with the widespread interest France takes in Shakespeare. Even now as I am writing, another young producer, Jean Vilar, is reviving *Richard II* in the magnificent setting of the Château des Papes in Avignon.

Indeed, no theatrical season in France can be worthy of the name without some new Shakespeare production. The emulation between translators, producers, and actors is so great that they all want to improve upon each other. All French actors have dreamed of being Hamlet, Romeo, Othello. At one time there were two different productions of *As You Like It* on in Paris. The French public are sure to be the best audience possible for a good Shakespeare production. Shakespeare can provide them with food for thought and emotion and dreams. His success was as great as ever during the occupation, when the Germans dared not ban his plays even when they cleared all bookshops of English books. He stood then as a kind of symbolic figure, untouched by tyranny, supreme in his aloofness, and yet so near to our hearts, so inspiring. When Aragon wanted to express the heart-rending despair of a man whose country is torn to pieces and humiliated, to whom should he turn if not to Richard II, termed *Richard II Quarante*, the utter symbol of misery? And if we wanted to strengthen our confidence in victory, what speech should we read if not the dying words of John of Gaunt?

NOTES

1. In his *Lettres sur les Anglais* (1732), Voltaire wrote: "Shakespeare, que les Anglais prennent pour un Sophocle, créa leur théâtre; il avait un génie plein de force et de fécondité, de naturel et de sublime, sans la moindre étincelle de bon goût et sans la moindre connaissance des règles...."

2. In 1776, Voltaire wrote to d'Argental: "Auriez-vous lu les deux volumes de ce misérable [Letourneur] dans lesquels il veut nous faire regarder Shakespeare comme le seul modèle de la véritable tragédie? Il sacrifie tous les Français sans exception à son idole (il l'appelle le Dieu du théâtre) comme on sacrifiait autrefois les cochons à Cérès. Il ne daigne même pas nommer Corneille et Racine....Avez-vous une haine assez vigoureuse contre cet impudent imbécile? Souffrirez-vous l'affront qu'il fait à la France?...Ce qu'il y a d'affreux, c'est que le monstre a un parti en France; et pour comble de calamité, et d'horreur, c'est moi qui autrefois parlai le premier de ce Shakespeare, c'est moi qui le premier montrai aux Français quelques perles que j'avais trouvées dans son énorme fumier. Je ne m'attendais pas que je servirai un jour à fouler aux pieds les couronnes de Racine et de Corneille pour en orner le front d'un histrion barbare."

3. Here is the first paragraph of Taine's chapter on Shakespeare in his *Histoire de la Littérature Anglaise* (1865): "Je vais décrire une nature d'esprit extraordinaire, choquante pour toutes nos habitudes françaises d'analyse et de logique, toute puissante, excessive, également souveraine dans le sublime et dans l'ignoble, la plus créatrice qui fut jamais dans la copie exacte du réel minutieux, dans les caprices éblouissants du fantastique, dans les complications profondes des passions surhumaines, poétique, immorale, inspirée, supérieure à la raison par les révélations impro-visées de sa folie clairvoyante, si extrême dans la douleur et dans la joie, d'une allure si brusque, d'une verve si tour-mentée et si impétueuse que ce grand siècle seul a pu produire un tel enfant." Here again we have the 'romantic' view of Shakespeare, hardly made more serious by the pretendedly 'scientific' law of *la race, le milieu, le moment*. Taine's essay is a superb piece of eloquence, sympathetic and inspiring, with many pertinent remarks, not infre-

quently on the right track, but the approach is wrong from the start. The irrelevance of such statements as: "Le style de Shakespeare est un composé d'expressions forcenées. Nul homme n'a soumis les mots à une pareille torture", or "Shakespeare n'aperçoit jamais les objets tranquillement", or again "Il ne songe point à ennoblir, mais à copier la vie humaine, et n'aspire qu'à rendre sa copie plus énergique et plus frappante que l'original. De là les moeurs de ce théâtre, et d'abord le manque de dignité", is more indicative of passionate admiration than of mature and conscious criticism. The whole view is distorted by the tendency to gauge Shakespeare by French units. As, however, there is in him something which forces admiration, the only way out is to transform him into an 'extraordinary' genius, carried away by his passions, frantic like a mettlesome horse, which frets and chafes and leaps forward, only explained by his 'time', which is also 'extraordinary', and whose creations escape the common measure of mankind.

4. Alfred Mézières wrote three books, in the middle of the nineteenth century, on Shakespeare, his contemporaries and his successors.

5. See Albert Dubeux, *Les traductions françaises de Shakespeare* (1928) and my own article in *Le théâtre élizabéthain* (new ed. 1940).

6. Strangely, but also logically enough, Hamlet's silhouette became that of l'Aiglon, only paler and more effeminate, the pathetic figure of a forlorn, tortured, grown-up child.

7. *A la recherche de Shakespeare.*

8. *Shakespeare, poète tragique.*

9. Louis Cazamian, *L'humour de Shakespeare*, p. 226.

10. The translations referred to here are: *La Pléiade*, 2 vols., prefaced by André Gide; Messiaen's translation, 3 vols. ed. Mellottée, with introductions to each play; *Les Belles Lettres*, by different hands, with the English text, introductions and notes; *Aubier*, with similar contents; *Editions de Cluny*, F. Victor Hugo's translation, revised by René Lalou.

As has been noted previously, no attempt is made by Shakespeare Survey to provide either a complete bibliography of recent writings on Shakespeare or a catalogue of his plays in production. In the following pages selection has been made—chiefly from the reports of our correspondents—with the object of presenting a general picture of the Shakespearian scene and of stressing what appear to be the most interesting and noteworthy trends.

In reviewing the year's critical studies elsewhere in this volume, Professor Ellis-Fermor notes that "important volumes by Fluchère, Reyher and Schücking, supported by those of Kranendonk and Rubow, indicate that the continental scholarship we awaited last year is alive, and alive to some purpose". Once more vigorously active after the long travail of the war and despite the uncertainties of the present, this continental scholarship seems likely to present us with interesting and stimulating studies in the months to come. Shakespearian studies are once again being eagerly pursued in all the universities, including those that were forced for several years to abandon their regular curricula.

Shakespeare Yearbooks and Societies

Indication of the reawakened devotion to Shakespearian studies is provided by the fact that this year has seen the establishment of a new Shakespeare Yearbook, the revival of another the progress of which was interrupted by the war, and the inauguration of a new Shakespeare Society.

With the present volume (numbered 80/81) the *Shakespeare-Jahrbuch* endeavours to catch up where it left off in 1944. In the bibliographies and theatrical records an attempt is made to list activities of the years immediately preceding, while substantial contributions to scholarly investigation are provided by the editor (Max Deutschbein) and by Paul Meissner.

The reappearance of the *Shakespeare-Jahrbuch* shows that the Deutsche Shakespeare-Gesellschaft is once more resuming its activities, and now it is being given a companion in the newly established Österreichische Shakespeare-Gesellschaft, which, under the presidency of Raoul Aslan (acting manager of Vienna's Burgtheater), aims at doing for Austria what the other, through so many years, has accomplished for Germany.

From Mikhail Morozov comes a report concerning the new *Shekspirovski Sbornik* (*The Shakespeare Miscellany*) and concerning the activities of the 'Shakespeare Cabinet', a branch of the All-Russian Theatre Society (VTO). He points out that since the time of the nineteenth-century critic Belinski and the great actor Mochalov, Shakespeare studies in Russia have been very closely associated with the theatre and that this association is being still further strengthened under the Soviets. At the annual five-day Shakespeare Conference organized by the 'Cabinet' and at their twice-monthly meetings, papers on diverse aspects of the dramatist's art are companioned by analytical discussions based on recent productions. Actors and directors meet with scholars here.

The *Shekspirovski Sbornik*, a handsome volume, contains much material of vital interest. Not least valuable is the first part of an exhaustive bibliography, prepared by E. Subbotina of Soviet writings on Shakespeare during the thirty years from 1917 to 1947: the second part will appear in the next issue of the *Sbornik*. While it would be impossible here to list all the articles presented in this book, attention may be drawn to a few among the other contributions. The vivid popular interest in Shakespeare displayed by Soviet audiences is explained by Yu. Yuzovski as due to the synthesis in Shakespeare's art of realism and of vigorous 'romantic' aspirations; M. Zagorski examines the chief stages in the development of Russian Shakespearian studies during pre-revolutionary times; in "Shakespeare Dead and Shakespeare Living" V. Uzin animadverts on those recent English and American works which, in his opinion, overstress the medieval element in the dramas, and in another article the same author treats the late romances as Shakespeare's final effort to express his ideals; the roots of the tragic spirit are explored by V. Kemenov, these roots being found in the fact that, compared with the inexhaustible riches incorporated in human life, "the life of each of the Shakespearian heroes seems but an episodic role"; Yu. Semenov collects all the references, scattered throughout the text, to the outward appearance of the more important dramatic characters, while M. Morozov (in an essay reproduced in this issue of *Shakespeare Survey*) treats of their inner concepts.

Nor does *The Shakespeare Miscellany* by any means exhaust the year's contributions to Shakespeare study in the U.S.S.R. The 'synthesis' that is dealt with in his article by Yuzovski gains fuller treatment in his new volume, *Obraz i epokha* (*The Image and the Epoch*). Morozov himself has added a study of Shakespeare's life and times to the popular series entitled 'Lives of Great Men' and has produced a book devoted to *Othello* —one of a set of volumes specially designed as guides to those numerous Russian stage-directors who are currently engaged in producing Shakespeare's plays.

New Translations

Part of Morozov's volume is taken up with a literal version of the tragedy, and other Soviet writers are actively seeking means of bringing Shakespeare's works close to the public. S. Marshak has composed a fresh rendering of the *Sonnets*, while all the Pasternak trans- lations are being published together in two volumes.

From nearly all countries come records of similar attempts to refashion the poet's works in other tongues— some endeavouring to provide as exact a rendering as possible, others seeking to recreate the spirit of his verse in poetic terms.

Particularly worthy of remark here is the effort made by so many countries to prepare or to bring to con- clusion complete versions of the works. In some languages, such as Hungarian and Czech, there is a peculiar necessity for the making of new translations, since the tongues themselves have so altered during the past fifty years as to make older translations relatively useless; but even where such pressing necessity is not present we find an urgent desire to improve on past effort and to reach toward a finer rendering of the English text. These collected translations extend all the way from the Portuguese project, sponsored by the Faculty of Letters at Coimbra (which has not as yet pro- duced any published results) to the finally accomplished Italian *Teatro di Shakespeare*, edited by Mario Praz, a truly monumental work. Italy, indeed, has two ventures of this kind, since the volumes containing *La Tempesta*, *Il sogno d' una notte d' estate* and *Il mercante di Venezia*

bring Vincenzo Errante's verse translations to a total of nine. In Hungary a new complete works was planned in the midst of war (1942) by Gabriel Halasz; after his death, in 1944, Ladislas Orsagh was appointed editor; and now he has succeeded, with the assistance of Kalman Ruttkay, in putting the entire four volumes of the 'New Hungarian Shakespeare' into proof. Just as in Hungary, such extreme alterations have occurred in the Czech language as to make earlier translations either incompre- hensible or hopelessly old-fashioned and consequently considerable excitement has been aroused in Czecho- slovakia by the inauguration of a new version by Erik Saudek, a distinguished poet whose aim it is to render Shakespeare's works into a modern idiom. With the *Songe d'une nuit d'été* the Piachaud translation has brought the Cailler edition (Lausanne and Geneva) to its com- pletion. The importance such volumes may have is well illustrated by the phrase used by Marco Mincoff to describe the announcement by the Bulgarian State Printing House of a comprehensive series of versions by Lyubomir Ognyanov; this, he says, marks "a landmark in the literary history of Bulgaria".

Apart from these vaster efforts, there are many others of more restricted scope. At Geneva a new French version of *Antony and Cleopatra*, by Maurice Oberli, was produced on the stage by Robert Speaight; from the Bern publisher Scherz comes a new German rendering of the *Sonnets*, by the poet Walther Freund; in its pro- duction of *Richard II*, the National Theatre of Greece used a new text by K. Kartheos—and the list might be extended indefinitely.

No doubt some of these new attempts are not thoroughly satisfactory. Some of the translators have found it difficult to combine faithfulness to the original with poetic fire; a few versions, on the other hand, are described as too 'scholarly' in their meticulous endeavour to follow Shakespeare's lines literally; in others our correspondents deplore the fact that 'smoothness' and 'actable dialogue' have been bought at too high a price. It is, however, the endeavour itself that is of paramount interest: hardly any year in the history of Shakespearian translation has shown such a widespread desire to find perfection in the transmutation of the Elizabethan blank verse and prose into other tongues.

A Play on 'The Tempest'

The inspiring force of the plays is demonstrated, too, in such an event as the appearance of a kind of sequel to *The Tempest*—*Caliban délivré*—written by one of Switzerland's most famous authors, Gonzague de

Reynold. Although already produced on the stage (privately) in Geneva, it has not yet been published. "The author", writes Georges Bonnard, "wishes to see it performed again and to revise it, if necessary, again before sending it to the press." By imagining that Caliban, reformed after he realizes Prospero's superiority over his drunken companions, is made lord of the island, the author provides a kind of political allegory of man's present state. "*Caliban délivré*", remarks Bonnard, "is a good instance of the profound influence exerted by Shakespeare on modern minds anxious for the future of the values to which he has given shape and form for all times."

Shakespeare on the Stage

It would, of course, be fruitless here to attempt a mere listing of all the many productions of divers plays in many lands. Some countries have had hundreds of these; others—and among them, regrettably, must be noted the Dominions—have had few: but hardly one has been without Shakespearian performances of some kind. Where professional presentations are lacking, the universities and colleges have sought to remedy the defect. Thus in South Africa *The Merchant of Venice* was given under academic auspices at Cape Town, Natal and Bloemfontein, *Love's Labour's Lost* at Cape Town, *King Lear* at Johannesburg and *Macbeth* at Natal. Even in far-off China, writes the producer Yui Shang-Yuen: "whereto the Western drama has been introduced only less than forty years the production of Shakespeare's plays is no more a novelty, since many of these works in translation and in original texts are already familiar to educated people. For the present year a production of *The Merchant of Venice* was presented by the National Academy of Dramatic Arts at Nanking. Although only four performances were given to a public audience of about 2,000 each night, the play was so well received that demands have been made for more Shakespearian performances next season."

In some countries, so many are the performances of his plays that Shakespeare takes rank as the most popular of non-native dramatists. This is true, for instance, of Hungary, where between 1945 and 1948 no less than 300 performances out of a total 4,000 in Budapest were of his works.

Among the plays most frequently and widely performed the name of *Othello* is prominent. The success of a production at Lodz in Poland has been such that the editors of *Łódź teatralna* have been stimulated to devote an entire issue of their journal to Shakespeare's tragedy.

(A particularly interesting article here is one by Stanisław Dambrowski on performances of the play at Lodz in the nineteenth century.) Other successful presentations of *Othello* have been given in Finland at the Suomen Kansallisteatri (The National Theatre) and at the theatre of Tampere.

Many reports of productions on the Continent indicate that the more labour and time and money are devoted to the devising of impressive settings the less appealing often is the total result. This, according to Karl Brunner, was true of the *Hamlet* presented by the film producer Leopold Lindtberg of the Vienna Burgtheater in Austria and of *A Midsummer Night's Dream* as produced by Herbert Wanieck. Significant, too, is Lorentz Eckhoff's report on two productions in Norway, one by the National Theatre and the other by the young vanguard theatre called 'Studio teatret'. The Director of the National Theatre, who is a Shakespeare enthusiast and wishes to produce at least one Shakespearian play each season, selected *Julius Caesar* for 1947 and obviously tried to use every means in his power to make the performance a theatrical event. There was rich use of music, lights and choreography: the battle scenes were accompanied by oversized shadows of warriors flitting across the sky and preceded by an impressive vulture dance. The result was a *succès d'estime*, hardly more. The settings were pretty but not very suggestive and the scene-shifts were painfully long. Despite the interesting portrayal of Caesar by Johan Norlund, the drama failed to yield a strong impression. The second presentation was that of *The Comedy of Errors* under the direction of a Danish producer, Sam Besekow. "Like Max Reinhardt in days gone by, Besekow took liberties with the text, cut out passages here, added others there and styled his new drama *The Twins*. The stage *décor*, designed by Guy Krohg, was worthy of note, gay and fanciful; in mid-stage stood a high narrow house that turned on a revolving platform and displayed a number of façades representing diverse localities in Ephesus. The costumes, too, were good, and the whole milieu had something southern and lively. If only the actors had equalled the designers...."

Shakespeare in the Open Air

There are Shakespeare students in all countries who realize that the days of this overburdening of the text with scenery are gone, and because of that it is interesting to observe the several attempts to present some of the plays either in open-air settings or with the use of platform stages. In Denmark *As You Like It* was given in the Deer Park, just outside Copenhagen, while a company of Finnish actors presented *Hamlet* in the National Open-air Stage at Kronberg (Elsinore). At the Place du Château at Lausanne in Switzerland, an interesting production was that of *Romeo and Juliet*, the text used being the version, mentioned in last year's *Shakespeare Survey*, prepared by P. L. Matthey, whilst a truly notable production of *Richard II* was presented by Jean Vilar at the Palais des Papes in Avignon. For the annual meeting of the Deutsche Shakespeare-Gesellschaft the same play, *Romeo and Juliet*, and *Richard III* were acted in a hall, great intimacy between audience and actors being gained by the transference of the play from peep-show proscenium-arch conditions into a freer structure. From Italy comes news of a *Richard II*, produced in Milan by Giorgio Strehler on an Elizabethan-type stage inspired by the film of *Henry V*, of a *Tempest* presented by Giovanni Ratto in the Boboli Gardens at Florence, with the famous Vasca dei Cigni as the principal element in the open-air stage scene, of a *Romeo and Juliet* production where Renato Simoni placed a medieval simultaneous setting under Verona's starry sky, and of *A Midsummer Night's Dream* given in the courtyard at the Castle at San Giusto in Trieste.

Among the most interesting of all these experiments is one that comes from Dallas, Texas, U.S.A., where Margo Jones has established a professional repertory company for the purpose of presenting plays "in the round"—or, to be exact, in the diamond. The auditorium is small, seating about 200 persons, and the actors appear on the floor in their midst, utilizing for entrances and exits gaps at three corners of the room. Here in 1948 *The Taming of the Shrew* was given with marked success. (See Plate IX B.) The properties consisted of a long table, two benches and a few stools—shifted into various positions for successive scenes, the changes being made by those taking minor roles. Except for a single intermission, the action was continuous. Those who have witnessed this and other productions of "Theatre in the Round" testify to their impressiveness and to the way in which fresh values become apparent when the performers are taken out of the often over-loaded picture-frame. Perhaps in such experiments lies the hope of remedying a defect noted in many countries —the dearth of histrionic talent for Shakespearian roles and the lack of suitable training-grounds for players who seek to accomplish something more than is called for in the realistic dramas of to-day.

SHAKESPEARE IN NEW YORK: 1947–1948

reviewed by ROSAMOND GILDER

Again I must report the not too surprising fact, considering the economic conditions of the New York stage, that Shakespeare has not been among the season's major dramatists. To be sure, the incidence of professional productions here has risen one hundred percent, but truth compels me to add that this represents an increase to two productions in contrast to one last year. Then we saw *Henry VIII* given as the American Repertory Theatre's first offering. This year we have had *Antony and Cleopatra* produced by our leading actress-manager, Katharine Cornell, and *Macbeth* produced by Theatre Incorporated with Michael Redgrave and Flora Robson in the leads. Outside New York there have been the usual college and university showings but none of a nature to attract very wide attention, nor did that staunch upholder of the Bard, Maurice Evans, tour through the country as he did the year before, carrying an amiable *Hamlet* to an enthusiastic hinterland. Evans deserted Shakespeare in favour of Shaw and has devoted his season to a highly successful run of *Man and Superman*—which is reputed to be driving the author mad because of the giddy flights of income tax to which its revenue subjects him. Shakespeare, who need not concern himself with income tax, has not this year contributed as generously as last to his producers' exchequer. *Antony and Cleopatra* was an expensive and weighty production, and probably did not do much more than "pay off"; and the *Macbeth*, though cordially received, had only a short run.

The most interesting element in Katharine Cornell's production of *Antony and Cleopatra* was the effectiveness with which it accentuated what one might call the political aspects of the play. Shakespeare's mighty drama must always be pre-eminently a tragedy of passion, the story of a world conqueror fallen victim to an all conquering love—"The triple pillar of the world transformed into a strumpet's fool." But the play has another major theme, which this production and perhaps the mood of the moment emphasized, the theme of power politics, of the battle for supremacy in the Mediterranean basin. The theatregoer to-day is especially conscious of this phase of the play. We ourselves have lived through just such epic battles as that of Actium. We have watched the ebb and flow of conquest as armies and navies manoeuvred for position on the war-maps and news-reel screens of our embattled days.

Shakespeare shows us the same type of struggle with only the spoken word and the masterly use of brief scenes in sharp juxtaposition as his tools. It is difficult to convey the swift movement of thought from one battle front to the other when realistic—or even semi-realistic—scenery is used, but everything that could be done by the ingenious use of permanent stairs and acting platforms combined with painted back-drops and swiftly changing scenes was accomplished. The text was given with a minimum of cutting; and the direction, in the hands of Guthrie McClintic, Miss Cornell's husband and long-time director, was smooth and competent. Miss Cornell's interpretation of the leading role was particularly happy in the gayer, kindlier scenes between Cleopatra and her handmaids and rose to truly noble heights in the majestic closing passages. The mercurial, playful, violent phases of Cleopatra's character were not as convincingly portrayed. Godfrey Tearle's Antony was robust and rollicking. He gave the impression not so much of a great man deflected from his course by an overwhelming passion, but rather of a lusty, vigorous fellow whose character had already begun to deteriorate through unrestrained self-indulgence and self-conceit.

If the production as a whole did not have the glow, the directorial and acting fire which distinguished the Cornell-McClintic *Romeo and Juliet* of some years back, the play itself with the generous production given it was so full of richness and beauty, so interesting in its implications and arresting in its inferences, that it brought a great deal of pleasure to those theatre lovers in and out of New York who have been too long deprived of this noble 'Egyptian dish'.

The Michael Redgrave *Macbeth*, staged by the American director Norris Houghton, was given first in London with Enid Burrell as Lady Macbeth and an English cast. Transferred to the American stage, with a largely American cast, except for the principals, Redgrave and Miss Robson, it brought to New York audiences a fresh interpretation of this tense and violent drama. *Macbeth*, like *Antony and Cleopatra*, is near and comprehensive as never before, though for entirely different reasons. Its gory and inexorable pace, its picture of murder piled on murder as tyranny seeks to consolidate its ill-gotten power reflect a world we know only too well. Norris Houghton in his direction and Michael Redgrave in his performance, while not in any sense offering a 'modern' *Macbeth*, let this aspect of the drama have full play. The only considerable deviation from accepted tradition in the production was Houghton's treatment of the scenes of the witches. In addition to the three squeaking and gibbering old women usually used for these scenes, he introduced three tall masked figures, as it were the supernatural Powers of which the human witches were only the pitiful earthly vessels. Awe and doom are in the words they speak, while the old hags dancing about in their fluttering rags, casting spells and raising ghosts whose dangerous property and essence they in no way understand, are merely reflections of these larger forces. The innovation was effective, and the direction of the play as a whole was interesting if not always as arresting as in these scenes. Both Miss Robson and Michael Redgrave brought moments of remarkable insight and feeling to their roles, providing as fine an interpretation of the play as New York audiences have seen in many years.

These two productions remind us once again that, though America has much potential talent, it still lacks a training-ground for Shakespeare actors. Miss Cornell had to go to London for her Antony, the *Macbeth* was primarily an English production. Last summer Orson Welles produced *Macbeth* at Salt Lake City, Utah, with a cast recruited in part from Hollywood, in part from the students at the University of Utah. Reports from this event, spectacular as all Welles' undertakings tend to be, were glowing. The attempt was in itself interesting and hopeful, but such sporadic flurries cannot take the place of a well-founded organized repertory theatre such as the old Old Vic, where young actors can get their training in an arduous and exacting craft.

THE YEAR'S CONTRIBUTIONS TO
SHAKESPEARIAN STUDY

1. CRITICAL STUDIES

reviewed by UNA ELLIS-FERMOR

There has been a rapid increase this year in the number of books published and in the proportion of these available for review, and the trends of current criticism stand out the more clearly.

In last year's survey of criticism I suggested that we had reached a pausing-place in Shakespeare studies, the turn of the half-century and the end of the war alike making a revaluation of the twentieth-century's findings and a fresh direction, or at least a modification, probable. A notable feature of that year's critical work was the tendency of its writers to turn back to the contemplation of Shakespeare as an artist and a poet and to indicate, even when primarily concerned with some other theme, that the essential Shakespeare is to be found in the poetic content of the plays. Some critics, clearly aware of their position, stated it explicitly; one almost in the form of a manifesto. Others, though less conscious of the novelty of this return to the imaginative tradition of the nineteenth century, nevertheless tended instinctively to the exploration of aesthetic or mainly aesthetic problems.

It was clear that the next few years would be crucial in determining whether or not there would be a change in direction strong enough to discover fresh lines of criticism, lines as boldly independent, perhaps, of what had gone before as those that mark the transition from the nineteenth century to the twentieth. I do not think we can yet say that this has happened; but we can point to indications, to certain tendencies that another decade may recognize for its 'hoved-strømninger'.

One of these is the preoccupation with Shakespeare's art and with his thought, whether the approach to their study is historical, philosophical or aesthetic. Another is the number of complete volumes devoted, after the manner of Granville-Barker's later 'Prefaces', to the close analysis of single plays. Another is the wholesome reaction already setting in against the false direction sometimes taken by the criticism of imagery when it escapes from the category of strict aesthetics into fantasy. All these are important, the first two showing an ever-deepening sense of the value of the content and of the art of the plays, and the third promising that the new-old interpretative criticism knows the nature and the need of discipline. The prospect is not unhopeful.

Still notable, as I have said, is the emphasis upon the interpretation of Shakespeare's thought and art; six volumes, five of them of considerable size, and some dozen pamphlets and articles indicate the growing importance of these two groups. Studies of individual plays usually make the largest list of essays in such a survey as this, but this year marks a sudden increase in the number of full-length studies; beside some twenty-five articles that should be recorded, there are five volumes, each analysing a single play, three of them on *Hamlet* alone. The examination of sources and comparative studies of Shakespeare's work and his contemporaries', though these enter incidentally into several general works, are, on the other hand, fewer than in some years.

Among the studies that survey, from one or more standpoints, the whole or a great part of Shakespeare's work, four full-length volumes stand out: Henri Fluchère's *Shakespeare, Dramaturge élisabéthain*;[1] Hardin Craig's *In Interpretation of Shakespeare*;[2] Paul Reyher's *Essai sur les idées dans l'œuvre de Shakespeare*;[3] and Sister Miriam Joseph's *Shakespeare's Use of the Arts of Language*.[4] A number of the articles and essays in collections are also general in scope. Henri Fluchère's volume arrived too late for a detailed notice to be given this year. Its significance is considerable: a substantial study of Shakespeare the artist in relation to the art and thought of his time.

Hardin Craig, acknowledging that "Shakespeare needs a good deal of interpretation if he is to be understood and appreciated by modern readers", sets out with the modest intention of giving information about the meaning of Shakespeare's work. But his book does more than this. It offers, as he says himself, prevailingly historical criticism (though never such as to lose sight of the enduring significance of Shakespeare's thought and poetry). But, subtly combined with this appeal to the historical imagination of his readers, is a large body of fact about the plays, their background (particularly the thought and mental habits of the age), the positions reached on doubtful issues by modern scholarship and some acute summaries of or comments on the trends of modern criticism. The plan is straightforward, treating the plays chronologically with an introductory chapter on "Shakespeare as an Elizabethan" and a conclusion on "Shakespeare as a Citizen of the World". It is thus a book which every student could use as an introduction to Shakespeare studies and as a companion during their progress. Lucid in expression and mature in reflection, easy and economical in the handling of fact and hypothesis, it is a happy reconciliation of the historical and the interpretative approach by one of the few living scholars who move freely in both.

Paul Reyher is concerned with the thought underlying the plays, with its significance and above all with its continuity, and this despite variety and modification of the thought and despite the paradox of its revelation in the impersonal form of drama: "A suivre la progression de la pensée, on se rend mieux compte de l'unité de l'œuvre....Mais on ne tarde pas à discerner les rapports entre les idées, des tendances et une orientation communes; peu à peu aussi l'on constate que, par leur concordance générale, et dans leur ensemble, elles forment une pensée et une pensée qui, en toute vraisemblance, est celle de l'auteur." In setting himself this investigation he thus tackles one of the most difficult underlying problems in dramatic aesthetics: the legitimate deduction of the poet's own thought, not from specific passages (which, if he be a dramatist, should give us no clue) but from the total effect of what is often implicit. After an introduction which sketches some of the ideas current in Shakespeare's age, Reyher groups his material according to kinds, finding in the comedies the presence of much that belonged to the common fund of ideas, transmuted by genius into originality; in the histories a concern akin to Plutarch's with the graver material of fact and the reality of life; in the tragedies a further progression into a *drame intérieur* whose problems are those of the conflict between will and destiny.

Reyher's method may be studied in any one of these sections. In the one hundred or so pages which he gives to the histories he not only analyses and elucidates the thoughts—easier, indeed, to isolate here, as they are often made explicit in argument and debate—but builds up a picture of the body of thought which supports the ten plays and shows that these ideas are fundamental

[1] *Cahiers du Sud*, 1948.   [2] New York, The Dryden Press, 1948.
[3] Paris, Didier, 1947.   [4] New York, Columbia University Press, 1947.

not only to the individual plays but to the sequence, and not only as ideas but as vital and indispensable links in the continuity of a series in which action and event exist for the presentation of ideas: "Son premier soin est de marquer l'enchaînement des faits, d'en indiquer les causes et les effets."

Sister Miriam Joseph examines a field from the complexity of which many readers and most writers would shrink. One of the most valuable contributions of historical criticism to our understanding of Shakespeare has been the examination of Elizabethan thought and learning, including their critical theory and their educational system. Sister Miriam Joseph combines the findings of these two and puts before us, in an extensive volume, a detailed analysis of the current theory on the art of composition, derived ultimately from Aristotelian logic and rhetoric with its Classical Latin, medieval and contemporary Ramist modifications. This intricate 'material she considers to have been substantially taught in the Elizabethan Grammar Schools, so that an educated Elizabethan man had a knowledge far beyond any but a specialist's at the present day. Regarding the curricula of these schools as standardized in Shakespeare's youth, she then proceeds to assume this as his training and to trace the results of such an education in his work. The body of her book demonstrates his knowledge and use of the elaborate system of figures and positions by means of detailed quotation and analysis. She argues that Shakespeare was, unlike us, at all points aware of his technique, having been made so by a continuous training in a form of mental agility long unpractised among us. Whatever we may think of the nature of the poetic process implied, her argument, resting as it often does upon the authoritative work of Baldwin, must be considered.

Most of the essays and articles that contribute to this section come from two sources, the Memorial Volume to J. Q. Adams[1] and C. F. Tucker Brooke's posthumously published *Essays on Shakespeare*.[2] In the first, Hardin Craig's "Shakespeare and the History Play" traces the evolution of this kind from the Senecanism of *Titus Andronicus* to the dramatic history characteristic of Shakespeare's mature work. This process is mirrored in his treatment of rhetoric in the Yorkist plays, where it is gradually modified or subdued as he "learned from his own experience a new kind of dramatic interest, an interest which resides in history itself". In "Shakespeare's Ideal Man" Alfred Harbage meets the accusation of "absence of religion" in Shakespeare brought by Santayana and implied by Mazzini before him. Judged by the comments on the plays a good man must be scholarly, soldierly and honest; he need not be pious, overscrupulous or much moved by abstract principle. But only in the substitution of action for abstraction does Shakespeare's moral system really differ from ours, and the explanation may well be that "We take pleasure, as Shakespeare refused to do, simply in righteous sensations", and that the balance is in favour of Shakespeare, not against him. Hereward T. Price, in his "Mirror Scenes in Shakespeare", indicates that the occurrence of a certain kind of scene may serve as evidence of authorship: these are scenes which reflect "in one picture either the main theme or some important aspect of the drama", where "Shakespeare invents something unique in order to form an incident which will mirror the whole play". In the second of his essays, "Shakespeare Apart",[3] Brooke, unlike many modern critics, argues that Shakespeare was not a characteristic Elizabethan but, as a man and an artist, often of paradoxical normality; one who

[1] *Joseph Quincy Adams: Memorial Studies* (Washington: The Folger Shakespeare Library, 1948).
[2] Yale University Press, 1948.   [3] *Op. cit.*

cannot be closely related to any of his great contemporaries. He finds that "Wisdom is perhaps the only attribute which we can apply to him without need of qualification" (p. 16), "A wisdom so deep that it concealed his plentiful lack of knowledge—a humanity so immense that few could note how completely he had failed to be Elizabethan".

Studies of the art of Shakespeare and of special aspects of his technique form an important group. There is some notable work on character, in which John Palmer's posthumous *Comic Characters of Shakespeare*[1] stands out. In the introduction to this all-too-brief volume he describes, with some penetrating analysis of the nature of the problem, the mood and underlying implication of Shakespeare's comedy and goes on to trace its operation in a series of characters (Berowne, Touchstone, Shylock, Bottom, Benedick and Beatrice) in each of whom we find our point of reference for the humorous values of the play. This, in its easy and unassuming demeanour, is first-rate criticism and it is matter for deep regret that the remainder was never written. The study of Bottom alone, taking its stand against a false traditional interpretation still in possession, would have justified the volume. There are several acute pieces of analysis in essay or article form, the Memorial Volume to J. Q. Adams contributing three. Lily B. Campbell, in "Polonius: the Tyrant's Ears", after noticing briefly various estimates and mis-estimates of the character and function of Polonius, shows him to be in fact a natural busy-body taking on himself the office of Claudius's spy, the tyrant's indispensable agent in a suspicious court. She finds here a consistent piece of character-drawing with a consistent function in the play. Donald McGinn's "The precise Angelo" examines Shakespeare's alteration of and additions to his sources in *Measure for Measure* in the light of sixteenth-century religious thought and finds in the severity and hypocrisy of Angelo's character a study of an Elizabethan puritan whose part in the action is clearly contrasted with the liberality and benevolence of the representatives of the Old Faith, thus resolving certain problems of the play. Elkin Calhoun Wilson analyses the character of Enobarbus at some length ("Shakespeare's Enobarbus") and, noting that this figure is substantially Shakespeare's addition to Plutarch's material, sees in him the equivalent of a classical chorus who is yet an individual in his own right. At once soldier, humorist, half-poet and ironic commentator, his function also is indispensable to the play. In a clearly-reasoned article on "Character in Relation to Action in *Othello*",[2] Moody E. Prior starts from the position that, though character may remain static in comedy it never does so in Shakespeare's major tragedy, and proceeds to demonstrate the reciprocal relationship between character and action in *Othello*, "so that character is continually being revealed by the course of the action and the action, in turn, is continually being restricted and governed by revelations about the character which increase the probability of subsequent episodes". Finally, C. F. Tucker Brooke[3] gives an original reading of the character of "The Romantic Iago", finding in him an honest and even charming man, the mental and moral counterpart of Falstaff in his youth, whose "diabolism is an accident thrust upon him early in the play and whose progress thereafter does indeed show something of demoniac possession". The source of his ruin is the materialism which "corrodes the imagination", lays him open to envy and blinds him to ideal beauty.

The study of other aspects of Shakespeare's technique, of his language, imagery and prosody, continues and works for the most part along already established lines, but it occasionally

[1] Macmillan, 1946.   [2] *Modern Philology*, XLIV (May 1947), 225–37.
[3] *Op. cit.*

manifests disturbing tendencies; it is one thing to welcome the return of interpretative criticism and quite another to watch it straying towards those excesses which formerly earned it discredit. Oscar James Campbell, in "Shakespeare and the 'New' Critics",[1] surveys the recent work, deriving originally from T. S. Eliot's view of the function of imagery as "a part of an architectural structure", from G. Wilson Knight's methods of interpretation and from C. F. E. Spurgeon's statistical investigations. Campbell's sane, conservative estimate of the limitations of the function of interpretation in the study of imagery (whether or not one always agrees with his choice of the individual critic to receive admonition) comes at a moment when it is needed, if not overdue. "His [Shakespeare's] figurative language is designed to reveal and to intensify the comprehensiveness and complexity of human life, and not to adumbrate a gaunt, metaphysical, ethical or sociological proposition as the scaffolding on which his drama has been built." Francis R. Johnson's "Shakespearian Imagery and Senecan Imitation"[2] is a work in a specific field, associated on one side with the conservative modern criticism of imagery and on the other with important recent investigations of Renaissance educational ideals and practice and their bearing on literary craftsmanship. Choosing the field of Senecan imagery, and assuming in Shakespeare a first-hand knowledge of Seneca's Latin text, Johnson proposes "to analyse what Shakespeare did with the training that he shared with his contemporaries" in this field. In a paper on the "Function of Imagery in *Venus and Adonis*"[3] Hereward T. Price demonstrates that Shakespeare in this poem devised for himself a new technique of imagery, a study of which throws light on the meaning of the poem, the aspect to which, in his view, adequate thought has not so far been given. "Shakespeare has based this one poem at least on a profound conception, held with passionate intensity and conviction, expressed in finely imagined symbols." Moody E. Prior's *The Language of Tragedy*[4] enters this field with its section on "The Elizabethan Tradition". Prior's purpose is to reveal the function of language in poetic drama, the essential relationship between the ways and the order in which words are used in verse tragedy "and the totality of the final product". The different results he finds for different periods are therefore an important part of his study. Elizabethan tragedy, contrasted with the Heroic Play, with nineteenth-century tragedy and with modern tragedy, was fortunate in its conditions and in its discovery of blank verse. Prior examines, in some thirty-five pages, the functional use of language in drama as it appears in Shakespeare. "Each mature play of Shakespeare", he concludes, "reveals the same closely integrated, dramatic way of handling language, of making, that is, the diction and imagery play an essential role in the scheme of necessity and probability which determines and shapes the action." The later sections of his work, and perhaps especially that on the problems of modern poetic drama, illuminate the distinctive function of language in the Elizabethan and Jacobean drama in general and in the work of Shakespeare in particular. A special section of this and of an adjacent field is examined in Audrey Yoder's[5] essay, *Animal Analogy*, which surveys and analyses, by means of lists and statistical tables, Shakespeare's use of animal comparisons in

[1] *Joseph Quincy Adams: Memorial Studies*, pp. 81–96.   [2] *Ibid.* pp. 33–54.
[3] *Papers of the Michigan Academy of Science, Arts and Letters*, XXXI, 1945 (publ. 1947), 275–97. Mention should also be made here of J. C. Maxwell's "Animal Imagery in *Coriolanus*", *Modern Language Review*, XLII (Oct. 1947), 417–21, and of R. D. Altick's "Symphonic Imagery in *Richard II*", *P.M.L.A.* LXII (June 1947), 339–65.
[4] Columbia University Press, 1947.
[5] New York: King's Crown Press; London: Cumberlege, 1948.

character portrayal, relating the findings derived from some four thousand allusions to certain well-defined groups of traditional material.

The number of essays and articles on special aspects of single plays is so great that, important as are many of them, no detailed account can be given in this short summary. At least eighteen plays appear, many of them treated twice or three times by different writers. From this body of scholarship, two groups may perhaps, without depreciation of others, be chosen: the full-length studies of single plays and the series of books and articles—nearly a dozen in all—on *Hamlet* alone. The two categories overlap, as three of the first fall into the second.

Hamlet, as might be expected, has produced some independent and contradictory interpretations; it is matter for sober reflection that all its critics substantiate their directly conflicting readings by close reference to the text; a reviewer, reading them all in succession, notices with some disquiet how often a line which is the keystone of one argument slips past unchallenged by the next. Señor Salvador de Madariaga [1] presents, with logic the lucidity of which is itself a source of delight, a direct attack on the sentimentality of the traditional interpretations of Hamlet's character and of the implications of the play. He considers the egotism often shown in Hamlet's behaviour—and he perhaps finds it more frequently than some of us—to be the key to his character and not a symptom of his nervous condition. If Hamlet is a callous, vital, somewhat foul-mouthed and crude Elizabethan, by nature and not simply by disguise, much that has puzzled commentators becomes plain. If Ophelia is a similar product of a similar court, maidenly demeanour covering a wanton mind (and Hamlet's mistress to boot), more mystery disappears. This brief summary does wrong to Madariaga's argument, which is self-contained and firm. But his inferences sometimes rest upon interpretations an Englishman would not make: he sometimes seems to overlook, for example, the presence in Hamlet of that tiresome English attribute, a sense of humour. But the case he makes should not be put aside because it is startling or unfamiliar. [2] It is such a reinterpretation as might be expected from a poet bred in a different culture and should be taken seriously, whether it is ultimately accepted or not. It is from such directions that fresh wisdom may always come.

I. J. Semper presents, [3] as nearly as is possible, the opposite interpretation in a study whose seemingly frivolous title belies its earnestness. His Hamlet is a philosopher-prince, the cast of whose thought is determined by a medieval outlook upon life, Thomist in its main positions. "The main issues of the play are theological", and Semper dispatches the conception of Hamlet as a Renaissance sceptic and demonstrates his Catholic orthodoxy. The cosmic philosophy of the play, including the presentation of the Ghost, is substantially that of St Thomas Aquinas and its dominating concern is with life in the next world. The position is clearly put, but there is nothing controversial in the tone of the book; its weaknesses spring from what the author does not take into account, not from the use he makes of what he does.

Roy Walker, [4] differing as nearly as is possible for a third writer from either of these, offers an interpretation that seems, to the average Englishman, more probable; his Hamlet is a man of imagination whose imagination leads him to the perception of spiritual truth in terms of which

---

[1] *On 'Hamlet'* (Hollis and Carter, 1948).
[2] Parts of it have been proposed from time to time, though not recently.
[3] *Hamlet Without Tears* (Dubuque, Iowa: Loras College Press, 1946).
[4] *The Time is Out of Joint* (Dakers, 1948).

he is thus, by this perception no less than by the ghost's admonition, commanded to live. The essential conflict of the play is clear: the world of the imagination and of the spirit is in deadly conflict with the almost overpowering forces of unimaginative materialism. Walker makes a systematic study of the play which is full of thoughtful analysis. If it seems sometimes vehement and not always lucid, this is rather from fecundity of idea and sincerity of conviction than from vagueness of thought. There is much in the detail with which many readers will disagree; but there is much to consider.

This diversity of criticism would not be fully demonstrated if we did not mention that Ernest Jones,[1] bringing to bear the criteria of psychoanalytic criticism, finds in Hamlet "no question of insanity in the proper sense of the word; Hamlet's behaviour is that of a psycho-neurotic" and his relations with Claudius, Gertrude and Ophelia more complex than have generally been supposed. *Hamlet* is concerned with "the deepest problem and the intensest conflict that have occupied the mind of man since the beginning of time". Emerson Venable,[2] by contrast, reads the play as the record of Hamlet's moral progress, and W. W. Lawrence[3] traces certain problems of Ophelia's character and conduct to the influence of Shakespeare's sources. It is peculiarly suitable that Paul S. Conklin should complete this account with *A History of 'Hamlet' Criticism*;[4] though his careful and thorough compilation only covers the years 1601–1821, the volume of material that he has assembled and classified reminds us that our diversity of voices is no new thing.

Two other plays have received a volume each. Harley Granville-Barker's posthumously published *Coriolanus*[5] is, like all its predecessors in the series, shrewd and penetrating in its commentary, full of memorable summaries, with a fine opening section in which the nature of the play is defined. As always in his work, the notes on problems of staging are accurate and practical; the probable technique of the Globe managers in handling awkward battle scenes; the significance of the stage directions in the play; the details of producing and interpreting, whether on the Globe stage or on the modern—all this makes the study valuable. His reading of the character of Coriolanus is conservative and some modern scholars will not necessarily agree with it. But it is consistent and maintained throughout with close reference to the text. The study of the character of Menenius and of the possibilities it offers the actor is illuminating.[6]

---

[1] *Hamlet...with a psycho-analytical study by Ernest Jones* (Vision Press, 1947).

[2] *The Hamlet Problem and its Solution* (Cincinnati: Kidd, 1946).

[3] "Ophelia's Heritage", *Modern Language Review*, XLII (Oct. 1947), 409–16. A note should also be made of Kenneth Muir's "Portents in Hamlet" (*Notes and Queries*, 7 Feb. 1948); of John W. Draper's "The Tempo of Hamlet's Role" (*Rivista di Letterature Moderne*, Firenze, Sept.-Dec. 1947, 193–203) and of Robert Adger Law's "Belleforest, Shakespeare and Kyd" (*Joseph Quincy Adams: Memorial Studies*), also noticed, below, among the works on Shakespeare's sources.

[4] New York, King's Crown Press; London, Cumberlege, 1947.

[5] *Prefaces to Shakespeare*: Fifth series (Sidgwick and Jackson, 1947).

[6] Two articles on *Coriolanus* help to show the increasing interest in this play. G. B. Harrison, in "A Note on Coriolanus" (*Joseph Quincy Adams: Memorial Studies*), discusses the verse of the play, showing the damaging effect of "editorial tinkerings" and correction of supposed mislineation in the Folio text; their effect has been to prevent sound judgment on the verbal music of the play. J. C. Maxwell finds more cohesion than has been supposed in the "Animal Imagery in Coriolanus" and assigns it a function in the play.

S. L. Bethell interprets the peculiarities of the *Winter's Tale* [1] and other late plays as a conscious, indulgent mockery of technique which nevertheless serves to disengage, as perhaps no other method could have done in Shakespeare's time, those overtones of spiritual thought which enable us "to perceive at the same time, beyond time, a changeless, divine order". This is a serious piece of thinking, even if at times it seems to insist too much upon symbolic intention in Shakespeare's structure or to imply that criticism is in part at least disputation. But the book is characteristic of its time: the author's conclusion is that, in the late plays, the peculiarities of technique are intentional, the profundity of thought real and that the first exist to serve the purposes of the second.

No other play receives a volume to itself, but *Henry IV* has three articles. M. A. Shaaber [2] considers the arguments in favour of the unity of the two parts, points out their weaknesses and adduces others that point to independent origins. The fact that the two plays, though linked, are artistically independent is corroborated for him by practical theatrical necessity. D. A. Traversi, in a pair of essays,[3] discusses the "unfolding of a personal interpretation of his inherited theme" in Shakespeare's two plays. In the first part he finds in Prince Henry a typical member of the House of Lancaster in whom "the only true *moral* criterion is *political* success", whereas Falstaff, whose presence balances the play, represents the humanity which "politicians bent on the attainment of success must necessarily exclude". In the second part, the differences in outlook between the older and the younger statesmen of that House have widened and the growth of the tragic mood, reflected in the imagery, the integration of the structure and the greater profundity of the underlying thought, mark a further stage in Shakespearian development.[4]

The tendencies noted above may be traced, even in this year's contributions to the study of Shakespeare's sources. Selma Guttman's [5] valuable contribution to the bibliography of Shakespeare's sources will be welcomed by all specialists in that field. Not only does she give lists, clearly classified for reference, of the foreign sources which have been considered (together with summaries of the commentary), but she gathers together in one group lists of "Certain Translations available to Shakespeare". Her volume thus constitutes a guide to that research in sources which is tending to correlate and draw together the findings of specific investigations, so that the study of his treatment of sources may itself throw light upon his art. Three articles in the Memorial Volume to J. Q. Adams offer instances of such specific research: John Elson [6] finds in Bale's *Kyng Johan* a possible source (together with Foxe's *Actes and Monuments* and Polydore

---

[1] *The Winter's Tale: A Study* (Staples Press, 1947).

[2] "The Unity of *Henry IV*" (*Joseph Quincy Adams: Memorial Studies*, pp. 217–28).

[3] "*Henry IV*—Part I" and "*Henry IV*—Part II", *Scrutiny*, xv (1948), 24–35, 117–27.

[4] Other articles which deserve mention and, but for lack of space, should have longer notice are two on *Lear*: J. A. Chapman's in *Nineteenth Century* (Aug. 1947), 95–100 and Evander Milne's ("On the death of Cordelia") in *English* (Summer 1947), 244–8; two on *Macbeth*: John Arthos's ("The Naïve Imagination and the Destruction of Macbeth") in *E.L.H.* xiv (June 1947), 114–26 and J. W. Draper's ("Patterns of Humor and Tempo in *Macbeth*") in *Neophilologus* (Oct. 1947), 202–7; J. C. Maxwell's "*Troilus and Cressida*" (*Times Literary Supplement*, 2 Aug. 1947) and E. C. Pettet's application of historical criticism to *Timon* and consequent elucidation of some of the values of the play in his "*Timon of Athens*: The Disruption of Feudal Morality", *Review of English Studies*, xxiii (Oct. 1947), 321–36.

[5] *The Foreign Sources of Shakespeare's Works: An Annotated Bibliography of the Commentary Written on this Subject between 1904 and 1940* (New York: King's Cross Press; London: Cumberlege, 1947).

[6] "Studies in the King John Plays."

Virgil's *Anglica Historia*) of the source-play *Troublesome Reign of King John*. The examination of the sources of the source throws light upon the dramatic capacity of its author and that in turn upon the art of Shakespeare's *King John*. Robert Adger Law[1] examines Belleforest as a source of *Hamlet* in the light of Shakespeare's "known habits of composition from extant material" and finds that "many situations in Shakespeare's version that are commonly attributed to Kyd might have sprung from sheer inventiveness of the author". It would be gratifying to be again allowed to credit Shakespeare with that. M. W. Black,[2] after some clear generalities on Shakespeare's methods of choosing and handling his sources, examines, in the light of his conclusions, J. D. Wilson's theory that *Richard II* is a revision of an old play. Black considers that Shakespeare was working directly from the chronicles, and, moreover, that he "prepared himself more thoroughly for the writing of *Richard II* than of any other play in the canon". Again, a sidelight on Shakespeare the artist.[3]

Three comparative studies, those of Kranendonk, Schücking and Thaler,[4] are again concerned to varying degrees with Shakespeare's thought and art, this time in relation to that of his contemporaries. Kranendonk, writing what is manifestly a general study of Shakespeare and his age for Dutch students, nevertheless finds room not only for the necessary matter on Shakespeare's England, on Stratford, London and the theatre and textual problems, but, in his chronological survey of Shakespeare's work, refers continually to contemporary drama and gives one chapter (xi) to a comparison with Ben Jonson's Roman plays and comedies. Schücking, as his title suggests, is concerned with the likeness in difference, the reciprocity between Shakespeare and the other dramatists, with the transmutation in Shakespeare not only of common material, but of common dramatic traditions and conventions, of psychological assumptions common to both, and of the characteristic, ever-recurring human types and motives which result.

Thaler, prompted "to put together Sidney's precepts and Shakespeare's practice", reaches, after careful collation, the conclusion that "Shakespeare—for whatever reason—casually or causally—'executed' what Sidney had 'outlined'" and further indicates "not only that Shakespeare illustrated Sidney, but that he remembered him". Thaler's method is to proceed through the topics of the *Defense* (though not, mercifully, in Sidney's order) and lay beside each precept related or illustrative passages or references. In the nature of things only general harmony of principle can be expected between a work of criticism and a body of drama, but his results offer matter for consideration.

Paul V. Rubow's volume[5] is not, as its title might suggest, a comparative study like Schücking's, but, as the author himself says, "en raekke kritiske Studier"; two of these handle the problems of *Henry VI* and the *Sonnets*, and most of the rest those of the work of Kyd.

[1] "Belleforest, Shakespeare and Kyd."

[2] "The Sources of Shakespeare's *Richard II*."

[3] Mention should be made, before this section is closed, of Michel Poirier's "Sidney's Influence upon *A Midsummer Night's Dream*", *Studies in Philology*, XLIV (July 1947), 483–9, and of P. D. Westbrook's "Horace's Influence on *Antony and Cleopatra*", *P.M.L.A.* LXII (June 1947), 392–8.

[4] A. G. van Kranendonk, *Shakespeare en zijn Tijd* (Amsterdam: Querido, 1947); L. L. Schücking, *Shakespeare und der Tragödienstil seiner Zeit* (Bern: Verlag Funke, 1947); A. Thaler, *Shakespeare and Sir Philip Sidney* (Harvard University Press, 1947).

[5] *Shakespeare og hans Samtidige* (København: Gyldendal, 1948). This volume belongs, in so far as it touches Shakespeare, mainly to the bibliographical section; it is only briefly noticed here.

Can we draw any general conclusions from this hasty survey of this year's vigorous output? One or two, perhaps. A tendency, already noticed last year, to return to the earlier preoccupation with the content and the art of the plays is steadily increasing. The English and American criticism has, moreover, ceased to issue even the gentlest and most courteous of manifestos. Assured now of its own right, it appears to occupy the greater part of the territory without deprecation and almost at unawares. And its strength is not in its bulk only but in its quality. But again, as last year, something like a manifesto is uttered and again the voice comes from one of the Latin civilizations: "Le problème critique essentiel me paraît donc être, non pas le classement en genres littéraires pour la satisfaction de la critique universitaire, ni l'étude théorique des diverses formes dans lesquelles l'apport poético-dramatique a pu s'insérer, ni même l'analyse dite psychologique des personnages, qui apporte à l'esprit l'illusion de se saisir d'un réel complexe et fuyant, mais bien l'étude de l'expérience humaine réfractée à travers le drame, et façonnée par l'instrument d'expression....Nous prenons le théâtre de Shakespeare tel qu'il se présente...et nous l'examinons du simple point de vue critique et esthétique."[1] This does not sum up all the tendencies revealed in this year's work, but it indicates certain of the strongest directions. Finally, the volumes of Fluchère, Reyher and Schücking, supported by those of Kranendonk and Rubow, indicate that the continental scholarship that we awaited last year is alive, and alive to some purpose.

2. SHAKESPEARE'S LIFE AND TIMES

reviewed by D. J. GORDON

An article in last year's *Shakespeare Survey*, examining twentieth-century studies on the Elizabethan stage, indicated the profits gained by the discernible movement away from the sweeping treatment of the general theme towards the detailed investigation of special problems. Capital instances were of course the volumes by J. C. Adams on the Globe theatre and by George F. Reynolds on the Red Bull. And this year we have from these scholars studies of just such a kind as were called for in this article: an essay by Adams on "The Original Staging of *King Lear*" and one by Reynolds on "*Troilus and Cressida* on the Elizabethan Stage".[2]

Adams goes through *King Lear* scene by scene, showing how he believes it must have been staged at the Globe. We cannot here attempt a précis of his paper but some of his generalizations startle one into a fresh realization of the latest changes in our conception of the Elizabethan stage, of how far the traditional notions of its 'bareness', of its 'restricted range', of its use have been modified—this, for example:

It is a basic principle of Elizabethan drama that a given stage may not be used in two successive scenes to represent two essentially different or widely separated places.

Or this:

Now the Elizabethan drama from beginning to end tended to support stage illusion by scenic realism.

[1] Henri Fluchère (*op. cit.* pp. 23 and 11). Cf. Napoleone Orsini, "La Critica Shakespeariana", quoted in *Shakespeare Survey*, I, 118.
[2] *Joseph Quincy Adams: Memorial Studies*, pp. 229-38, 315-35.

The moral of it all is the complexity and subtlety of the arrangement of spaces that made up the Elizabethan stage, and the control that Shakespeare had over this medium: the last a remark that has been made often enough but one which hardly has much meaning until the precise nature of the medium and of this 'control' has been clarified. Reynolds, too, takes us a long way from the bare stage. The generalization he begins from is: that Elizabethan plays may have been given "with very different stage arrangements but without any difference appearing in either the text itself or in the stage directions". He takes *Troilus and Cressida*—the problem of whether or not it was publicly performed is familiar—and suggests ways in which it could have been given on the public stage or privately—on, for instance, a stage erected in the dining hall of one of the Inns of Court. A bare stage with the curtained space and two unconcealed stage doors would have sufficed. But Reynolds asks if there was any reason why such austerity should have been sought for either at the Globe or for a private performance. And he envisages a setting constructed on the same principle as the Renaissance Terentian setting which provides as background a series of 'cells', and which depends on the medieval principle of symbolism and 'simultaneity'. Thus he envisages the play given at the Globe with two tents or structures, one serving as the tent of Achilles, one for that of Agamemnon and Calchas, the rear-stage serving for Pandarus' house, and two stage doors indicating Troy and the Greek camp. The tent structures could have been multiplied on a private stage. Such a setting would have clarified the movement of the play; and Reynolds argues in an interesting way that the need for clarity may well have demanded the use of signs—an old convention—indicating the occupants of the structures.

Both essays confirm the justness of another contention expressed in the *Shakespeare Survey* article: they cry aloud for testing on an actual stage.

Nothing has been more marked in recent years than the growth of interest in the 'ideas' expressed in Shakespeare's plays or the intellectual assumptions that underlie them. Attempts to state these ideas, to relate them to current doctrines and, more ambitiously, to recreate the 'intellectual background' of Shakespeare and his age multiply and increase. All of them are not so judicious and interesting as three which may be noticed here: R. C. Bald's "'Thou Nature, art my Goddess': Edmund and Renaissance Free-Thought",[1] John F. Danby's "*King Lear* and Christian Patience"[2] and W. A. Armstrong's "The Influence of Seneca and Machiavelli on the Elizabethan Tyrant".[3]

Studies in Shakespeare's 'ideas' and in the 'intellectual background' of his age suffer less from lack of attention than from a certain misdirection of energy, and, too often, from a certain simple-mindedness. Here, as elsewhere, in the field of literary history, a few minutes spent reflecting on method, on the precise nature and scope of the activity undertaken might bring in dividends and save a good deal of trouble. The vice of these studies is the production of specious abstract schemes presented as statements of "what people thought about a given subject". It is too often forgotten, for one thing, that every discourse or statement used as document was made with a purpose: that the 'idea' does not exist pure and naked: that its context is part of it. Important, therefore, is Lawrence Babb's essay "On the Nature of Elizabethan Psychological

[1] *Joseph Quincy Adams: Memorial studies*, pp. 337–49.
[2] *The Cambridge Journal*, I, no. 5 (Feb. 1948), 305–20.
[3] *Review of English Studies*, XXIV (Jan. 1948), 19–35.

Literature"[1] with its much needed warning about the dangers involved in setting out charts of Elizabethan theories of psychology and using them as guides to the interpretation of characters and action in Elizabethan drama. It is—the principle should be too commonplace to require emphasis—necessary to realize the nature of the documents with which one is dealing. And Babb points out what confusions are likely to result when we bring modern notions of 'science' and the 'scientific approach' to the reading of such treatises; for these treatises show none of the desire for consistency and order which we equate with the 'scientific approach'; they were eclectic in method, they were deliberately literary and—which is very important—they were hortatory treatises ethical in aim, discourses aimed at showing men how to lead the good life and not manuals describing man's psychological make-up in a detached, neutral, comprehensive way: the end, which is hortatory and ethical, controls the choice and presentation of material. Babb also makes some sensible suggestions about how far we can use this literature for the interpretation of the drama.

But other histories than that of ideas can be written. There is a history of the narrative material, fable and characters used by Shakespeare—for these had often been shaped before they came into his hands. W. W. Lawrence's *Shakespeare's Problem Comedies* remains the most notable example of this approach. He has now attempted in "Ophelia's Heritage"[2] a brief study of the figure of Ophelia as shaped by the tradition of the Hamlet story which Shakespeare received. And how a historical figure was shaped by tradition into legend is the subject of L. M. Oliver's "Sir John Oldcastle: Legend or Literature"[3] a re-examination of the prehistory of Falstaff.

It is perhaps strange that considerations of Shakespeare's imagery have not provoked a wider interest in his use of the language of visual imagery. An example of this kind of study is Samuel C. Chew's immensely learned iconographical study of "the seven ages of man" according to Jacques.[4] Chew relates this handling to the whole body of literary and visual representations of the notion, which was common enough. There is if anything perhaps too much material in this essay; but the ground deserves further cultivation.[5]

The famous question of the 'pessimism' of the early seventeenth century and the controversies on this subject illustrate the difficulties inherent in the attempt to define the 'temper' of the age in which Shakespeare wrote. Again, it may be suspected that some reflection on method, on the nature of the question being asked and of the possible replies to it, might serve a useful purpose. At any rate Theodore Spencer returns to the subject with a paper on "The Elizabethan Malcontent".[6] He finds that the Elizabethan melancholy men fall into five categories which he proceeds to set out. And, even admitting the existence of a great traditional body of thought

---

[1] *Joseph Quincy Adams: Memorial Studies*, pp. 509–22. With this article compare Louise C. Turner Forest, "A Caveat for Critics against Invoking Elizabethan Psychology", *P.M.L.A.* (Sept. 1946)—noticed in *Shakespeare Survey*, I, 126–7.

[2] *Modern Language Review*, XLII (Oct. 1947), 409–16.

[3] *The Library*, 5th ser., I (December/March, 1947), 179–83.

[4] "This Strange Eventful History", *Joseph Quincy Adams: Memorial Studies*, pp. 157–82.

[5] Willard Farnham's "The Medieval Comic Spirit in the English Renaissance" (*Joseph Quincy Adams: Memorial Studies*, pp. 429–37) attempts to set Shakespeare in a wide historical context. What he says about Falstaff is interesting; he does not, however, mention Miss Welsford's *The Fool*, which is very relevant.

[6] Much of this material had already been brought together by L. C. Knights in his "Seventeenth Century Melancholy", reprinted as an appendix in his *Drama and Society in the Age of Jonson*.

that condemns the world, and admitting that Elizabethan melancholy may often have been a matter of words, an attitude for which an available language existed, he would hold that there is in this period an obvious stress on melancholy and that this stress must bear some relation to certain factors in the state of culture and society. He indicates some of these factors: the ambitions and frustrations of the courtier's life; the troubles and uncertainties of the professional writer's position; economic strains. Economic changes at work in English society in the early seventeenth century and their cultural effects lie behind *Timon of Athens* if we accept E. C. Pettet's analysis of this play in his "*Timon of Athens: the Disruption of Feudal Morality*".[1] The title shows the direction of his thesis: the money-dominated society of Athens is the projection of this time when "Feudal morality" was being replaced by the morality of an "acquisitive society"—to use words of Tawney's, on whose work this essay largely depends.

There is no end to exploration of the age in which Shakespeare lived out his life. But to write of this life itself or of the 'personality' of Shakespeare is now it seems reserved for the bold, the crazy or the amateur: it requires the courage of great knowledge or the courage of little. C. Martin Mitchell's *The Shakespeare Circle* is typical of the amateur's work.[2] Officially its centre is the life of Shakespeare's son-in-law, Dr John Hall, and a statement of Hall's place as physician. But the author wanders here and there, and into places where his knowledge of the history of medicine or of the social and political history of the age does not serve him as a reliable guide. However, Mitchell explicitly warns the professional scholars off. And indeed such a book, innocent, amiable and enthusiastic, reflects the spirit of a local *pietas* that produces all sorts of manifestations, the good and the powerful as well as the curious and the merely tiresome, its chapter one of the most difficult to write in that impossible work, the history of Shakespeare's *Nachleben*.

Strangely innocent, too, in its way, is Eric Partridge's essay on Shakespeare's 'bawdy'[3] with its hearty and soothing insistence that it is quite permissible to talk of Shakespeare's treatment of sex. And, after all, little comes out of this "literary and psychological essay" except the reassuring news that Shakespeare was not a homosexual, that he—the 'myriad-minded'—knew all about sex (Partridge devotes space and ingenuity to piling up antitheses descriptive of Shakespeare's attitudes), that he was extremely clever at creating or using sexual imagery, that he uses more of it than any of his contemporaries, and more skilfully; and that—this is 'basic, significant, supremely important and most illuminatingly revelatory"—for Shakespeare writing and lovemaking are acts of creation, acts of release, spiritual or physical, with writing the more satisfactory of the two. Of the value of Partridge's glossary the lexicographer must speak. We may note that the author does not try to relate Shakespeare's language to the usages of his contemporaries; and that the general impression received is that it is startlingly easy to give almost any word at all a sexual connotation; and this we knew already.[4]

[1] *Review of English Studies*, XXIII (Oct. 1947), 321–36. On this essay see also the preceding section, "Critical Studies".

[2] C. Martin Mitchell, *The Shakespeare Circle* (Birmingham: Cornish Brothers, 1947).

[3] Eric Partridge, *Shakespeare's Bawdy. A Literary and Psychological Essay and a Comprehensive Glossary* (London: Routledge, 1947).

[4] G. M. Young's *Shakespeare and the Termers. Annual Shakespeare Lecture of the British Academy*, 1947 (Oxford, The University Press; London, Cumberlege) is a sketch of how Shakespeare may have been influenced by his contacts with the young gentlemen of the Inns of Court. H. D. Gray's "The Chamberlain's Men and *The Poetaster*"

3. TEXTUAL STUDIES

reviewed by JAMES G. MCMANAWAY

The New Cambridge Edition moves one volume nearer completion with the publication of *Macbeth*, a play that challenges and receives John Dover Wilson's best efforts. Textually the edition has the same virtues—and faults—that W. M. T. Dodds describes so acutely in the first four pages of a memorable review [1] of two earlier plays in the series, pages that should be read by every Shakespeare specialist, particularly those who contemplate editing one of the plays. Miss Dodds points out what has long been realized, that the fourfold aims and methods of the edition are mutually incompatible. These are, in Miss Dodds' words:

(1) To advance textual study.

(2) To advance the literary appreciation of the general reader.

(3) To present to the general reader a text embodying the results of specialist methods at present beyond that reader's ken.

(4) To give due weight to literary considerations, as well as to strict textual analysis, in arriving at an established text.

The matter of prime importance [Dodds continues] is the incompatibility of the first and third aims when handled in the way here chosen. A little reflection on the immediately practicable as distinct from the ultimately desirable makes plain their incompatibility within one and the same edition, were both to be *consistently* pursued: one cannot simultaneously advance an unfinished study and present its final or even its agreed results to a public to whom textual study must be rather mediated than laid out for scrutiny....As long as critical method kept within the comprehension of the general reader, and editors were in fact required to be no more than especially gifted general readers, they could in one and the same edition appeal to scholar and general reader alike. But the new critical methods of the scholar are beyond the ken of the ordinary reader; therefore, what must be offered him is decision. One cannot at the same time offer the scholar what he needs: the material for decision (the presentation of alternatives, specialized debate, the tentative solution submitted for consideration).

But to assert that a New Cambridge text, "is highly controversial and carries no guarantee by textual scholars" (Dodds, p. 373) is not to deny the brilliance of many of the editor's observations and conjectures or the eloquence of his aesthetic appreciation. The New Cambridge continues to be the most stimulating as well as the most controversial of editions.

Wilson conjectures boldly that *Macbeth* was first written next after *Hamlet*, about 1601 or 1602, and performed in Edinburgh, where he supposes Shakespeare to have taken refuge after the

in *Modern Language Review*, XLII (April 1947), 172–9, is an attempt to identify members of this company satirized in Act III, scene 4 of Jonson's play. He suggests that Aesop is Shakespeare, and, boldly, that Jonson was angry because Shakespeare had prevented *Cynthia's Revels* from being produced at court on the ground that certain treasonable allusions to the Essex affair could be read into it. In Tucker Brooke's *Essays on Shakespeare* (New Haven: Yale University Press, 1948) several papers are reprinted which may concern us here: "Shakespeare Remembers his Youth in Stratford", "Shakespeare's Dove-House", "A New Life of Shakespeare" (a review of J. Q. Adams' *Life*), "Willobie's 'Avisa'".

[1] '*King Henry IV: Parts I and II*', *Modern Language Review*, XLII (July 1947), 371–82.

Essex revolt. In the second detail he was admittedly anticipated by Fleay; in the first, though the fact is not mentioned, by J. M. Robertson in *Literary Detection* (1931), who employed, among other proofs, the evidence adduced by J. M. Nosworthy and accepted by Wilson.

The full-length text, Wilson believes, was abbreviated by Shakespeare himself for use in a performance in 1606 before James I and King Christian of Denmark; later (about 1610 or 1611) it was altered by Thomas Middleton, two of whose songs are partly quoted in III, v and IV, i.

In the confidence that a transcript of the prompt-book of this truncated and altered version was used in the printing of the Folio, Wilson feels free to regularize the lineation throughout the text, and though he is more conservative than his predecessors, the first Cambridge editors, he underestimates the closeness of his basic text to Shakespeare's intention. As an example of the many passages in *Macbeth* which by their lineation indicate how a sensitive actor would read the lines, consider II, ii, 64–74, which are thus printed by Wilson:

> *Lady M.* My hands are of your colour; but I shame
> To wear a heart so white. (*knocking*) I hear a knocking
> At the south entry: retire we to our chamber:
> A little water clears us of this deed:
> How easy is it then! Your constancy
> Hath left you unattended. (*knocking*) Hark! more knocking.
> Get on your nightgown, lest occasion call us
> And show us to be watchers: be not lost
> So poorly in your thoughts.
>   *Macbeth.* To know my deed, 'twere best not know myself. (*knocking*)
> Wake Duncan with thy knocking! I would thou couldst! (*they go in*)

This is not one of the illustrations cited by Richard Flatter in *Shakespeare's Producing Hand* (to be mentioned below), but as the lines have been normalized it shows how scholarly editors have been imbued with the notion "that it is a poet's chief aim to write regular verse" and that "they seldom tried to find an explanation from the theatrical angle (still less did they think of any histrionic meaning)" (Flatter, p. 73). How great has been the loss in emotional intensity and theatrical effectiveness, one may discover by comparing the lineation of the Folio. Lady Macbeth's speech begins with a regular line,

> My hands are of your colour: but I shame
> To weare a Heart so white.   *Knocke.*

The pounding at the gate interrupts her. After a pause, she whispers in alarm,

> I heare a knocking at the South entry:
> Retyre we to our Chamber:

Then a break, as both listen anxiously. When nothing happens, she resumes, with confidence,

> A little Water cleares us of this deed.
> How easie is it then? your Constancie
> Hath left you unattended.   *Knocke.*

But before she can finish the third line, the dreadful knocking begins again, and speech is suspended.

> Hearke, more knocking.

A half line, followed by more anxious listening. Then, swiftly,

> Get on your Night-Gowne, least occasion call us,
> And shew us to be Watchers: be not lost
> So poorely in your thoughts.
> *Macb.* To know my deed,   *Knocke.*
> 'Twere best not know my selfe.

His first line is interrupted by the insistent pounding at the gate, and only after a pause can he complete the sentence in another short line. Then defiantly he breaks out,

> Wake Duncan with thy knocking:

but before a full line can be spoken his mood changes again, and he concludes almost prayerfully,

> I would thou could'st.

Audiences will hear the lines thus from the lips of good actors, and readers will be stimulated by finding them so printed on a page.

The editor of *Macbeth* cannot evade three questions: (1) what, if any, scenes have been lost; (2) to what extent did Middleton contribute to the text; and (3) is Simon Forman's account a forgery? Wilson's answers to the first were in many instances anticipated in the edition of J. Q. Adams (Houghton Mifflin, 1931), which "did not come into [his] hands until November 1946, when [his] edition was already in the press". And if, as both editors believe, Shakespeare altered a full-length play for a court performance, these two scholars are doubtless right in their conjectures about omitted and truncated scenes. Nosworthy points out, however,[1] that in his use of sources Shakespeare "has woven all the tractable material into his main plot, and left it at that" (p. 108); "if the cumulative evidence can point to any conclusion it is that *Macbeth* was never anything but a short play" (p. 115). This thesis becomes the more acceptable when we recall that Shakespeare constantly imposes upon his audience a belief in the actuality of his *dramatis personae* by having them allude to incidents that are not represented on the stage. Thus, after we have heard Lady Macbeth unsex herself in preparation for Duncan's murder (I, v, 39–54) and promise her husband that if he will "only look up clear" he may "leave all the rest to [her]" (I, v, 71, 73), we really do not need to *see* her go armed to the King's chamber to accord her full belief when (II, i, 12–13) she mutters: "Had he not resembled My father as he slept, I had done it."

Middleton's part in *Macbeth*, which is limited by Sir Edmund Chambers to three passages, II, v; IV, i, 39–43; and IV, i, 125–32, is scarcely augmented by Wilson (cf. p. xxiv). On this subject, too, Nosworthy, who at all points is conservative, has several interesting observations.[2] It is his opinion that the Hecate speeches were introduced only to smooth the insertion of

---

[1] "*Macbeth* at the Globe", *The Library*, 5th ser., II, 108–18.

[2] "The Hecate Scenes in *Macbeth*", *Review of English Studies*, XXIV (April 1948), 138–9. See also his "Shakespeare and the Siwards", *op. cit.* pp. 193–241.

Middleton's two songs, and, poor as the links are, he would not deny them to Shakespeare. His suggestion that "possibly [Hecate] had encroached gradually on the territory of the Weird Sisters for years", involves him in all sorts of difficulties. It implies that theatrical manuscripts of *Macbeth* bearing successive alterations were in existence in or about 1663 or 1664, when Davenant staged his adaptation, a supposition for which there is only one shred of evidence: the inclusion of the full texts of Middleton's songs in the first printing of this version.[1]

The genuineness of Simon Forman's *Bocke of Plaies* was called in question many years ago, but despite A. K. McIlwraith's emphatic rejection of S. A. Tannenbaum's contention that J. P. Collier forged it, it was eminently worth while for Dover Wilson and R. W. Hunt to search out the history of the manuscript and state at length the reasons for accepting it as genuine.[2] At the request of Wilson, I examined the *Bocke* in the summer of 1947 with the proofs of his and Hunt's notes before me, and I think it would be sheer perversity to question the document further.

The search in Shakespeare for allusions to contemporary events continues, for it is undoubtedly true that if we knew more than we do about the personalities at the courts of Elizabeth and James we should enjoy many oblique hits that were penned for the understanding auditor. Working along identical lines with Dover Wilson, H. N. Paul agrees with him that four lines in *Macbeth* (IV, iii, 97–100) are an interpolation.[3] In Holinshed, Malcolm tests Macduff's fidelity by accusing himself falsely of voluptuousness, avarice, and falsehood. Shakespeare's Malcolm uses the same device, but for the third vice he substitutes the sin of desiring to

> Pour the sweet milk of concord into hell,
> Uproar the universal peace, confound
> All unity on earth.

Later, in lines 129–31 as Paul notes, "Malcolm retracts the charge of false-speaking, although as the text now stands he has not charged himself with this vice."

The precise occasion of the change, according to Paul, was the "distemperature of the unrulie multitude" of Londoners at the pegme in Cheapside, where Marston's Concordia descended in a cloud and tried to deliver to King James I and King Christian IV a Latin oration on Concord, Peace and Unity. Now, riding in procession with their sovereign on this 31 July were the "Kinges Groomes and Messengers of the Chamber", among whom should have been William Shakespeare. It is tempting to join Paul in believing that Shakespeare's indignation caused him to substitute the passage in question, which echoes the words Concord, Peace and Unity, that Marston had emphasized, so that Burbage (if he played Macbeth) might speak them before

---

[1] Only the initial phrases of the songs are printed in the Folio (III, v, 33, S.D., and IV, i, 43, S.D.), yet when the operatic *Macbeth* was presented in 1673, their complete texts were somehow available. The success of the revival prompted William Cademan to issue a quarto with the Folio text which he seems to have attempted to pass off as the operatic version by inserting one of Middleton's songs and as much of Davenant's lyrical interpolations as could be pirated. In 1674 Philip Chetwind, publisher of the Third Folio, printed the Davenant alteration in full. Yet the only MS. of Middleton's *Witch*, from which the two songs were extracted, is non-theatrical—it is a transcript in the hand of Ralph Crane which the author presented to his friend, Thomas Holmes, and which, presumably, always remained in private hands. How did Davenant recover the two Middleton songs?

[2] See *Review of English Studies*, XXIII (July 1947), 193–200.

[3] "The First Performance of *Macbeth*", *Shakespeare Association Bulletin*, XXII (October 1947), 149–54.

the Kings one week later at Hampton Court. The King's Men had already presented two plays for the entertainment of visiting royalty, and Paul comes as near proof as we shall ever be that *Macbeth* was the play enacted on the seventh of August. Although this could hardly have been the *première* of the tragedy, as Paul conjectures, it was almost certainly the first performance of Shakespeare's abbreviated version.

Thirty years ago there was general agreement about the chronological order of Shakespeare's plays and their approximate dates of composition. Many of these assumptions have been called in question in more recent years, especially by the editors of the New Cambridge Shakespeare with their notions of continual revisions. In a weighty volume, *William Shakspere's Five-Act Structure*,[1] T. W. Baldwin gives support to several of the newer hypotheses and provides evidence to bolster the argument that more than once Shakespeare took up a play he had written a decade before and refurbished it. His chapters on the early comedies and tragedies, the structure and incidents of which are examined laboriously in relation to their Terentian models, propose the following order of composition: *Love's Labour's Lost*, *All's Well that Ends Well* (?= *Love's Labour's Won*), *Comedy of Errors*, *Two Gentlemen of Verona*, *Romeo and Juliet*, and *Rape of Lucrece*, with *Venus and Adonis* apparently fitted in before *Romeo*. Contemporary allusions convince Baldwin that *Love's Labour's Lost* was given its first form between August 1588 and August 1589 and its final form in time for a performance at Christmas, 1598. *All's Well* he would presumably equate in its earliest version with Meres' *Love's Labour's Won*, on account of its theme, the opposite of that of the other play, and structure, and also on account of the fact that it seems to have been written for a company of the same composition as *Love's Labour's Lost*.

Baldwin thinks that in *Errors* Shakespeare attained to initial mastery of Terentian structure. This he demonstrated again by combining plots and incidents from Lyly in *Two Gentlemen*; soon after came the earliest version of *Romeo*, which borrows much from it; and then *Lucrece* (1594), whose date of publication provides a terminus.

If these dates be accepted, several questions require answers. Why, for example, should the young gentlemen of Gray's Inn, when they broke with precedent by hiring a cry of common players to assist in their revels in 1594, select as the play of the evening one that had been performed publicly some years earlier (I assume that the play was performed shortly after being written)? Would they not rather have chosen something fire-new? Or is it possible that a modernized version of this old play was the only available piece that smacked enough of the classics to satisfy their fastidious tastes? Again, if *Love's Labour's Lost* was composed in 1588–9, why did Shakespeare decide to revamp it, and how did he point up the topical allusions enough to recommend it for performance at court ten years later? And yet again, if *Romeo* was written about 1592 or 1593, how did it pass more or less unnoticed until revised in 1597, at which time it became so popular that Danter published a pirated version? (Incidentally, I am troubled by Baldwin's treatment of Q1 and Q2, which he discusses at times as if the former represented the supposed version of 1592–3, and the latter that of 1597.)

It is easy to offer objections, as I have done; but Baldwin presents so many new details and deals with such an important body of hitherto neglected material that his theses must be given very careful attention.

[1] *William Shakspere's Five-Act Structure. Shakspere's Early Plays on the Background of Renaissance Theories of Five-Act Structure from 1470* (Urbana: University of Illinois Press, 1947).

One further detail must be considered. In discussing *Two Gentlemen*, Baldwin comes to this conclusion (p. 724):

Shakspere had been brushing up on Terentian structure also as he studied the plays of Plautus for *The Comedy*, and there had learned such things that he could not thereafter have constructed a play so clumsily as did the author of *Love's Labor's Lost*. The construction of that play is certainly earlier work than that in *The Comedy* and the *Two Gentlemen*.

This is dangerous argument. It ignores differences in genre and difficulties of subject-matter, and it is based on the assumption that in the attainment of literary skill the road winds uphill all the way, that a playwright who has written one well-constructed play will never thereafter produce a 'flop'.

In discussions of Shakespeare's text it is customary to speak of the reading of the First Folio, but in reality the text of this literary monument has never been established; nor can it be, until every extant copy, however fragmentary, has been minutely collated. This would be a prodigious labour, even if all the copies were housed together, as they are not. In 1941 C. J. K. Hinman began collating the text of *Othello* in the Folger Library collection of First Folios and, coming upon a page that bears the original proof reader's marks, was enabled to explain a crux that had previously baffled editors.[1] Convinced by this experience that his text could not be sound if he relied upon the collation of a limited number of Folios and well aware of the time and labour required to collate the some 230 extant copies, Hinman set about devising a machine that would throw upon a screen alternate images of the same page in two copies of a Folio in such a way as to disclose the slightest variation in the types. A preliminary account of this device was read at the Modern Language Association meeting in 1946.[2] The working model, which uses micro-film copies, speeds up collation fifty times. A variant of the device now under construction will permit the direct comparison of pages of a book without recourse to photography. With these two machines a scholar may with some confidence undertake the collation of all the surviving copies of the Folio. Not until his bibliographical work shall have been completed will it be legitimate to speak of the reading of the First Folio.

A fresh approach to some of the textual problems in Shakespeare is found in *Shakespeare's Producing Hand*.[3] Certain technicalities of versification, rhythm, diction, and punctuation that are rarely commented upon by Shakespearians have forced themselves upon the attention of the author, Richard Flatter, while he has been engaged in transcribing and translating into German the *Sonnets* and eighteen of the plays. And though there will be disagreement about some of the details, Flatter is sound in his insistence upon the restoration of much of the original lineation and punctuation that was 'improved' by the eighteenth-century editors in the interest of correctness.

In "A Note on Coriolanus",[4] G. B. Harrison employs similar methods to show how modern

[1] See *The Library*, ser. 4, XXIII (September–December 1942), 101–7.

[2] See "Mechanized Collation: A Preliminary Report", *Papers of the Bibliographical Society of America*, XLI (1947), 1–8. See also his "Why 79 First Folios?" a paper read before the Bibliographical Society of the University of Virginia on 6 June 1947 and later distributed by the Society in mimeographed form.

[3] London: William Heinemann, 1948.

[4] In *Joseph Quincy Adams: Memorial Studies*, pp. 239–52. Harrison finds additional evidence for dating the play about 1609 in a hitherto unnoted allusion at III, i, 93 to Hugh Middleton's project for bringing water from Hertfordshire to London.

editions sacrifice much of the dramatic value of certain scenes by retaining the regularized line-ation of the early editors and thus obscuring Shakespeare's revelation of character and mood by his fluent accommodation of the verse to the passions of his *dramatis personae*. "The result", for readers who have not ready access to facsimiles of the Quartos and the Folio, "is to destroy most of Shakespeare's subtle touches; to abolish the pauses, the silences, and the rushes.... The gain is that with a little forcing we can now recite [the] speeches to the accompaniment of that inspiring instrument—the metronome."

Several welcome notes[1] on cruxes in the text have come from the pen of Helge Kökeritz, whose familiarity with Elizabethan phonology enables him to dispose of such difficult passages as Nym's "The Anchor is deepe" (*Merry Wives*, I, iii, 57) and Hamlet's "I know a Hawke from a Handsaw" (II, ii, 397). Kökeritz chides the literary scholar of to-day who edits Shakespeare for taking Elizabethan spellings as his only guide, "blind to the fact that English spelling and pronunciation often have little in common...and that what really matters is the spoken form, very rarely its graphic representation".

Another form of attack on the verbal cruxes in Shakespeare is illustrated by Leslie Hotson's note on "The prenzie, *Angelo*".[2] Hotson turns to John Florio, whose dictionaries must have been known to Shakespeare—but who, in any case, is an authoritative repository of current usages—and finds 'Prenze' defined as 'Principe', a prince. Hotson notes nearly contemporary support for this gloss in F2's 'princely', and points out that the punctuation of F1 should be restored: "The prenzie, Angelo" = the prince, Angelo, 'Prenzie gardes', he would gloss as 'prince-robes'. Marie C. Stopes rejects the suggestions and insists that 'prenzie' is the usual corruption in fencing of 'prenez'.[3] And in another connection,[4] Donald J. McGinn turns to the *ductus litterarum* for confirmation of his belief that 'prenzie' is a misreading of 'precise'.

In "'What's that *Ducdame*?' (*As You Like It*, II, v, 60)", J. T. Jones[5] rejects the suggestion that the word is a nonsense coinage, for the reason that "it is more satisfying to the writer of non-sense verse, whether he be Lewis Carroll or Jacques, to base the apparent nonsense on some meaning which he can enjoy whether his listeners can or not". Accordingly, he proposes a derivation from the Welsh *dewch 'da mi*, "Come with me", a close enough translation of "Come hither" in Amiens' song, and one that rhymes with "come to me", as *dewch yma* ("come hither") does not.

A. P. Rossiter's emendation[6] of *Troilus and Cressida*, V, vii, 10–11, is plausible. F1 reads "double-henned sparrow", which is nonsense as applied to Menelaus, and Q, "double-hen'd spartan", which is little better. Rossiter's "double-horned Spartan" fits Menelaus exactly and prepares the way for 'bull' and 'horns' which follow closely. His attempt to eliminate Hector's inadequately motivated *volte face* at the end of II, ii requires serious consideration. The difficulty, he suggests, may be removed by supposing that a disorder in the manuscript misled the com-

---

[1] "Five Shakespeare Notes", *Review of English Studies*, XXIII (October 1947), 310–20.

[2] *Times Literary Supplement* (22 November 1947), p. 603. See *ibid.* (11 October), p. 521, for reliance upon Florio in glossing *Twelfth Night*, I, iii, 45.

[3] *Ibid.* (6 December 1947), p. 629.

[4] "The Precise Angelo", in *Joseph Quincy Adams: Memorial Studies*, pp. 129–39.

[5] *Modern Language Notes*, LXII (December 1947), 563–4.

[6] *Times Literary Supplement* (28 May 1948), p. 261.

positors of Q and F into printing the last twenty-five lines of the scene in their present order, whereas Shakespeare intended Troilus to interrupt Hector at the middle of line 188 (Globe text) with the second half of his next speech, beginning "But, worthy Hector" (ll. 198–206). Then Hector was to resume with "Hector's opinion" (ll. 188–93); and Troilus was to reply, "Why there" (ll. 194–8). This is indeed complicated, but possibly not too much so if Greg is correct in thinking that Q was set from a private transcript of Shakespeare's foul papers.

Raymond A. Houk continues his detailed textual studies [1] of A Shrew and The Shrew. It is his belief that Shakespeare wrote an Ur-Shrew about 1592–3, of which A Shrew is a bad quarto and The Shrew a later Shakespearian revision. In a comparison of the Shrew texts with Alleyn's player's part of Orlando and the quarto of Orlando Furioso (1594), Houk notes similarities and attempts to isolate the borrowings from Greene; some of the similarities are valid, but a few details appear to be no more than commonplaces, and in the case of several the indebtedness may run in either direction. The study of Faustus is intended to eliminate Samuel Rowley from consideration as a collaborator in that play and A Shrew and to prove that the latter contains elements of Marlowe's play that were present in a version different from and anterior to that published in 1604 but accessible in some form for the edition of 1616.

A proposed addition to the Shakespeare canon is advocated by George C. Taylor in his contribution [2] to the memorial volume for J. Q. Adams, after a study of the diction, grammar, and versification of a number of speeches in Jonson's Every Man in his Humour. He finds close parallels to lines in Merry Wives and observes that in preparing the text of the play for his Folio of 1616 Jonson eliminated some of the bold figures in the questioned passages.

The literary scholar whom Kökeritz would require to master Elizabethan phonology before he ventures to edit Shakespeare must also become a specialist in "The New Bibliography", as F. P. Wilson called it in Studies in Retrospect.[3] Two of the principal contributions to the bibliographical study of Shakespeare in the past year stem from Greg's monumental study, The Variants in the First Quarto of King Lear. In "An Examination of the Method of Proof Correction in Lear",[4] F. T. Bowers takes issue with some of Greg's conclusions about the precise method employed by Nicholas Okes in printing and proof-reading Lear, and in a long-needed companion study, "Elizabethan Proofing",[5] he attempts a generalized description of how Elizabethan printers proofed their books. Bowers applies to Lear the method employed in its elemental form to a simple textual problem in Middleton and Dekker's Roaring Girle,[6] in which by identifying the various settings of the running-title and tracing their reappearance in the Quarto he is able to bring to light hitherto unnoted details about the sequence of formes in the press. Since both Greg and Bowers are "dealing only with probabilities and trying to demonstrate that one set of assumptions is more normal and thus more in accordance with the evidence than another", their expositions require the reader's closest attention. And if in the light of newly

[1] "Shakespeare's Shrew and Greene's Orlando", P.M.L.A. LXII (September 1947), 657–71; "Doctor Faustus and A Shrew", ibid. (December 1947), 950–7.

[2] "Did Shakespeare, Actor, Improvise in Every Man in his Humour?", in Joseph Quincy Adams: Memorial Studies, pp. 21–32.

[3] London, for the Bibliographical Society (1945), pp. 76–135.

[4] The Library, ser. 5, II (June 1947), 20–44.

[5] In Joseph Quincy Adams: Memorial Studies, pp. 571–86.

[6] See my "Thomas Dekker: Further Textual Notes", The Library, ser. 4, XIX (September 1938), 176–9.

discovered facts Bowers has been able to modify certain of Greg's conclusions, it is likely, I think, that further study may lead to modification of several proposals by Bowers, who tends, for example, to assume that when Okes was printing *Lear* all the employees and facilities of the shop were continuously available for this one book, whereas in all likelihood the printing of a small play quarto was only one of a number of jobs in progress.

After a careful examination of the bibliographical peculiarities of the Second Quarto of *Othello* (1630), C. J. K. Hinman disposes finally of its pretensions to textual authority.[1] He demonstrates that the compositor of Q2 worked from a copy of Q1 containing the inner forme of sheet I in the uncorrected state into which had been written numerous corrections and short additions derived from F or from a conflation of Q1 and F. And interleaved in the copy were slips of paper on which were transcribed the longer insertions from F. Incidentally, the copy of F used by the editor of Q2 contained one uncorrected forme. The independent readings in Q2 may in future be treated as variations introduced by the compositor or as the emendations of a not too careful Caroline editor.

The punctuation of the *Sonnets* (1609) is considered in a novel study by A. H. Carter,[2] who comments on the fact that the reason the "enthusiasts who find great beauty and great significance in some of the marks of punctuation...have failed to convince is that they failed to see that this great beauty and this great significance are to be found in only *some* of the marks". He concludes that the system of punctuation in the book is such that "the reader must in most cases rely on the words or at best on the words and what punctuation he finds rather than upon the punctuation alone to determine the meaning of the sonnet or directions about oral delivery".

The publication of four volumes of the Yale Shakespeare (*Hamlet, Lear, Othello,* and *1 Henry IV*) in revised editions[3] is a reminder of the loss to Shakespearian scholarship in the death of C. F. Tucker Brooke. His colleague, Benjamin Nangle, has piously taken up the plays at the point Brooke left them and seen them through the press. There are many good things in Brooke's notes and comments, but I cannot agree with his discussion of the text of *Lear*.

Three more volumes of The Penguin Shakespeare (*Winter's Tale, Troilus and Cressida* and *Coriolanus*)[4] under the editorship of G. B. Harrison, are now available. Priced at one shilling, each item contains a brief account of Shakespeare, a description of the Elizabethan theatre, and a short introduction. In *Coriolanus* Harrison has an opportunity to print the kind of text he advocates in the essay that has already been commented on.

Another series of single-volume texts, "Crofts Classics", began in 1946, priced at thirty cents. Six plays have thus far appeared: *1 Henry IV*, edited by R. C. Bald; *Othello*, by Mark Eccles; *Tempest*, by Alfred Harbage; *Hamlet*, by R. C. Bald; *Romeo and Juliet*, by H. R. Hoppe; and *Much Ado*, by Charles T. Prouty.[5] Each volume contains an easily read but meaty introduction, a tabular record of Shakespeare's life, a carefully prepared text, and a selective bibliography.

[1] "The 'Copy' for the Second Quarto of *Othello*", in *Joseph Quincy Adams: Memorial Studies*, pp. 373–89.
[2] "The Punctuation of Shakespeare's *Sonnets* of 1609", in *Joseph Quincy Adams: Memorial Studies*, pp. 409–28.
[3] New Haven: Yale University Press, 1947.
[4] Harmondsworth, Middlesex: Penguin Books, 1947.
[5] New York: F. S. Crofts, 1946, 1947, 1948.

BOOKS RECEIVED

ALLEN, PERCY. *Talks with Elizabethans, Revealing the Mystery of 'William Shakespeare'* (London: Rider, n.d.).

BETHELL, S. L. *The Winter's Tale: A Study* (London: Staples [1947]).

CONKLIN, PAUL S. *A History of 'Hamlet' Criticism* (New York: King's Crown Press at Columbia University. London: Geoffrey Cumberlege, 1947).

DELATTRE, FLORIS and CHEMIN, CAMILLE. *Les Chansons Elizabéthaines*. Bibliothèque des Langues Modernes II (Paris: Didier, 1948).

ELLIS-FERMOR, UNA. *The Study of Shakespeare*. An Inaugural Lecture Delivered at Bedford College, University of London, on October 28th, 1947 (London: Methuen, 1948).

EVANS, B. IFOR. *A Short History of English Drama* (Penguin Books, 1948).

GILBERT, MARK (edited by). *The Short Story Shakespeare. The Story in Prose with Dialogue from the Play*. (i) *Julius Caesar*; (ii) *Macbeth* (London: William Earl, n.d.).

GRANVILLE-BARKER, HARLEY. *Prefaces to Shakespeare. Fifth Series. Coriolanus* (London: Sidgwick and Jackson, 1947).

GUTTMAN, SELMA. *The Foreign Sources of Shakespeare's Works. An Annotated Bibliography of the Commentary Written on this Subject between 1904 and 1940 together with Lists of Certain Translations Available to Shakespeare* (New York: King's Crown Press. London: Geoffrey Cumberlege, 1947).

HARRISON, G. B. (edited by). *The Penguin Shakespeare*. (i) *The Tragedy of Coriolanus*; (ii) *The Tragedy of Troylus and Cressida*; (iii) *The Winter's Tale* (Penguin Books, 1947).

JOSEPH, SISTER MIRIAM, C.S.C. *Shakespeare's Use of the Arts of Language*. Columbia University Studies in English and Comparative Literature, no. 165 (New York: Columbia University Press, 1947).

KRANENDONK, A. G. VAN. *Shakespeare en zijn Tijd* (Amsterdam: Querido, 1947).

MADARIAGA, SALVADOR DE. *On Hamlet* (London: Hollis and Carter, 1948).

MITCHELL, C. MARTIN. *The Shakespeare Circle. A Life of Dr John Hall, Shakespeare's son-in-law, with glimpses of their intimate friends and relations* (Birmingham: Cornish [1947]).

NORMAN, CHARLES. *So Worthy a Friend: William Shakespeare* (New York: Rinehart, 1947).

PALMER, JOHN. *Comic Characters of Shakespeare* (London: Macmillan, 1947).

PRIOR, MOODY E. *The Language of Tragedy* (New York: Columbia University Press, 1947).

REYHER, PAUL. *Essai sur les Idées dans l'Œuvre de Shakespeare*. Bibliothèque des Langues Modernes I (Paris: Didier, 1947).

RUBOW, PAUL V. *Shakespeare og hans Samtidige. En raekke kritiske studier* (Copenhagen: Gyldendal, 1948).

SHAKESPEARE, WILLIAM. *The Complete Dramatic and Poetic Works*. With General Introduction, Biography, and an Introduction to Each Play by Frederick D. Losey (Philadelphia: Winston, n.d.).

SHAKESPEARE, WILLIAM. *Hamlet*. With a psycho-analytical study by Ernest Jones, M.D. Drawings by F. Roberts Johnson (London: Vision Press, 1947).

TAYLOR, GEORGE COFFIN. *Essays of Shakespeare. An Arrangement* (New York: Putnam, 1947).

THALER, ALWYN. *Shakespeare and Sir Philip Sidney. The Influence of 'The Defense of Poesy'* (Cambridge, Mass.: Harvard University Press, 1947).

BOOKS RECEIVED

WALKER, ROY. *The Time is out of Joint. A Study of 'Hamlet'* (London: Andrew Dakers, 1948).

WILSON, J. DOVER (editor). *The New Shakespeare: Macbeth* (Cambridge: The University Press, 1947).

WOOD, STANLEY. *The New Teaching of Shakespeare in Schools* (London: George Gill, n.d.).

YODER, AUDREY. *Animal Analogy in Shakespeare's Character Portrayal* (New York: King's Crown Press at Columbia University. London: Geoffrey Cumberlege, 1947).

YOUNG, G. M. *Shakespeare and the Termers*. Annual Shakespeare Lecture of the British Academy, 1947. From the Proceedings of the British Academy, vol. XXXIII (London: Geoffrey Cumberlege).

INDEX

INDEX

INDEX